THE INNER BELOVED

The Heart's Journey to Divine Unity

. . . . .

A. H. Almaas
FOREWORD BY RAM DASS

SHAMBHALA

Shambhala Publications, Inc.
2129 13th Street
Boulder, Colorado 80302
www.shambhala.com

© 2026 by A-Hameed Ali
Page 313 constitutes a continuation of the copyright page.

Cover art: Cursedesign/Shutterstock and -strizh-/Shutterstock
Cover design: Daniel Urban-Brown
Interior design: Kate Huber-Parker

All rights reserved. No part of this book may be reproduced in any form or by any means, electronic or mechanical, including photocopying, recording, or by any information storage and retrieval system, without permission in writing from the publisher.

9 8 7 6 5 4 3 2

Printed in the United States of America

Shambhala Publications makes every effort to print on acid-free, recycled paper. Shambhala Publications is distributed worldwide by Penguin Random House, Inc., and its subsidiaries.

Library of Congress Cataloging-in-Publication Data

Names: Almaas, A. H. author.
Title: The inner beloved: the heart's journey to divine unity / A. H. Almaas; foreword by Ram Dass.
Description: First edition. | Boulder, Colorado: Shambhala [2026] | Includes index.
Identifiers: LCCN 2025012231 | ISBN 9781645474319 (trade paperback)
Subjects: LCSH: Love | Spirituality | Self-acceptance
Classification: LCC BF575.L8 A449 2026 | ddc 152.4/1—dc23/eng/20250724
LC record available at https://lccn.loc.gov/2025012231

The authorized representative in the EU for product safety and compliance is eucomply OÜ, Pärnu mnt 139b-14, 11317 Tallinn, Estonia, hello@eucompliancepartner.com.

"This exquisite book guides us—clearly, systematically, beautifully—along the path of love all the way to its ultimate source. It calls us from our usual, fickle, fragmented passions through multiple stages of healing and opening to the boundless love-bliss that has always been our deepest desire, our deepest nature, and the source of all. What a gift!"

—ROGER WALSH, MD, PHD, professor at University of California and cohost of the "A. H. Almaas Wisdom Dialogues" on the *Deep Transformation* podcast

"Almaas has given us a luminous guide to the devotional path of the heart. Rooted in his own lived realization and enriched by poetry and story, this book speaks directly to our innermost longing. Reading *The Inner Beloved* is like being invited into a private conversation between the soul and its deepest yearning. Almaas unfolds the path of love with honesty, precision, and tenderness, showing both its heartbreak and its ecstasy. In doing so, he offers not just teachings but an embodied transmission of the sacred eros that calls us Home. Almaas leads us from the discontent of ordinary love into the luminous mystery of the one Beloved who is the source of All. A profound contribution to contemporary spirituality."

—SEAN ESBJÖRN-HARGENS, PHD, Dean of Integral Education, California Institute for Human Science

Dedicated to my friend, Karen Johnson, my companion on this path since its inception. Sharing my experience of the journey to the Beloved with her—and her confirmation and amplification of it through mirroring it in her own experience—has made it possible for these discoveries to become a significant thread in this teaching.

Contents

Series Foreword by Ram Dass   IX
Editor's Preface   XI
Acknowledgments   XV
Introduction   XVII

1. The Discontent of the Heart   1
2. The Divided Heart   17
3. Names of the Beloved   40
4. Fidelity of the Heart   65
5. Beyond Divinity   81
6. Poverty of the Heart   97
7. Yearning for the Beloved   115
8. The Primal Cavity   137
9. The Death Wish   154
10. Stupa Love   167
11. Luminous Night   183
12. Secrets of the Heart   197
13. The Beloved   213
14. Bedazzlement   227

15. Divine Darkness   247
16. Wholeness   269
17. The Unity of Love   285
18. Intimacy   302

About the Diamond Approach   311
Credits   313
Index   315

Series Foreword

The three books in the Journey of Spiritual Love series by A. H. Almaas offer an excellent road map for bringing you to inner love... spiritual love.

When I met my guru, Neem Karoli Baba, my perception of myself—and the universe—changed. He mirrored my soul back to me. Prior to that, I had known my soul, but my guru helped me to shift my perception in order to see that the soul itself is love.

Now I love everyone and everything. Being love is a matter of perception. The trees, the clouds, and everything are all made up of love. I love the floor and the ceiling... which are also made of love. I even work on loving the souls of difficult people. The only thing that has to shift for us to see love in everything and everyone is our perception.

The soul is love, wisdom, compassion, peace, and joy. I drop inward to move from the mind down into the spiritual heart. The spiritual heart is the doorway to the next plane of consciousness... "soul land."

May these books offer a blessing to you as you make that journey—from the mind into the soul...

The journey home.

With love, Ram Dass
Maui, Hawaii
August 2019

Editor's Preface

Fundamental to the Diamond Approach is the recognition that ultimate reality, the underlying ground of being, is the deepest truth of what we are. We are but a form manifesting out of it, and so the human soul expresses the depth, richness, and ultimate nature of that ground. As such, the pursuit of what is true in a person's experience cannot help but lead eventually to the ultimate mystery of our innermost nature.

This guiding principle of loving the truth for its own sake is central to the practice of inquiry, the core method of the Diamond Approach. By discerning what is true in our own experience, we invite our beingness—our true nature—to reveal itself. Often this involves going through many layers of belief and conditioning that obscure this underlying truth. There is no rush or pressure to get to the bottom of things but rather a simple willingness to allow and be with the truth in any given moment. We learn to trust that if we can be open, nonjudgmental, and nonreactive, the immediate truth—whether it manifests as emotion, thought, or sensation—will reveal something deeper that has been hidden. As we inquire in this way, ever deeper truths will continue to be revealed.

The guidance for this exploration and discovery of our personal truth lies in our heart. The mind may discriminate our experience, but it can only speculate and reason, without knowing directly what is real. The heart, on the other hand, listens, tastes, and knows what is true by being one with the experience, staying closely in touch with and touched by life. As such, the personal, spiritual journey of inner realization relies on the heart knowing what is real and following its guidance.

The heart relates to experience through feeling, and when it senses the truth, it is naturally drawn to it. To describe this experience of attraction in our soul, we use words like "wishing," "wanting," "longing," "desiring," and most basically, "loving." Love is a force that connects one soul with another, the heart with what moves it, and even the absolute source or mystery with what it has manifested. It is this profound force of love in our heart that drives our inner journey by drawing us deeper as we seek what is most true in our nature. True nature is drawing us through love. Without recognizing it, we are being drawn toward home, where we will feel undivided, whole, contented, and fulfilled because we will know ourself in our deepest nature.

The search for the inner Beloved is the purest expression of this journey toward home. It is motivated by the longing to be with our inner truth and become an authentic expression of it. Before we recognize this desire, our inner search is generally driven by a feeling of discontent and dissatisfaction with our life and what we know. Even as we love many specifics in our life, including lovers, friends, and family, we do not feel content. This is only natural when the heart does not yet know its deepest truth. Once we have fully recognized this, the path of the heart is to follow the desire for what will truly satisfy it, without needing to know what that is—all we know is that we have not yet found it. Missing what we love may bring sadness and heartache and at times a deep emptiness. Along the way, we may attempt to soothe the ache or fill the void by discovering new forms, people, and qualities to love. Whatever joy they bring does not last, however, and the search continues.

This is the journey that this book takes us on, as we follow our heart toward the deepest mystery of existence, recognizing that nothing else will satisfy our profound longing for the truth of what we are. It involves learning to listen to the heart—listening to that inner sensitivity that lets us know whether we are nearer what we seek or farther away. We can do this without needing to know or name what it is that we seek or why things unfold in ways we cannot comprehend—the inner Beloved is by its nature an unfathomable mystery that resists labels and concepts, names and images. We simply learn to be loyal to the truth compass we each carry in our heart. At times we may settle for some immediate truth or love object, but loyalty to our inner truth means always coming back to what the heart truly loves.

This is not to deny that our mind can be of service on this journey. The mind can help us to discern elements of our experience as they arise, making connections and revealing meaning. However, it cannot be the means by which we set goals, define outcomes, or make plans for how to proceed on this inner journey. The best the mind can do is help us clarify what prevents us coming nearer to the mysterious Beloved. And at some point, the mind must surrender completely to the endless mystery, as the path will take us beyond all concepts, words, and efforts to understand.

A. H. Almaas offers all spiritual seekers the necessary wisdom to support this path of the heart. He describes all the stages of this journey in great detail, presenting insights and revelations that can fuel our personal process and invite us to stay the course. This challenging journey is not for the faint of heart, but by defining the territory so clearly, Almaas encourages us to not give up on what our heart loves most. May this book be a companion for your heart in pursuing its deepest desire for true contentment and uniting with the inner Beloved.

BYRON BROWN
Editor

Acknowledgments

I would like to thank my students and their dedication to the truth as it is revealed in their personal journeys following the Diamond Approach path. Without their presence and participation in this teaching, this book would not have been possible. I also feel deep appreciation for Evelyn Birnbaum, who has been my chief transcriber for many years and did the demanding work of translating the recordings onto the page for editing.

I feel much gratitude to Paul Hancock, who has become the primary editor for this series of books on love. He was impeccable in his efforts to bring forward the precision and clarity of my teaching, first by comparing all the transcripts with the original recordings to clear up places that originally appeared unintelligible or were at times misheard. Then he outlined the whole retreat to get a sense of how to develop and present the chapters. And finally, with the help of my chief editor, Byron Brown, he brought the original text into a much cleaner and clearer form most appropriate for a book, as opposed to what worked in the retreat itself where the Beloved journey was first taught.

It is with great satisfaction that I am able to complete this series that presents the perspective of the Diamond Approach on the topic of love in the spiritual path. For this I am as always most grateful to Shambhala for being a dedicated presenter of my work in book form. Liz Shaw has been my editor there for many years and has shepherded many of my books into publication, this one being the latest. I am most thankful for her consistent and reliable support each step of the way in publishing this book, from reviewing the manuscript, offering suggestions, working with others at Shambhala to finalize both the title and the cover, and making sure that we get the best support in making this book available to the public.

Introduction

When I talked to Ram Dass in 2019 about writing a foreword for a trilogy of books about love and the heart, he was happy to contribute to this project since his teaching was primarily about love and the way of the heart.

This is the third and final volume of this series on love. In the first two volumes I discussed how spiritual love manifests in the everyday personal sphere, and then how it can take us into the boundless dimension of Divine Love. Those books paved the way for this one and prepared the ground for its theme—the central journey of the heart. This journey is not simply about love; it is actually more about the way of the heart, the path that leads to the realization of the mystery that many teachings regard as the ultimate nature of everything and the source of all that we experience.

All genuine spiritual paths are oriented toward the realization of this ultimate source. In Kashmiri Shaivism it is known as Shiva; in Advaita Vedanta it is Parabrahman; and in Mahayana Buddhism it is Dharmakaya. For Kabbalists it is Ain Sof, for Christian mystics it is the Father, and for Sufis it is the divine essence or the mysterious essence of God. In this teaching, we refer to this fundamental truth as the Absolute, recognizing that it is pure mystery. This is not to imply that all these names refer to the same experience, for the ultimate mystery reveals itself in different ways in different paths, and in different individual beings. There are, hence, many paths to the awakening to and realization of the ultimate. Some are yogic and meditational paths. Some are devotional and employ the heart. In our own teaching, we can arrive at this realization through different pathways, the path of the heart being a major one. I have discussed the other ways this teaching reveals the mysterious essence of reality in other books; this book is dedicated to the teaching as it manifests in the devotional path of the heart. We can see similarities to other devotional paths, and I borrow poetry from some of them. Poetry is the natural language of the heart, and I begin most chapters with a poem written by a well-known lover of the truth.

The spiritual stirring that initiates the search for the ultimate truth also arises in different ways in different individuals. Some people experience a lack of meaning in their life and are therefore searching for the meaning of life and the point of existence. Some feel they don't know themselves, and so the stirring appears as the desire for self-knowledge or enlightenment. Some feel their life is inherently one of suffering and discontent, and are seeking to end the suffering and find true and lasting happiness.

For some the search is felt directly as a passionate desire to be one with the divine, and that is the nature of the path expressed in this book. This search is powered by an intense yearning for something not yet known or understood, and the growing recognition that the heart will not be satisfied except by finding this hidden mystery and becoming one with it.

The book comes from a teaching I originally gave in a series of talks to the Ridhwan School, and the chapters are basically transcripts of those talks edited to suit the written form. This direct teaching to actual students is the best way of communicating the path of the heart. Because I am speaking from the heart to the heart of the listeners, it is a personal and direct expression of the different stations of the heart. What I say is what I happen to be experiencing at the moment of utterance, which makes it a faithful expression of the heart. In this teaching, I use my own experience as well as the experience of my companions and students in detailing the stages of the path.

We begin the journey by exploring the ordinary human love of the divided heart for its different earthly beloveds. We all love, and we love many people and many things, but the path of the heart begins when we understand that this is only a partial and incomplete function of the human heart. As the spiritual stirring arises in us, we recognize the incompleteness of such loves and the unsatisfactory nature of our lives. The heart is the organ of consciousness that knows this, without being told. It has an innate sense of the truth, and the heart's discontent informs us that we are not yet real and that our lives and endeavors are off the mark. As we listen to the heart and its guidance, we recognize that our experience of satisfaction and fulfillment will always be incomplete until we have found the treasure hidden in our soul, in our consciousness, and primarily in our heart.

I detail all the stages of the path that the heart must follow to find its true love. It is a journey on which the heart learns to shed its ordinary beloveds in order to become so empty that its passionate love is directed purely toward the one Beloved that truly belongs in the heart. This shedding of the heart's familiar loves happens naturally; as the passionate longing and love for the Beloved intensifies, our other loves are set aside and dissolved by this intensity. The natural process of emptying the heart of absolutely everything, good or bad, eventually takes us into mystical poverty, as described by St. John of the Cross in his treatise *The Dark Night of the Soul*.

The passionate love, as we experience and allow its power, thus empties the heart of all loves and desires except for the one that it intuits but does not yet know. The resulting emptiness of the heart is an important station on the path of love. Only when the heart becomes completely empty, and therefore completely pure, can it become the place of revelation of the mystery of existence. The heart is then shown to be the throne of the Beloved, the rightful sole occupant of the heart that is its true abode and the center of its revelation and radiance. Without our knowing or anticipation, and without any effort or striving, the majesty and beauty of the true inner Beloved reveals itself as the unseen nature of the mystical poverty—a scintillating nothingness that has the radiance of the luminous night. We see that this unfathomable mystery is what underlies all of existence and experience and is the source of all revelations and awakenings. This mystery is usually veiled by all the manifestations of reality we experience, both mundane and spiritual. As the last of these veils fall away, we enter a state of intoxication, revelry, and ecstasy, dissolving completely into this luminous darkness. The union we have longed for turns out to be nothing but the cessation of the individual soul and its dissolution into this majestic beauty, leaving only the absolute Beloved to shine as the only and singular reality.

This singularity reveals that the manifest world of form and the nonbeingness of the Beloved are one and the same. From this realization we see that our ordinary loves are simply particular manifestations of the mystery, in forms we have come to love and treasure. The inner Beloved is the source of all, the truth of all, and the complete fulfillment of heart and life. This is how our heartfelt love can be in this world but not of it, when we truly know where this love comes from and what all our loves are beckoning us to.

A. H. Almaas
June 2025

ONE

The Discontent of the Heart

I often say that if the spiritual journey is to be sustained, it needs to be a love affair. In this book we will be looking at the spiritual path as a path of love, a journey of the heart. It's not that I'm going to focus on love itself here—that was the focus of the first volume in this series on love, *Love Unveiled*, which looked at the different aspects of love experienced by individuals in their everyday lives and how they can be gateways to a deeper spiritual awakening. The second volume, *Nondual Love*, took us into the boundless dimension of Divine Love, where all sense of individual boundaries dissolve and our consciousness knows itself to be an expression of a shoreless ocean of love. In this third volume, the path of love and its yearnings will take us even deeper into the mystery. We will be focusing on how the path of love appears and unfolds in relation to the ultimate truth, and it will mean leaving behind all the forms and concepts of divinity that we have previously known and cherished.

The primary method we use on the path of the Diamond Approach is inquiry, which means observing and exploring our own felt experience in the moment and seeking to discriminate what is true in it. Even though inquiry is always focused on the love for truth and the love for realization, its use of the discriminating mind means that people often don't recognize how much this path is a journey of love.

Inquiry was actually a late arrival in my own personal journey, which was above all a journey of the heart, a journey of love. At some point the love became specifically a love of truth, and that opened up the path of inquiry. But love remains the underlying current that drives the path of inquiry, and it is always the primary motive and feeling on our spiritual journey.

Indeed, love plays a fundamental role in all areas of our lives because it is such an inherent and central part of being human. If we look at ourselves and humanity in general, it's clear that we cannot but love. It's not an accident that we love, and it's not as if only some people love and others don't. Yes, we may differ in terms of our capacity for love, but even the most hardened human beings love. We might not think of their love as love in the way that we understand it, but it is still love.

Love is always there in the sense that we always love something. It's not possible to live and not have objects of love—it's universal. The objects of love can be human beings or they might be animals; some people don't love other people, but at least they still love their pet. Objects of love can be activities—sports, watching movies, stamp collecting, photography—and they can also be actual objects. Some people might not love any living things, but they love ice cream or fast cars. Maybe they love their gun. They polish it every day and kiss it, and put it in its nice velvet case—they really do love it. It's hard to recognize that as love, but it is. Some people love hurting other people, but even that's still love. So people differ in their objects of love, the degrees of love they're able to experience, and how mature or immature their love is, but we cannot escape the fact that human beings love.*

We won't focus here on the more unusual and strange manifestations of love. Instead, we'll look at the normal love for human beings and things that is common to most people. And I want to focus on two central features of the way our heart expresses its love.

The first central feature is that we have many objects of love—we don't only love one thing. It would be very difficult to find a human being who only loves one thing, and generally our love is for many different people, things, and activities.

The other main characteristic of love is that the objects of our love are always changing; it's rare that our objects of love stay the same. It's easy to see this by looking at how they have changed since childhood—we've loved so many people since then, one person after another, and we've loved a succession of many different activities and things. What this shows is that the human heart is typically both polygamous and fickle—it has many objects of love, and these objects are always changing. This polygamous and fickle quality of human love is normal, and we have come to accept it as being so natural that we can't imagine how else it could be. We think of it as a healthy thing; some people say that the more things we love, the healthier we are, because that means our heart is more open.

But that's not the whole story, and we can learn more about this polygamy and fickleness particularly in the context of our

---

* See chapter 1 of *Love Unveiled* for more on the different kinds of love and the degrees of maturity of the heart.

relationships. No matter how intense our capacity for love is, at some point we might decide to settle on one person as our primary object of love. That's often difficult for us, to finally settle on one person. And when we do, there is then the next and even bigger task—to remain with that one person. Once these two tasks have been accomplished, a human being is considered to have matured and be capable of a more real and mature love relationship.

For some people, the primary love object they settle on may be something other than a human being—their work or a sport, perhaps—but either way there will still be many other love objects too, and the search for new and different ones will continue. This shows us that it is very difficult for human beings to feel completely satisfied by their love objects—there is a persistent nagging feeling that the heart is not completely contented yet. If we recognize that some level of dissatisfaction and discontent always remains, and nothing turns out to provide the completely fulfilling experience of love that we hope for, it can lead us to an important insight. It begins to explain the polygamy and fickleness of the heart, because we can see that the reason we move from one love object to another is largely because our search for love is never completely satisfied by any of them.

If there's no object of love that completely satisfies us, the heart will never be totally at peace, totally contented and fulfilled in its love, and so it's inevitable that we will have many different love objects and continue to seek out new ones. We might be blessed with some periods in our life when we feel contented in a way that feels complete for a while—perhaps when we've fallen in love and just got together with that person, or when we've found our dream house or our dream job and everything feels perfect. But it's realism rather than cynicism to acknowledge that such phases don't last, and that the nagging sense that something is missing in our life gradually returns.

So discontent and dissatisfaction are clearly prevalent characteristics of the human heart. Even when we love someone or something dearly and we're committed to them, it's very rare that we say, "I'm completely happy—there's no dissatisfaction, no complaint, and my love is complete." If we go into it further, we'll find that in truth, complete satisfaction is not actually possible, and the extent to which we recognize that is a measure of our maturity. It's a sign of immaturity if we're still searching for the right person, the right house, or the right job and thinking that one of these days it's going to happen and we're going to find "the one"—the object that will completely satisfy our heart's longing. When we recognize that our relationship with earthly objects of love will *never* feel complete, we mature. Only then do we become more able to settle into a more real and satisfying relationship with the things we love.

When we inquire into, explore, and wonder about this discontent of the heart, this lack of a sense of complete satisfaction and closure regarding the question of love, we recognize that it is a very deep and profound discontent. It's this discontent that has driven many of us to keep looking for the perfectly satisfying object, and we will do this until we are mature enough to see that the heart's discontent has nothing to do with any imperfection in our love objects. Their apparent flaws don't explain the mystery of why, after so long, the heart still hasn't found what it's looking for. It can take a long time to recognize that the depth and profundity of our dissatisfaction means it's not going to be resolved by finding the right person, the right object, or the right situation. The real reason for it is that all these love objects, all these beloveds, are just stand-ins for what the heart is really looking for—its true Beloved. They may come close sometimes, but they will never completely do it for us. So we mature by realizing that there is no new object to be found that will finally prove to be the true Beloved, because the true Beloved is not an object that we can find on Earth. It's unlike any earthly beloved that we're familiar with.

When we recognize that, two things tend to happen. We become more mature in what we expect from our earthly loves, more accepting of them, because we recognize that the imperfections in them and our lack of total satisfaction with them is natural and normal. At the same time, our love goes inward; the heart turns inward, looking now for its true Beloved. Having seen that the discontent we often feel with our love objects is an expression of a larger underlying discontent, we recognize that it has to do with our fundamental alienation from our inner nature. We do not behold our true nature completely, so our knowing of what we are is incomplete. Not knowing our own depth means our experience of life is not complete, so we feel discontent. How can it be otherwise when we don't really know what the Beloved is, and haven't even glimpsed it yet? We've thought it was this person or that thing, and the heart has gone from one thing to another, looking for it here and there, but after each one the heart has said, "No, that's not it."

So people get confused and make mistakes about this. They say to their lover, "No, I'm sorry, you're not the one for me. I've found someone else." And it's true—maybe for some of us there is the question of finding the right person to be our partner. But that doesn't resolve the question fundamentally, and if we think it should, it's because we've confused looking for the true Beloved with looking for the right person. We've been looking for the person who's going to fulfill all the needs of our heart, but there is no such person. No human love, no earthly love object, can satisfy the love of the heart because the true object of its love is within.

So the story of the inner journey of love has been there from the beginning, but now we're becoming more aware of it. With a certain degree of maturity in the heart, we begin to understand that love is not only about external objects. We become more conscious that resolving the question of love is actually an inner journey toward an intangible object of love, and so our inner journey is a question of love. We can say that our heart graduates as it moves from a focus on tangible external objects to an intangible inner one—to something we might call God, true nature, truth, freedom, or liberation. Whatever we call it—here we are referring to it as the Beloved—it is only this that will satisfy the heart's longing.

But this is just the beginning. These are just the first stirrings of a recognition that the discontent we feel in our love relationships is an expression of a larger discontent, which in turn is an expression of our alienation from reality. We will see that the inner journey of love has to go much deeper, and the heart has to mature much more before it can find the complete satisfaction of its love and arrive at its true Beloved. We might call it by that name, but as I said, in truth we don't really know what it is at this point, and we don't know what it is for various reasons, which will become clear as we continue to explore.

For now, we'll look at a poem. This poem also appears in my book *Luminous Night's Journey*, and it will give us an idea as to what we will be learning about on this journey of love.

The Guest Arrives Only at Night

Annihilate mind in heart,
Divorce heart from all relationships,
And then love,
Love passionately,
Consume yourself with passion
For the secret one.

When you are absolutely poor,
When you are no more,
Then the Guest will appear
And occupy his place,
In the secret chamber,
His abode,
The heart he gave you.

He is the inner of the inner,
He is the secret,
He is the Guest,
And he arrives
Only at night.

So the poem talks about having passion for "the secret one." But why is it secret? Well, that's because we don't know what it is. In some sense, this book is all about understanding this poem, going deeper and deeper into it until we really know what it means. But we need to start at the beginning, and we're doing that by exploring the condition of our own heart now, particularly its polygamy and fickleness. Not in a judgmental way but just to recognize it, because we will see as we go on, this polygamy and fickleness of our heart is only natural and normal, and it does in fact express a deep truth. But it also expresses an ignorance, a lack of understanding about the nature of our heart.

The fickleness and polygamy of the heart with its multiplicity of love objects will continue even when you have turned toward the inner path. It will take a long time to understand and fully recognize how the heart is divided, and what that actually does to the heart, which naturally seeks unity. But we'll make a start now, because the beginning of the possibility of unification comes through the recognition that the true Beloved of the heart is something intangible, something that we don't even know yet. In truth, the heart does know it, but the eyes have not seen it. It's because the heart knows its true Beloved that it is still discontented—it feels the pain of not being united with it.

In time we'll learn what it really means to be united with the Beloved and how this affects our relationship with our earthly loves. We'll learn how to unify our love and harmonize our heart, but we can't do this until we recognize that it is divided. That's why we're doing this inquiry into our personal experience of the discontent of the heart.

So now it's time for an exercise in which we can each explore our own heart and learn more about all this for ourselves.

Practice Session: Biography of the Heart's Loves and Discontent

· · ·

If you can work with other people, you should do this exercise in a group of three. If you're alone, you can do it in writing.

Each person will do a monologue for fifteen minutes. If you haven't done one before, a monologue is when you talk (or write) for fifteen minutes, and the idea is to express whatever comes up spontaneously, without censoring anything. You maintain an attitude of curiosity and interest in whatever arises in you, and you keep exploring it, seeing what you can notice about it. Whatever you notice—thoughts, feelings, physical sensations, or a combination of these—can help you to discover more about it. As each person talks, the other two just listen, without interrupting. They are witnesses to your inquiry.

In this monologue you basically want to uncover a biography of your heart. You want to explore its history of love, especially in relation to its contentment in love. How contented is your heart in its loves, and what keeps it from being completely contented? So it's a personal exploration of the love relationships in your own life—with people or things—and how contented your heart feels.

There will be something for everyone to find because this discontent is universal. Regardless of how happy we are with our different loves, the discontent will still be there one way or another. Each of us will know it in different ways and to different depths, so that's what we want to explore. Yes, some of us may have achieved various degrees of contentment of the heart through the loves we have found in life, but there will still be an incompleteness. When we see that incompleteness, we want to explore what's behind the discontent. Perhaps some of us still think it's because we haven't found the right person or the right job or the right house, or whatever. So perhaps we will see such things, and we don't want to negate these completely normal ways of feeling the discontent, because that will block the inquiry into where it is coming from. Don't say, "Okay, I realize those things are not important, so I'm only going to look at why I'm feeling discontent because of my disconnection from the inner Beloved." No, you want to make it personal to you, and just let it unfold as you notice whatever the source of your discontent seems to be. And *then* you can go deeper into it: "Is that really the only reason why I'm still discontented?"

. . . . .

Questions and Comments

Student: I saw in the monologue how my history and the resulting object relations* have created a personality for seeking. And there is something specific about how my object relations direct me toward seeking out certain objects, but more than that, doing it in a certain way, and how deeply I believe that that's how I'm going to get what I want.

A. H. Almaas: So you saw that related to the discontent?

S: Yes, in the sense that I keep doing that, but it's not working.

AH: So do you think you're discontented because that's not working?

S: I don't know if that's the reason. I just know that that's what's happening.

---

* "Object relations" refers to the recognition that it is through one's earliest relationships with others that the basic impression of oneself (the perceived "subject" in the relationship) is formed, and that this is dependent on whatever impression one has formed of the other person (the perceived "object" of the relationship). The internalized memory of these early object relations is rarely a true reflection of the actual relationship. Nevertheless, the resulting fixed impressions of self and other, plus the emotional charge felt in the relationship between them (love, desire, frustration, etc.), are carried over into all subsequent relationships and interactions in life, acting as filters through which they are experienced.

AH: That's good, because we just want to see what comes up as we explore.

S: What became clear to me was the hunger, the looking for something, for the object that is what I hope will fill me, and that object was love and value. And being present in that, I realized that a place in me basically feels deficient and empty. And it's not only with regard to objects outside of me but also with regard to objects inside of me. What's constant is the place that gets visited, either by an impact from the outside or by an essential experience, which both come and go, and what's left is this place that is hungry and looking around for something. And that's the identity, which feels deficient, and it tries to deal with this deficiency by filling it or by hoping it can be filled. And there's hoping and rejecting involved—I hope for a better outcome in the future, and I reject what's there right now because it doesn't feel like it's doing it for me. That's the constant process as I'm evaluating my surroundings. I guess it's ego activity.

AH: So how did you see that connected to the love?

S: The love is supposed to be the remedy. And I've experienced it as a remedy, as a balm for that deep feeling of deficiency and all the activity associated with it—the pain basically.

AH: So you're talking about the hunger for love?

S: Yes, I am basically.

AH: So in that situation we're seeing the role of the identity and the role of the need for the object, which then become mixed in with the question of love. The focus of our work right now is not actually the need for love. We're just exploring love here in terms of the state of the heart. I explored the need for love in other books that deal with the love aspect and the love dimensions.* But we see that it will still arise here, because as we deal with the question of love, our own need for love will arise, and that becomes a strong and very important factor in our love relationships.

S: You mentioned the quality of polygamy as being part of love, and it seems to me that a good deal of my discontent comes from my ego wanting love to be safe, for the way I love in the world to be safe, so that life feels safe. That quality of polygamy in love means that love moves around a lot more than I'm often comfortable with. Can you say anything more about that?

AH: So you're saying there is a fear of polygamy?

S: Yeah, where maybe you want somebody to love you and you're afraid they'll love somebody else.

AH: So you're afraid of other people's polygamy?

S: Yeah.

AH: But not your own?

S: [*laughs*] Yeah. But in terms of just simple affection, it can be that way. It's sort of just being afraid of the freedom of love, where love loves many things and many people.

AH: So that's true. Other people do that. How about you?

S: Yeah, me too.

AH: You too. And are you not scared of that?

S: Well, I guess my own image of myself is that I'm a bit more stable than that.

AH: Yes, I'm sure many of us think that. And you know, it's true; some of us are more stable than others in terms of staying with

---

* See *Love Unveiled* and *Nondual Love*, the first two volumes of this series on love.

certain objects of love. But the thing about love, when you talk about safety, is that there is no such thing as safety when it comes to love. And that's true for any kind of love. The only way you can be relatively safe in love is to love an inanimate object, and even that can be broken or disappear. So really, when it comes to love, you have to be prepared to be vulnerable. In fact the best way to go about love is to not care about safety. If we care about safety, love simply won't happen. We're talking about the heart, and the heart can't function without vulnerability. It's as simple as that.

S: In looking at the biography of my heart, I became aware of all the losses, all the blockages, all the experiences of love and all the experiences of pain. And then of having encountered a period of time when I actually felt a complete lack of love—to myself, from myself to the world, and from the world to me. Nothing. A flower wouldn't bring a smile. My job, my achievements, my creativity, whatever. And so I decided that since it felt like I was dying, I would go to Hawaii and experience this dying there for a week. And nothing there cheered me up—not the ocean, not the turtles, not the sky, not the sun, nothing. I just felt a lack of love, and I never thought it would ever come back or that anything would interest me at all. Everything felt empty, and there was no love. Then little by little, and all by itself, came a different experience of love than I'd had before. And . . . there's pain, and there's love. There's sweetness and there's poignancy and there's a flowingness without attachment at times, and the heart feels soft. I thought that if you experienced love, it would be a certain way, but this movement in love, can you talk more about that, the vulnerability part? Because it's new to me. I'm just discovering it and feeling it.

AH: It's a characteristic of the heart that it's always changing. The heart can't stay in the same condition. So it's the same thing with love. It's always transforming from one thing to another. It's not just the objects of love that change; the kinds of love change too, all the inner states of the heart keep changing. That's why the Sufis like to use the Arabic word for the heart, *qalb*, which comes from the word *qalab*, meaning "turn over" or "change." That comes from the fact it's an organ that is always changing or transforming, and that's part of the need for vulnerability, the fact that it can never stay the same. But that also expresses our true nature, our true condition, which is always changing and transforming, bringing many kinds of experiences and impressions. So there are many ways of experiencing love, and many ways of experiencing things around love. There are many kinds of hurt, many kinds of sadness, many kinds of loss, many kinds of pain. But for the person who loves, who is a true lover, these are not of any concern. Hurt, sadness, rejection, fear, terror—these are not the concern of the lover. The concern of the lover is whether the Beloved is there or not. All these other things are just side effects. If we're willing to go through them, as many of them as possible, then fine, if it gets us closer to what we love. Hurt and sadness and longing, they are just part of it. So if we don't want to feel hurt or sadness, rejection or abandonment, then we're not lovers yet—we haven't really started the path of love yet. On the path of love, sadness, hurt, rejection, and pain are all a large part of that path. For those who are on it, it is completely acceptable, part of the natural course of things. There's nothing unusual about it, that's how it is. So there is no safety, no stability, no constancy, no predictability. That's the case with any kind of love, whether it be in terms of the inner path or normal human love.

TWO

The Divided Heart

We'll begin with a poem. I'll begin most chapters of this book with a poem that relates to the subject matter. This one is by Kabir, an Indian poet, and it's from *The Kabir Book*, translated by Robert Bly.

> Inside this clay jug
> there are canyons and pine mountains,
> and the maker of canyons and pine mountains!
> All seven oceans are inside,
> and hundreds of millions of stars.
> The acid that tests gold is there,
> and the one who judges jewels.
> And the music that comes
> from the strings no one touches,
> and the source of all water.
> If you want the truth, I will tell you the truth:
> Friend, listen: the God whom I love is inside.*

* Kabir, *The Kabir Book: Forty-Four of the Ecstatic Poems of Kabir*, ed. Robert Bly (Beacon Press, 1977), 6.

When it says "inside," it doesn't mean just inside us. It means beyond the apparent, so inside of everything. Of course, the way to approach it is inside ourselves—it's difficult to approach it by going inside somebody else, though some of us may try to do it that way.

And just a reminder that in our exploring of love, we don't want to get hung up in thinking purely in terms of human relationships. The moment I mention the word "love," many people automatically think only of their experience as it pertains to other people: Do they have a lover or not? Yes, human relationship is a major and important expression of love, but love can be expressed in many other ways too. As I said before, some people don't love people—maybe they don't even like people. Some people love ice cream more than anything else.

When I talk about love, some people say, "Well, I can only feel love when I'm feeling safe enough to allow my vulnerability." But do you need to feel safe to love ice cream? And when you're excited about your new phone and all the things you can do on it, do you worry about feeling vulnerable? Because that's all love too. So issues around safety and vulnerability might come up in certain situations and limit our capacity to feel love, but our love can still be free to manifest in other areas of life. So let's not get fixated on human relationships and therefore think we don't really know what love is. Some people love food above all—they adore different kinds of foods. Some people love clothes, some people love art. And some people love technology and gadgets—judging by the amount of time some people spend looking at their phones, you might easily think they love them more than they love other people!

Love includes a range of feelings, including appreciating, enjoying and taking pleasure in something, as well as giving and sharing in an outpouring of affection and generosity. It also includes desire, longing, and yearning. Some people tell me, "Well, I don't experience love. I only experience desire." But why would you desire something if you didn't love it? If you really love something, you will feel a desire to be close to it. And if you want to be so close to something that you want to become one with it, why is that? It's basically inspired by love.

This brings in another characteristic of love, which is that it is orgiastic—it has an energy that can easily become unrestrained and uncontrollable, more so than with the mind or even the instincts. We usually think that the instincts, especially those arising in the genitals, are the most orgiastic part of human nature, but in fact the genitals are not as orgiastic as the heart. If you look at it more closely, the genitals actually have a narrow range of experience, and also a very short memory. The genitals would happily do pretty much the same thing every day—that would be fine for them. The heart is different. The heart is more fluid and changeable, and it has a much wider and more open range of expression. The mind tends not to be so orgiastic, but when the heart is involved, it seeks by its very nature to dissolve the boundaries and limits in our experience. Love seeks to overflow and break down any dams and barriers so that it can flow with abundance. So when our genitals do find a wider range of expression, it's usually because our heart is more involved. It's only when the heart is not involved that we see how limited the instincts are—without the heart, we are biologically hardwired to follow fixed patterns of instinctual behavior.

And that's the defining characteristic of human love—its expression is not governed purely by biological imperative. It is governed by biology to some extent; just as with animals, loving our mate and loving our children helps to further our survival and the propagation of the species. But by its very nature, human love can inspire behavior that goes counter to our own survival and convenience, and even counter to the propagation of our genes. In fact what most captivates people about love stories is how the lovers often show a total disregard for the consequences of their passion. And really, if you care about the consequences of your love, then your behavior is still being determined by your instincts rather than love. True lovers aren't interested in the consequences—they just want to be with their beloved, whoever or whatever it happens to be. So love does have mind in it, and it does have instinct in it, but there is also love that goes beyond those and is free from both. Love, as we know, can be very strange, weird, and odd, and it can also be very beautiful, wonderful, and glorious.

Being orgiastic, love doesn't like boundaries and barriers. It doesn't like separation, and it makes us want to bring things together. So when you love ice cream, for instance, it's not enough to just look at it through the window. Notice that. You stand in front of the ice-cream parlor and see all the different flavors of ice cream, and your love of ice cream will push you to want to go inside and buy a few scoops and make sure you get completely, thoroughly united with them.

Now, in human love relationships we might control ourselves sometimes because of the fear of vulnerability and the issues it brings up. But most of us don't keep control of our love in all areas of life. When it comes to the dessert menu, many people are not so controlled. Some people are not able to control their love of shopping: With other human beings they're always well behaved and they try to be more mature and adult, but when it comes to shopping, they lose it.

It is in the nature of the heart to lose it. If it doesn't lose it, it's not heart, it's something else. And losing it means losing control. It means losing defenses, losing limitations, losing discrimination, losing all consideration of consequences—ultimately it means losing anything that can be lost and completely given up. So that's why the heart is orgiastic; it's where there is a flooding of spirit through the soul, seeking unity no matter what. And that's why love frequently appears as desire, as longing and yearning. These are all expressions of wanting to be near, wanting to be as close as possible to what we love. We all have experience of that, so we all know the power of love in some way. Yes, we might not know it in its purity, and we might not know it in its maturity, but we do know it in some of the various ways it manifests.

We've talked already about how our love can mature, and how the key feature of that maturity is recognizing that the Beloved that will truly satisfy the heart is something intangible—something inside, as Kabir says in the poem. So when I talk about mature love, I don't mean that the love is more controlled and restrained. Nor do I mean that it is better behaved and more mundane. Mature love can be just as orgiastic, just as flooding in its manifestation, as we see in the ecstatic poems we're reading here. But the ecstasy they express isn't just the blissful kind. Yes, it's an orgiastic ecstasy that brings a flooding of pleasure and joyfulness, but it also brings yearning, longing, pain, and burning—all this is included in the ecstasy. For the lover who really wants to be with the Beloved, feeling this yearning, feeling this longing, feeling the agony of separation, feeling all the pangs of love, is just as important as feeling the love itself.

For the true lover, the only possible respite from feeling these pangs of love is to be with the Beloved—to feel the closeness, the nearness, and ultimately the union with the Beloved. So when we talk of following the path of love, it doesn't mean that the goal is to learn about love itself. Nor are we talking here about developing our capacity to love or a search for enlightenment. We're not on this path because we feel we are ignorant and need to learn more. The path is simply a search for the Beloved we feel separate from. And it's because we feel separated from it that there is the yearning, the longing, the pain, the wounding, the hurt, and the emptiness. We feel all of these—for the lover, well of course, how else could it be? In fact, the lover doesn't want those feelings to go away unless it's because the Beloved is there. You know how it is when you're deeply in love and you're separated from your beloved; you don't really want to make the longing and the pain go away and just forget about it all. The pain is a testament to your love for what you are separated from, and the only way you want it to go away is by your beloved being there. It's the same thing with the inner Beloved.

So it's not a bad thing when we're in love and we're feeling the intense pain of separation, or we're afraid we won't get to be with the one we love and feel a deep longing and emptiness. These are normal things for a lover to feel—they're an essential part of the way of love, the way of the heart. If we don't have those things, we won't have love itself, and we won't therefore have the Beloved. So to be brokenhearted is not a bad thing for a lover. In fact a true lover wants to be brokenhearted as many times as possible. If pining away with a broken heart is what it takes to keep your heart alive, then that's much better than not feeling anything at all for your beloved.

We can see then that the heart has a flexibility that allows it to feel this mix of agony and ecstasy in both the outer and the inner world, and that's because the heart is the locus of the soul where true nature penetrates and comes through into the realm of embodiment. It is the meeting place of the tangible and the intangible. It's where the intangible manifests within the tangible.

We'll return now to the polygamous and fickle nature of the heart, which we discussed in the first chapter. Actually, it's not just polygamous; it's what Sigmund Freud called "polymorphously perverse," which means that it can love absolutely anything, anywhere, anytime. It can even love any part of anything, which is how fetishism develops. So it's natural for the human heart to end up with many loves, many beloveds, many objects of love, and that's why it is so divided in the beginning. We've seen how the heart will focus more at first on the tangible—the physical and external. As we mature, however, we recognize the inevitable sense of incompleteness and discontent that this focus on the outer world brings. So the heart begins to turn. It begins to change direction and look inward, looking beyond the veils of appearance for the inner Beloved that will satisfy it.

We will see later how the polygamous and fickle nature of the heart is actually expressing a deep truth, but it is not possible to see this truth until we truly behold the ultimate Beloved. In the beginning, because we can't see the underlying truth behind it, our polygamous and fickle behavior is a barrier to beholding the Beloved, bringing frustration and dissatisfaction. Naturally we think the dissatisfaction is a problem, but it's not in truth; it is simply evidence of the fact that the heart knows its Beloved. It doesn't know it consciously or conceptually but primordially. It knows it in the sense that when the Beloved is not there, it knows it isn't there. And when the Beloved is there, it knows it is there. However, if we ask the heart, "What is it that you know?"—it's got no idea.

That doesn't stop us from giving it a name, such as God, the divine, spirit, or truth, although having a name for it doesn't alter the fact that for a long time we don't really know what it is. But then the heart does not need to know. It doesn't need to have any name for it to love it, want it, and long for it, and to burn with that longing. The heart doesn't need explicit words, images, concepts, or forms to feel its love—it just loves.

Regarding my own journey, I can say that for about ten or twenty years I went through this process of constantly loving and wanting something, feeling a deep yearning and desire for it, without really having any idea what it was that I was looking for. I knew it wasn't something that the eyes can see or the hands can touch. So if somebody had asked me, "What is it? What does it look like? How does it feel?"—I wouldn't have been able to answer, because I didn't know. But that didn't stop my heart from passionately loving and desiring this unknown something, and feeling whether I was near to it or distant from it. Deep down, the heart has this primordial capacity to know unconsciously, or rather preconsciously, what the Beloved feels like, so it knows whether it is close to it or not. I remember times when I had the definite feeling that I was far away from it. But again, if somebody had asked me what I was far away from, I would have had to say, "I don't know." It's just a simple and undeniable fact that the Beloved feels near sometimes, and when that happens, the heart feels happy and becomes ecstatic. The sense of nearness is a very particular and unmistakable experience, and when it comes, we know it immediately. Something inside us says, "Yeah, it's here," and there's a feeling of celebration. But it took many years before I could recognize it well enough to say, "Ah yes, this is the Beloved." When the Beloved finally shows up, we recognize it—it is one hundred percent clear and certain, make no mistake about it. It doesn't matter what anybody says, the heart knows it for what it is. And the more we know and recognize the inner Beloved, the more our heart moves inward toward it and our love for it increases.

However, the heart is still divided. We may have discovered our love for the inner Beloved, but naturally, for a long time most of us remain more preoccupied with our love for all manner of things in the external world, so there are still many beloveds. It's very rare for someone's love for the inner Beloved to swiftly take precedence over all the other love objects. There may be moments of orgiastic experience of the heart, when our love for the inner Beloved becomes more intense and we feel that the inner Beloved has revealed itself to us more fully. But if we look more closely at these occasions when our love is more intensely focused on the inner Beloved and we feel more unified with it, we can see that we usually only allow this to happen to the extent that it doesn't challenge our other love relationships too much. That means we can still have the same relationship with our other loves as we move toward our realization. Otherwise, we get anxious: "What happens if I commit myself fully to my relationship with the Beloved? Can I still have my relationship with my partner? Can I eat ice cream? Can I love my children?" These are the kinds of questions that come up. "Can I go running? Is it okay to go skiing if I'm enlightened?" People ask, "So if I'm enlightened and I'm realized, do I have to just sit there and meditate?" That's what many people think, you see—they're worried about what will happen to all their other loves. And indeed, understanding how we can relate to our external love objects as the heart focuses ever more exclusively on the inner Beloved is far from easy.

So our heart continues to be divided after we've become more aware of the inner Beloved, and as well as the competition we've always felt between the many different people and things that we love, all these loves now appear to be in competition with the inner Beloved too. All of our love objects are continually vying for our attention; they compete for our energy, for our time, and for space. And for a long time the inner Beloved becomes just one of those objects of love, also competing for our attention.

Perhaps when we've had a good time with somebody who's loving toward us and we're feeling secure in their love, maybe then we'll devote ourselves fully to our practices and have some good meditations. We feel with great sincerity, "I really love the truth. I really love God. I only want to see God." But the rest of the time, we're more preoccupied with other things.

So becoming aware of the inner Beloved is just the very beginning of the journey of the heart. The heart's polygamy and division continue to act as a barrier on that journey because we can never forget all those other beloveds. It means that our energy, our libido, is continually parceled out and divided among so many things that there's only so much left for the inner Beloved, who we sometimes forget altogether. Once we get to know the inner Beloved better, we'll see how impossible this situation is. It takes us a long time to appreciate some important characteristics of the inner Beloved and understand why they mean that having many loves just does not work at this stage of the journey.

Most important of these characteristics is that the inner Beloved is completely polygamous but requires monogamy from us.

That's the first thing; it will love everybody, but there's a sense in which it wants you to only love it—nobody and nothing else. If we see it in human terms, we could say that the inner Beloved is one hundred percent possessive and completely jealous. If you so much as look at somebody else, it says, "See you next time." It can't share the heart with anybody else. It says, "The heart is my place. If you put anybody else there, you'll never find me."

But it's hard for us to avoid doing that when we have so many objects of love, because with any object of love, what do you want to do? When you feel the love for it, you want to take it and put it in your heart. You want it to be so close to you, to be at the center of your being. You want the center of your being to be completely inseparable from the center of the being of that beloved, completely united, whether the beloved is a human being, a horse, or ice cream. Well, at least God is merciful by putting the stomach not too far away from the heart, so uniting with ice cream is pretty straightforward. However, love for a human being is a little more complicated. We have to get somewhat entangled with each other in order to get close, don't we? And even if we don't get entangled physically, there's the emotional entanglement.

The problem is, the more we pay attention to our other loves, the less the inner Beloved will appear to us. Fortunately, the converse is also true—the more we pay attention to the inner Beloved, the more we value it and give it precedence, the more it will reveal itself. It will manifest itself in various ways in the heart, and the more unified the heart becomes in loving the inner Beloved, the less it will focus on other objects of love. But the hard truth is that we will not get to the ultimate point where the inner Beloved reveals itself completely, in the way that will fully satisfy the heart, unless our heart becomes one hundred percent empty of all other beloveds. It simply won't. It has to become the only Beloved for that to happen, and that is quite a challenge for us, as we know.

So we're acknowledging that this challenge needs to be fully faced at some point on the path of realization, with no compromises. We might still be trying to make accommodations up to that point, perhaps saying, "Okay then, I'll limit it to just one person I sometimes focus all my love on." And then, "Well, of course I can also love my cat. And my hats, ice cream, and my afternoon stroll—I think I can love those in ways that won't distract me from the Beloved too much." But in the end, the inner Beloved will say, "No, it doesn't matter what it is. If you love it, it's in competition with me. You say you're just keeping a little bit of love for it, but that means your heart is a little bit divided. It doesn't want just me, and it's only when you want just me that your heart is undivided. And it's only then that I'll show myself fully." This is why the polygamy and the fickleness of the heart becomes an issue and a barrier on this journey.

Many of us will be familiar with this dynamic, perhaps from experiencing our love for the truth, for Being, for God, for the divine, or simply for love itself—all ways of referring to the Beloved. Whatever we may have called it, we know the experience of our love going through vicissitudes—always fluctuating, always going back and forth. At times this love fades, and so our commitment to make it primary gets forgotten. We get involved with other loves, and abandon it in some sense. But then we remember, and the love for the Beloved comes back. Sometimes it reappears as a quiet yearning—there's a gentle burning in the heart that leaves the soul feeling a little bit of yearning for the

Beloved. The love that is then reawakened might be gentle, sweet, and delicate, accompanied by a soft, quiet feeling of appreciation. That appreciation might then grow stronger; it becomes more powerful and the sense of value in it is heightened. And our love can then become passionate again, deep and intense, flooding the soul and overwhelming the senses.

Just as our love and appreciation for the Beloved can be felt in many different ways and to varying degrees, it's the same with the desire, the wanting, the yearning, the sense of separation, the pangs of love, and the feelings of hurt, abandonment, and emptiness. The range of the heart is infinite. Some languages reflect this by having different words for love, each referring to a certain kind of love, with a certain quality. The ancient Greeks, for example, had among other words: *eros*—romantic, passionate love; *philia*—friendly affectionate love; *storge*—unconditional familial love; *agape*—selfless, universal love. There are also many words in some languages for different kinds and degrees of longing, yearning, and feelings of separation. We don't have so many words for love in English, but the heart can know all these states and feelings with or without words.

It's also important to note that when it comes to love, we cannot be proud or arrogant and be a lover.* That's because to really be a lover means that when the Beloved is absent, we are willing to feel separated, to feel abandoned, to feel the unfulfilled desire and yearning, to feel the incompleteness, and to feel deficient. A proud person doesn't want to feel these things—how can pride tolerate a feeling of deficiency? So humility is

---

* As is expressed in the well-known letter of St. Paul to the Corinthians: "Love does not vaunt itself, is not puffed up," (1 Cor 3:4).

a very important quality for the heart. Humility, truthfulness, openness, vulnerability, a lack of control, and a lack of restraint. As we work through this material, you may experience some of these difficult feelings coming up around love—wanting it, needing it, missing it, and feeling the hurt and the abandonment of losing it. But we're not going to be focusing on these things. We just need to recognize from the beginning that they are part and parcel of the path of love. We can practice humility and just let them be there.

Many of us have already experienced what's called "the opening of the heart." There comes a time in our life when we experience the heart opening in a certain way, when it becomes able to feel things more intensely, more deeply. Openness of the heart sounds wonderful, because people often think it means only ecstasy and joy. And yes, it can bring ecstasy and all the orgiastic, rapturous feelings of love. But as we saw earlier, when the heart is open, it opens to the whole range of emotions, so we will also begin to feel more of our vulnerability, our sadness, our hurt, and our wanting and yearning. We feel the love and the deprivation, and both are felt in a deeper and more powerful way. This is the openness of the heart.

The mind would prefer to bypass these intensely difficult feelings, but we can't let the mind guide the heart. If the mind tries to guide what the heart feels, then it's a form of control—it means there is something from outside of the heart that wants to direct or contain it. And the simple truth is that by its very nature the heart knows the Beloved, and it doesn't need any guidance at all on what to feel about it. So if we feel a painful sense of distance, if we feel a sense of separation and abandonment, if we feel a sense of insufficiency and emptiness, a sense of hurt, desire,

The Divided Heart 31

longing, and yearning, then we are on the right track. We don't want to control these things. We want to let them be felt as freely, as completely, and as deeply as possible.

Of course, issues from our childhood around love and our various early objects of love will arise. That's fine, let them arise. Sure, you can try to understand more about them, but the most important thing on the path of love is that the heart continues to be open. You don't really need to keep analyzing how your mother didn't love you or how your father hated you—just feel the feelings. Let the feelings flood you. We tend to want to protect ourselves from these things, but if we do that, we protect ourselves from having a heart. And our love is not going to move to the spiritual dimension if we try to constrain it that way.

So there will be disappointments to be felt. There will be hurts, fears, and even terrors. But these are just fuel for the path. It doesn't mean something's wrong—it's what's supposed to happen. We need that to happen to get a deeper understanding of where we are with love and for the heart to move toward loving the intangible Beloved. If we want to stay safe, if we want a practical plan, if we only want immediate satisfaction, we won't be able to follow the path of love, the path of the heart. That path means years, maybe decades, of heartache. And to find what we are seeking, we need to be guided by something in us that really knows the ultimate object, and that is the heart. The mind doesn't know, nor do the instincts.

This is why complete freedom of the heart is necessary if it is to mature and grow, so that we come to see the limitations of its ordinary loves and our love begins to deepen. Only with this freedom will we begin to have moments when our love becomes so overwhelmingly strong and passionate, so intense and courageous, that we forget all about our other beloveds and all our other concerns. Sometimes we will just feel a complete love for the inner Beloved even though we don't know what it is. And we can't know for sure whether it's going to respond to this love in a way that brings the fulfillment we desire. So we need to get to some place where our heart is completely open, completely loving, and completely vulnerable, and then love passionately without any promise of a response. If we say, "I'm too insecure for that. I can't love like that without some guarantee that I'm not going to be hurt," the inner Beloved says, "Ah, sorry, no deal. I'm afraid you need some more time to get cooked by experience. You need to let your heart become like a shish kebab."

So it's by no means easy for the heart to fulfill the Beloved's demand to divest itself of all other beloveds, but we have to accept that this is the only way the ultimate Beloved can manifest itself fully, completely, and clearly to the heart. You see, sometimes true nature can manifest itself completely in ways that won't do it for the heart. The heart won't recognize its Beloved until it has manifested itself directly to the heart, and it can't do that if the heart is still divided and contains remnants of its other loves.

One of the stories that many Sufi schools use to illustrate this is the story of the Kaaba, which is said to be the house of God in Islam. It's a black stone building in the shape of a cube that was built by Abraham as the house of his God, and it became the place of pilgrimage for all who followed his faith.

Now, Abraham is significant in Western history because he brought a new concept to the world. Before him, it was common for people to have many gods. There were different gods for different areas of life—the god of fertility, the god of marriage, the god of rain, the god of floods, the god of agriculture, the god of the sea, and so on. But Abraham said, "No, there's only one God." He told people that polytheism—what we're calling polygamy—is wrong; monotheism (monogamy) is the only way when it comes to God. Many of you will be familiar with this as it was expressed in the first of the Ten Commandments later given to Moses: "You shall have no other gods before me."

Although Abraham built the Kaaba and made this stipulation, the belief in many gods persisted for hundreds of years in Mecca, the part of the Arabian Peninsula where the Kaaba was. In time, people brought statues and ornaments of their own gods and put them inside the Kaaba. So instead of being Abraham's place of God, it became a place of pilgrimage for people praying to many different gods.

The Sufis then tell the story of Muhammad, who had many battles with the people of Mecca before he finally conquered it. When he did, he went by himself to the Kaaba, took an axe inside, and knocked down all the statues and ornaments that represented the various gods. He threw them all out and said, "This is the house of God. And there is only one God. He is not going to appear if you have all these idols filling his place."

For Sufis, the Kaaba and the heart are the same thing, so on the inner journey of the heart we have to do the same as Muhammad—empty the heart by taking out all the idols that we worship, all the other things that we love, so it becomes one hundred percent available for the true God, the true Beloved, to appear and take its place there. So this story tells us something more about the heart—that like the Kaaba, the heart is created purely and solely for the ultimate Beloved, but we have filled it with many idols. For the heart, loving many things is like loving many gods, so polygamy and idolatry are the same thing.

Practice Session: The Divided Loyalty of the Heart

• • •

In this exercise you will work if possible with one or two other people. Each person in the group will do a monologue for fifteen minutes. If you are alone, write out your exploration for fifteen minutes.

Explore the situation of your heart in terms of its divided loyalty, its lack of unified faithfulness, its many beloveds. You want to consider the many objects that compete for your love with the Beloved—your inner truth—and how this competition manifests for you personally. We don't see it at the beginning as disloyalty or lack of unified faithfulness; we see it as ordinary human life. But let's look at it in light of the fact that we have become more aware of the inner Beloved. We want to see how all these loves compete with it in our heart and vie for our love.

• • • • •

Questions and Comments

Student: I'm just curious. I was struck by the apparent contradiction between Muhammad allowing men to have only one God but four wives. [*laughter*]

A. H. Almaas: That's good. Not only that, Muhammad had thirteen wives himself.

S: But doesn't that act as even more of a distraction and a dividing of the love?

AH: I think it does, yeah. At least these days it would. I don't know about those days. It's a good question, and a question, actually, that we won't be able to answer until later on. We need first to understand more about what the Beloved is.

S: I noticed that it seems like the effect of the competing love objects is to keep me safe and kind of reined in. If I go with the inner Beloved, all hell is gonna break loose, and so there's a feeling of tamping down and dividing myself in a way that kind of keeps me safe. It keeps me knowing myself, and it's the opposite of unrestrained and unleashed and uncontrolled.

AH: Right. So that shows that one thing that the division of the heart does is preserve our sense of self, so in that way we are not overwhelmed by the love.

S: What came up in my monologue was the realization of the love that's arising in my life, about having a personal life and the love of my family and becoming really engaged in life in a way that I've never been before. This feels like it brings up issues around my personal loves and a sense of preciousness and engagement that is very different from the experiences I've had of the Beloved, the single-pointed intimacy. Can you say something about that? Because it doesn't feel like . . . I mean, on the one hand, I could see that this engagement and love could separate me, it could take me away from the path you're talking about, and yet it's different. It's taking me into something in a different way.

AH: As we've already seen, when the heart matures, it recognizes the inherent limitations of our usual objects of love and that makes it possible to have true personal relationships and true love. But the other thing this maturation reveals is that as these earthly loves become more mature and complete, we experience them as expressions of our inner nature. The more they reflect and express our true nature, the more lovable our earthly loves appear—that's part of the maturity. The more we can see it that way, the less competition there will be between our beloveds and the inner Beloved. So that is one of the resolutions of this conflict that begins to happen along the way. However, for a long time there will always be an element of competition, and that's why we have to learn what it means to empty our heart completely of all other beloveds. But just as we saw with Muhammad, this complete focus on the inner Beloved does not mean totally abandoning our earthly loves—to do that would only mean that we haven't really understood what the inner Beloved is. The full resolution is to discover what the relationship is between the two. On the way toward that, the maturation of the heart can mean that, yes, you can also have earthly loves, but only as long as you truly understand that they cannot be the primary source of what the heart is missing and searching for. If they are, that makes them idols, and that's what needs to be renounced. Once we understand that and know that only the inner Beloved can satisfy the heart, our love for it keeps deepening, keeps intensifying and expanding, and at some point it completely eclipses our other loves, to the point that sometimes we completely forget about them. But of course, that doesn't mean we forget about them for a year or two. That's usually not what happens. But at least we have times when our inner love is so big, so overwhelming, that everything else fades.

S: I see how many things pull me away, but I've also got a similar question to the last one, where I feel like at the beginning when I started out, maybe as a teenager, to feel my own life, well, there was no concept of a Beloved or God. That felt totally alien to my life, so it was just like a yearning, a searching, a pulling, which I followed, and it attached itself to all kinds of people, things, work, and passions. And that's still how it seems now. For example, with the relationship to my teacher, or also to the teaching, that's still an object to some degree, but the object seems to become more transparent, and it becomes clearer that the love is inside. So if there's a particular object, and it evokes something, and it seems like the heart is turning to where the love can be found... Well, if true nature is at that point an abstract concept to me, what does it matter to me, if I can really love my teacher in that moment, or music, or a lover. That seems to still bring me closer to opening my heart to what might ultimately become the single-pointed orientation.

AH: As I've just said, that definitely is one of the main things that happens, that the heart develops and our ordinary love matures. But as we've seen, even when our ordinary love matures, regardless of how good it is, that ordinary love does not give the heart total contentment. That doesn't mean there is something wrong with ordinary love. It just means that there is something incomplete about that beloved. If we continue to believe that these external beloveds can provide what we truly seek, the inevitable discontent just points to the fact that there is an inner Beloved that we still don't see, that we don't experience. And of course, that love for the inner Beloved, at the beginning it attaches to so many things. But with the maturation we begin to recognize that these things are not what the heart is searching for. We see that these things are not to be rejected, but we recognize that our love is really looking for a Beloved that is intangible and invisible. And the heart can love that completely, fully, intensely, passionately, majestically, without having to give it a name or a word or an image. To say it's abstract means that we give it a concept, but the heart doesn't need that concept.

S: So it's all the same love. The love is just deepening and unfolding and opening, broadening, whatever...

AH: It is only one love, but what I'm saying is that it's divided usually among many things, and for it to move deeper, it needs to become more unified. In terms of human relationships, at some point the love has to become more focused on one person instead of many, and that makes the love mature and deepen. It's the same when it comes to the Beloved. The eventual true alignment of the inner and outer love isn't easy to grasp, and as I keep saying, the answers to some of these questions will not really become clear until we go further into understanding the relationship of the Beloved to all the other beloveds.

S: In my monologue I found myself talking about the animal soul, and the spiritual resolve—what the Sufis call *himma*—needed to not be dominated by it, and focus on the truth. Because it seemed to me that the kinds of loves that really seemed like they were in competition, the way I viewed that, were things like you were talking about—the pleasure and the love of sleep, and ice cream, and things like that. And that it would be himma that would once again realign me to focus on the inner Beloved.

AH: That's true. When it comes to the animal soul, himma is quite necessary, to be able to focus that love. Because much of our love, as I said, is motivated by the instincts, by the animal needs and drives. The heart needs to be liberated from that influence for it to really begin to realize what its true love is. We might sense there is a true Beloved, we might see it in different things, but for a long time we don't know what it is. And it is not something that the instinctual part, the animal part, is interested in. So if we allow our love to be dominated by the instincts, it will not move in that direction. The exact opposite actually. Because the inner Beloved is the most intangible, the most formless, while the animal soul wants to go to the most tangible, the most formed, the most structured kind of beloved.

THREE

Names of the Beloved

I 'll begin with another poem by Kabir.

> When my friend is away from me, I am depressed;
> Nothing in the daylight delights me,
> Sleep at night gives no rest,
> Who can I tell about this?
>
> The night is dark, and long... hours go by...
> Because I am alone, I sit up suddenly,
> Fear goes through me....
>
> Kabir says: Listen, my friend
> There is one thing in the world that satisfies,
> And that is a meeting with the Guest.*

As you see, Kabir uses names such as "guest," "friend," and "secret" to refer to the Beloved. He's one of the people I got some

---

* Kabir, *The Kabir Book: Forty-Four of the Ecstatic Poems of Kabir*, ed. Robert Bly (Beacon Press, 1977), 1.

of these words from, and he probably got many of them from Rumi and others who use the words "guest" and "secret." In this chapter we want to understand more about why such names are useful and in what way they are not.

We've seen that discussing the Beloved brings up the path of love and the question of love in our everyday lives. It can bring up issues around our need for love, our history around it, and the question of our love relationships, past and present. But the path of love actually has nothing to do with those things, and when the poets and mystics talk about the path of love and the Beloved, they're generally not concerned with personal relationships. Many of them were happily married, with children, and the issue of personal love wasn't a major consideration for them. This doesn't mean that our unresolved issues around personal love relationships aren't important and don't need to be dealt with; we need to understand how these issues block the heart's movement. However, the focus of our work here is not love in general, and it's not even the path of love. The focus is the inner Beloved, and the path of love is only relevant because it speaks to our ability to realize the Beloved.

If you read Kabir or Rumi, or even people like Dante, whose love of God was more explicitly connected with the love of another person, their poetry is not about human relationship but the relationship with true nature. It's about the inner work of realization and enlightenment—union with the Beloved as seen through the heart.

Describing inner work in the language of love is common to many traditions. We know it, for instance, in the Indian traditions that take the bhakti approach, the way of devotion, as Kabir does. Sufis are renowned for embracing the way of love, but there are also Christian mystics, particularly the Spanish ones that follow the path of love, as well as mystics in the Jewish tradition such as the Hassids. Each tradition may have a different flavor, but there are certain features, natural laws, and progressions that are common on the path of love.

So what we're really learning about here are the secrets of the heart that will connect us with our deepest nature. If this brings up issues around our personal love relationships, then yes, we can look at how that intersects and overlaps with our love for the inner Beloved. But discriminating the two is important. It's something we need to be very clear about because it's easy to confuse them in a way that can complicate both.

Obviously, many people can have a love relationship, be married, and have a family without having any spiritual orientation at all, so the question of the inner Beloved never arises. In fact most of humanity is like that, so you clearly don't need to be on the bhakti path or inner journey of the heart to be able to have a human love relationship. Being on the inner path will change the quality of those relationships, it's true, but it's not what determines whether they happen or not.

At the other end of the scale, some people try to make their personal love relationship into a spiritual path. There hasn't really been a path like that in any spiritual tradition, but it makes sense that people will think that way nowadays. It reflects the fact that love relationships in our Western culture have become so central to our lives. As a result, they've become more complex than they used to be, and therefore more difficult in some respects. In the past, love relationships were not such a big issue. Society took a more functional view of them—they needed to happen in order to produce offspring, and if they didn't happen, families arranged for them to happen. As we know, this is still the case in many parts of the world. But in our Western culture, around two hundred years ago, something changed in the way we live and the way we raise our children, and it changed the nature of our personal relationships. The change was that we started to have our babies sleep in separate bedrooms.

Having babies sleep in separate bedrooms created a whole new way of life that didn't exist previously and still doesn't in a large part of the world. It meant that infants didn't always have their mother nearby at all times, which created a need for what are known as transitional objects—things like teddy bears and security blankets, which comfort the infant as it's learning to cope with the absence of mother for longer periods. In cultures where this development has occurred, there's more separateness within the family, with couples spending more time together without the children present.

Along with that kind of separation within the family came the development of the nuclear family, whereby the couple and their children became more separate from the extended family and the surrounding community—no longer supported by a close network of parents, grandparents, aunts, uncles, neighbors, and friends. This has been aggravated with the advent of greater social mobility, which often leaves families spread out across the country, or even between countries. This has all led to couples becoming more isolated and therefore much more dependent on their own relationship for support. It means that in modern Western culture, much more emphasis is placed on the strength and quality of the love relationship between spouses, and this heavy burden of expectation often results in disappointment and frustration.

Other cultures don't always make such a big deal about personal relationships, because unlike us, they've never seen them to be such a burning issue. That is reflected in the spiritual traditions that arose in those cultures. Of course, people might look at Rumi and say that much of his realization and poetry came about through his close relationship with Shams al-Din. Rumi was happily married, with children, and already had a following of devoted students when he met this enigmatic Sufi nomad, Shams al-Din, who traveled around spreading his spiritual teachings. Shams showed Rumi that he still wasn't realized—that he didn't really know what the inner Beloved was and wasn't that near to it at all. A deep bond developed between Rumi and Shams, and it was after this, and particularly after Shams disappeared mysteriously, that Rumi came to be the mystical poet we know.

Some people might think this is an example of an intimate personal relationship acting as a medium for the Work, but the truth is, we don't really know what that relationship was like. And yet it seems pretty certain to me that when Shams al-Din and Rumi were sitting together, they weren't dealing with their projections of mother and father onto each other. And I'm sure they weren't making anguished pronouncements such as "Why don't you love me? I need you to love me. Why don't you see me?" It was a whole other thing going on between Shams and Rumi. I don't even know whether we could really call it a relationship, although it appears that way from the outside. Different people have different views on the nature of their interaction, and people have all kinds of stories about it.

The fact is, if you understand Rumi's poetry, it's clear that Rumi and Shams were not two people interacting in the kind of relationship we're familiar with. They were like two rays of light coming from the same sun. Though actually, that doesn't really capture the true nature of their relationship. It may be an accurate way to describe the relationship between some people who are somewhat spiritually realized, to see them as rays of light coming from the same sun. But with Rumi and Shams, it was more like they were two rays of light that have not yet left the sun.

So, how can we understand the concept of two rays of light that are still inside the sun? What do you call that kind of relationship between two people? It's a whole different order of things, and totally different from what most people mean when they think a relationship can be the vehicle for their inner work. A relationship like that of Rumi and Shams is about something so mysterious, it's unlikely we can comprehend it and know what the chemistry between them was. As I said, it's not like Rumi would say something and Shams would say, "I think that's a projection" or "Why can't you tell me that you love me? I think it's because you're afraid of being vulnerable." If anything, I imagine Rumi might say something like, "I feel that I love you totally," and Shams would reply, "What are you talking about? What's this 'I' that loves me? If you think you love me like that—as if there is such a thing—why don't you leave right now?" It would be something more along those lines, because Rumi and Shams were about eliminating relationship, not creating one. And that's really the kind of thing we're talking about here on the journey to the inner Beloved.

But eliminating the notion of relationship in that way didn't prevent Rumi from having a relationship in the external world—a wife and family and all of that. What's crucial is that he didn't confuse the inner and outer experience. We do tend to confuse them, and that can make our relationships much more complicated. It's as if we think we're going to be lovers with some kind of divinity—like we're going to marry God—and so we have to be some kind of divinity in our relationships. When the truth is, no, in our relationships we are normal human beings. We can be aware of our true nature when we're relating to others, but we also have to see our humanity, our own limitations and the limitations of the other. Human relationships usually involve learning a lot about that—it's not just a question of bathing in ecstatic love.

We can see that even though Rumi had such a profound teaching from Shams on these matters, it was only when Shams died that he could fully differentiate his inner relationship with true nature from this powerful outer relationship. Rumi did not become fully realized until that happened. He needed that separation, that loss, to recognize that the sun was not Shams—though ironically the name Shams al-Din means "the spiritual sun." Only then could he fully experience the truth that the real sun was inside him, and its manifestation didn't depend on the relationship with Shams. It was only after Shams died that Rumi began to write his poetry. This gives us some idea of how an external relationship and the inner path of love toward the Beloved are related, and how they interact, even if this relationship is a rather extraordinary example.

As you can see, if after such a long time even Rumi had problems differentiating the inner and outer relationship, it's not a simple thing. It's a very subtle matter, and that's why many of us remain confused about it for such a long time. I was confused myself for a long time, or maybe not so much confused as mixed up. I just didn't really understand how it all went.

Now definitely, the more we open to love with other human beings, the more our heart opens, and the more we can therefore engage the inner path of love. We clearly can't engage it if our heart is not open to love and willing to tolerate all the feelings that come with it, and those feelings usually emerge first in relation to other human beings, often intensely. When it comes to the inner Beloved the intensity is of a different order, though when the heart first opens, we tend not to be aware of the difference. So the opening of the heart is in some sense the beginning of the path of love, and often this is experienced when we fall in love with someone. However, the heart opening is not just a matter of falling in love, because people can fall in love before the heart opens. When we talk about the heart opening, we mean that the heart center is open and flooded with ecstatic love.

I fell in love several times when I was a teenager, which is easy to do, but having that happen doesn't mean that teenagers have their hearts open. I didn't have a true heart opening until I was in my late twenties. After that, I fell in love again several times, but there was a different quality to it—there was more recognition of a spiritual manifestation in the other person and in myself, something that was not present in me as a teenager. With this shift, the question of the inner Beloved became something palpable for me, and my relationship with it was full of intensity. At the same time, it was still easy for that intensity to get channeled to another human being, and I became aware of a movement back and forth between the two. This is the usual thing: Our heart opens, but it is difficult to stay with the inner Beloved, and our love gets attached to another person again. This is a natural tendency that we all have. We cannot prevent it, and we shouldn't. It's how we deal with it that matters, how we relate to it, and ultimately that brings in the central question of how the love we feel in external relationships relates to the love for the inner Beloved.

As I said, becoming aware of the spiritual source of love can add another dimension to our personal relationships. But in my experience, the external attachment to a love object was so strong that even though I would go back to the inner Beloved, it was a difficult struggle to do so, and the tendency was to forget the true source and take the outer form of it more seriously than I should. That continued until I was able to develop and realize what we call the personal essence, or the pearl beyond price. This development brings the individuation of the soul, which means we experience ourselves as the embodiment of true nature, an expression of Being. This means we have our own autonomy—who we are is not dependent on others or even on our mind or our history. Establishing this true autonomy is what makes it possible to engage in a relationship in a way that it is not an impediment to being faithful to the inner Beloved.

So although relationships with others can exist without spiritual realization, it is the realization of the personal essence in particular that helps to make our relationships more real, so they become an expression of our realization. With the essential autonomy of the pearl, we can be in true relationship with others, because we no longer depend on them to alleviate an emptiness that can only be resolved through the inner Beloved. In my case, this meant that basically I didn't commit myself to a long-term relationship until the personal essence was sufficiently developed in me, so I could know for sure that the relationship wouldn't take precedence over the inner Beloved.*

---

* See *The Pearl Beyond Price* for a detailed account of the development of the personal essence.

We saw in the previous chapter that the inner Beloved will not fully reveal itself in the heart unless we show complete fidelity to it. I'm sure a lot of us have been wondering what we can do about that. I mean, we do love other people, we do love other things. It's natural, and we can't stop it—and we shouldn't try to stop it. So what do we do?

We know it's not a matter of going to extremes—abandoning external relationships and remaining single, or becoming an ascetic and living in a monastery. That can't be the solution. So, what I found that works, a secret of the heart that I've already alluded to, is to be very clear about the question of priority: The inner Beloved must always be the primary Beloved. All other beloveds are secondary, always and with absolutely no exception. So with my deepest and dearest friend, or anyone that I love deeply—even with my partner—it doesn't matter how important the relationship is, it's not as important as remembering the inner Beloved. This is a practical way we can begin to deal with what we characterized in human terms as the jealousy and possessiveness of the inner Beloved—we may have other relationships, but we have to make it clear that the Beloved will always be number one.

How difficult we find it to remember the Beloved while we're engaged in external relationships depends on where we are on the path. And ultimately, what makes the key difference is whether we are on the path or in realization. If we are in the realized state, the connection between the inner Beloved and the outer beloved becomes clear and obvious; the conflict dissolves, and the resolution of the two is complete. It's a whole different story than seeing the situation from the path. We'll be looking at this question from the perspective of realization more and more as we proceed, but we're starting out by discussing our relationship to the inner Beloved from the perspective of the path, not from that of realization.

When we're still on the path, we're not completely unified with the inner Beloved, so I find that what works is to be clear that the inner Beloved is number one. The key principle is that loving somebody or something else can never be at the expense of the relationship with the inner Beloved. If it ever comes to a choice or a conflict—it's the inner Beloved.

This isn't a choice we make because we feel we "must" or "should," but because we recognize the fact that no other beloved can satisfy the human heart. The inner Beloved is therefore established as the primary love of the heart, the one that we will never betray—after all, this is the only Beloved that we're going to be with for eternity. The process needs to continue to deepen and expand in that direction, and that will happen naturally the more we keep our attention focused on the inner Beloved. We can't force it and try to make it happen by saying no to our other beloveds, because that means saying no to our love, and if we say no to our love, we block our heart.

My experience showed me that by making sure the inner Beloved was given primary value, and by always remaining open to it, the relationship with my other loves became much easier. When they took their proper place, they were more in harmony with my love for the Beloved, because there was no longer an inappropriate dependence on an external beloved. This is how the pearl quality manifests in our personal life, bringing us an inner independence—a true autonomy that is based on the inner fidelity of the heart. It brings a devotion and commitment to the inner Beloved that means we will never betray it by leaving it for any external beloved. It places quite a burden on our relationships if we don't have that deep committed relationship to the inner Beloved, because then we inevitably want the external beloved to fulfill our deepest longings. As we've seen, no external beloved can do that; so if we're trying to make that happen, our human relationships will always be troubled. Remember Kabir's poem—the only thing in the world that satisfies is the meeting with the Guest.

So while we may not need to liberate ourselves from our external attachments in any concrete way, the more our heart liberates itself from fixating on them, and the more it allows the inner Beloved to take precedence over them, the more clearly and fully the inner Beloved will reveal itself. There will then be occasions when we see for ourselves that it will only reveal itself fully in the heart when the heart loves only it and nothing else—when it completely forgets all its other loves in that moment. Sufis call that absence. It means being absent to the world, but it's actually presence and absence at the same time. You might be in the world, and you might be feeling present while engaging with a beloved you love very much, but in a sense you're also absent from them, because all that you are seeing is the inner Beloved. For that to become a more enduring state, the heart has to gradually disentangle itself from all its fixations on particular earthly loves—that's what we mean when we talk about emptying the heart. It comes from an inner dedication of the heart to becoming purely the house of the Beloved—or the throne where the Beloved sits, as some people put it.

So the understanding that only the inner Beloved can ultimately satisfy the heart is crucial to this process. But there's something else we need to understand and accept—that the journey will be a long and challenging one. This is another way the relationship with the inner Beloved is different from our earthly loves. In the early stages of falling in love with someone, or in developing a very deep friendship, there's usually a phase of intense burning and longing for the relationship to become established. Once it's established, it has a different quality. The burning and longing is over; the person is no longer such a mystery to you, and it's now a matter of getting to know them better so that the relationship can develop and deepen.

With the inner Beloved it's not like that. The burning and longing goes on for years, decades in fact. And far from getting to know the inner Beloved better, for all this time we still don't even know what it is. For years and decades we have to endure the fact that although we come closer to it at times, there are times when it seems to just disappear off the scene—gone, and for who knows how long. It feels to us as if the Beloved just decides that we're on a break for a while. Now, if a human being kept doing that in a relationship, after a year or two you'd say goodbye, no more—time for divorce. We tend not to tolerate it with other people, partly because there are alternatives—plenty more fish in the sea, as we say. But with the inner Beloved, you can't say goodbye. You can't say, "I'm getting divorced, and I'm going to find somebody else." There's no "somebody else" there. It would be the same if there was only you and one other man or woman in the world. What are you going to do if you feel rejected and don't want the relationship anymore? Marry a monkey? Well, some people might try that. But staying committed is the only option with the inner Beloved, if we recognize that it is the only beloved that can satisfy the depth of the heart.

That's why there's a need to be as vulnerable as possible every time the inner Beloved moves farther away or disappears—we still work to stay open, to stay devoted, to stay committed, to stay faithful, to stay loving. We continue to want, to yearn, and to desire, regardless of the separation, regardless of the loss, regardless of the feeling of abandonment. That's why there's a need for the humility we talked about before.

So the relationship with the inner Beloved is much more mysterious than our human relationships, and the sense of mystery in it continues throughout the relationship. Even when we finally behold the inner Beloved, the mystery doesn't diminish—in fact it deepens. There's a sense of going back and forth between closeness and distance, union and separation, and we need to accept that this can go on for years and years. Even though someone like Kabir might have reached a state of union with the Beloved, there was still this going back and forth for many years, and Rumi kept experiencing the yearning and longing almost to the end of his life. You see it in his poems—one day he's loving, the next day he's yearning. The Beloved continues to come and go mysteriously, and it takes a great deal of realization before our relationship with the inner Beloved feels more settled.

It's clear then that the level of love required, and the quality of pain to be endured, is of a different order with the Beloved than with a human being. Maybe we can understand better now why the more settled we are in our human relationships, the easier it is for us to sustain our relationship with the inner Beloved. It's not a necessity, but it makes for less confusion if we aren't experiencing the anguish of love externally too. In cultures and traditions like those of Kabir and Rumi, people had their personal love issues settled before they really embarked on the inner journey. That's less likely to be the case these days, because many people still aren't settled in a committed relationship when they're fifty or even older. The inner journey might begin decades before that, so both the inner and outer relationships can be going through significant turbulence over a long period of time. That's why we need a better understanding of how they are related and how to avoid confusing one with the other and complicating both.

We've learned that what helps most at the beginning is to become fully aware that the Beloved the heart longs for is intangible. The confusion begins to dissipate when we're wise and mature enough to recognize that what we're looking for is not in this world, the world of form. And that's why the mysterious inner Beloved has no name and no image. The heart is missing something. It knows it is separate from something, and it experiences the separation—its alienation from true nature—as the pangs of love. So the heart will yearn and long for what it knows is missing, burning and melting with its love and desire for it, and yet it doesn't have a name for it and no clear image of what it is.

As we grew up and discovered things, we learned to give them names, so of course it's inevitable that we will do the same now with this mysterious something. We might use one name or another for it depending on our background and culture. We might call it God, or we might call it Christ—the Christian mystics thought of Christ as the groom and the soul as the bride who needed to prepare herself for the groom. Different cultures have many different names for God, and for the mysterious inner Beloved. Perhaps we might decide to use a less culturally specific name and call it the divine, or truth, or love. But whatever name or image we use for the inner Beloved, it is always a dangerous thing for the heart. That's because a name or image can easily become another idol that fills the heart. It becomes an idea of what the Beloved is, and it makes us feel as if we know what it is. The truth is, we don't really know—certainly not consciously, not in our mind. We've seen that the heart knows it by intuitively sensing whether it's there or not, but the heart doesn't then make an image of it and give it a name. It's the mind that can't help doing that. And that's okay, we can have a name for it as long as we remember and remain aware that the name is just a label for the nameless, formless Beloved.*

That's why many mystics and poets give the Beloved names such as "the guest" or "the friend." "Guest" and "friend" are in some sense neutral names. They don't try to give us any specific ideas about what the Beloved is but simply evoke the notion of a mysterious stranger who is to be welcomed. Kabir would never have tried to name and describe the inner Beloved definitively because he understood that by giving it a name and then thinking the name really describes it, we create another idol—another exterior beloved in some sense. That's likely to happen if we call it God, or Christ, and even the divine, or truth. In fact any name can be latched on to by a mind that is always trying to reify everything.

Even as our heart becomes more faithful to the Beloved, and the Beloved reveals itself more and more in various aspects, it's inevitable that in remembering those experiences we will give them particular forms, specific images, and certain names. The problem is that once we've created these forms and images and given them names, we then seek them out again. We start loving

---

* The well-known invocation *Allahu Akbar* is usually translated as "God is great," but a more accurate translation would be "God is greater." And the true meaning of that is very relevant here: God is greater than any concept you might form of him. No matter what you might think you know God to be, the ungraspable truth will always be beyond that.

and looking for the Beloved we've experienced before, when in fact that was just one way the Beloved happened to reveal itself in that moment. And it was most likely not the essence of the Beloved but only a partial experience of it—just one aspect or quality. If we direct our love toward that particular experience, then the heart is no longer free, and it's not open. It can't then be an empty chamber for the Beloved, because it's been filled with an idol—a specific idea and form of the Beloved that it's now searching for.

Because these memories, ideas, and images are a creation of the mind, the mind is now directing the heart in its search, and that goes against what our first poem said: "Annihilate mind in heart." To annihilate mind in heart means to erase all our ideas, all our beliefs, and all our memories and images as to what the Beloved is, because these are all just creations of the mind. Even when the Beloved finally reveals itself fully, if we remember that particular revelation and decide this is what we love, it creates an idol, an image that takes us down the road of reification.

So we can have idols in our inner world as well as the external one. In both realms we create and become attached to forms that then fill the heart. Holding any image, name, or form for the Beloved constrains the movement of the heart. To know the Beloved, however, the heart needs complete freedom—complete liberation from all mind, all memory, all image, all positions and beliefs. It just knows that it loves, and it loves the Beloved without knowing what the Beloved is. All the heart needs is to be near the Beloved, close to the Beloved, in contact with the Beloved, and it is unwilling to believe any ideas about the Beloved. When the heart is free, it has no direction, no image, no idea where to go or what to do. It just melts.

When these images and the memories of them have become established, the way to deal with that from the perspective of the heart is not to try and do something to the images, but to simply allow the love itself to deepen and expand. Our passion and ecstatic love for the Beloved isn't actually diminished by us having images of it; it just gets obscured, covered up, constrained, and somewhat muffled. And our yearning can actually increase when we see how the images are separating us from what we love. If we then allow that yearning love to manifest itself strongly—if we burn with it and feel, "Yes, that's what I want!"—it will burn away all these images and memories of the Beloved, and the passion of the heart will dissolve the mind. So one of the secrets of the heart is that we don't need to meddle with these things. The heart divests itself of them through its own passion, through its own love.

Of course, inquiry and understanding can help us recognize that there are images and idols that we have created, some of them so subtly that we don't even realize they have become idols and images. So let's do an exercise to deal with that particular point.

Practice Session:
Images of the Inner Beloved
...

We'll do a form of exercise called a repeating question. If you have someone to do the exercise with, you will each take a turn for fifteen minutes asking the other person the first question:

Tell me what you feel your inner Beloved is like.

Each time the question is asked, the person responding answers spontaneously with whatever arises for them. Answers may be a few words or sentences—whatever needs to be said—but not going on for too long, as this is not a monologue. When the response is complete, the person asking says, "Thank you," and then asks the question again until the fifteen minutes are up. It's then the turn of the other person to ask the question for fifteen minutes. You then both do the same with the second question, but this time for ten minutes each:

What's right about believing you know your inner Beloved?

With the first question, you can see all your ideas and beliefs, all your images and memories, whatever has taken its place in your heart that makes you feel that you know your inner Beloved. Just let your heart open up and reveal these images—don't decide with your mind that it has to be only certain kinds of things.

With the second question you may be thinking, "Well, it's already been made clear that you can't know your inner Beloved, it's a mystery, so there's nothing right about me believing I know it." However, there is a part in all of us that believes it knows our inner Beloved; this is a time for that part to speak, regardless of what I have been saying in this chapter.

If you don't have a partner to do this with, you can answer in writing as many times as possible within the allotted time. Or you can record the question and have it spoken to you by your computer or device after you finish answering out loud.

. . . . .

Questions and Comments

Student: When I thought about how I experience or what I think the Beloved is, what came up for me is, it seemed to be similar to love itself, or to being love. I mean, as if that is my experience of myself, as love, and actually when that experience is there, it's as if the sun is shining in the heart. Then there is actually no Beloved, and it feels the Beloved is more between these experiences, as if it's the stretch between the points in time where I experience myself as love, or my identity as being love. Does that make sense?

A. H. Almaas: So definitely, being a lover and relating to a lover is a transitional way of looking at it. When you're finally connected with the Beloved, there isn't separation between you and the Beloved, and you don't say, "I'm relating to the Beloved." It doesn't make sense—you are the Beloved then. So what you say makes sense, yes. The idea that I'm working with here is that that happens in many ways. The Beloved reveals itself in many qualities, in many dimensions, getting deeper and subtler and less defined. So it changes in both ways, in terms of how near we are to the Beloved, until there is no distance at all. There are also changes in terms of what the Beloved is that is appearing—that also goes through transformations.

S: I started off the exercise, with the first question, feeling something very subtle and beautiful, and being touched with really sunshine in my heart, and I was surprised with my extensive facility to be delicately in touch with this. Because in exploring the divided heart, I wasn't feeling in touch with my heart at all. Then at the beginning of the second question, things really fell into place, because what came up was that the inner Beloved was absent. On a deeper level there was a sense of absence there, and in my object relation with God, there was no love—God was not a God of love. This linked up with a sense that's been happening in my life recently, of a very deep despair, which feels like it's to do with this, with the thread of what we're working on here. So that feeling of a lack of love, historically, has kept me away from even beginning to allow that possibility, because God was not a God of love. So I'm just feeling that at the moment.

AH: It's good that you brought that up. I'm sure many people have that kind of experience, the struggle with that, the relationship with a God that doesn't have love. Then we need to really explore and find out: How come? What makes it that way? Frequently it's not really the relationship with God but something overlaid onto that, some kind of projection going on that we need to see through.

S: In the first question it was really beautiful to recognize how inadequate language is. So when I experienced gentleness, it was like the words felt empty; it felt shallow to the depth of what I was experiencing. So there was a real tenderness to the first question, which I'm feeling right now. In the second question, I got very angry, and I'm still feeling a lot of anger. It was anger and disgust, and there was some anger at you, because "What's right about believing and knowing?" seemed like an unreasonable question, because of those three words: "What's right about . . ." And what I felt I was absorbing and feeling really good about was the knocking down of idols that you were doing so well. To me, any belief is an idol, and so I tried to cooperate with the question and come up with something, and I couldn't. It was like, "Damn it, there's nothing right about believing!" And then I feel like I'm flashing back to other times when I've had this experience, when I feel like I'm missing something. So I just wanted some feedback on that.

AH: Yes, it's a trick question.

S: It's a trick and I didn't get it.

AH: Right. In fact, all the questions we use are actually trick questions, but with some it's more obvious than others. So when we say, "What's right about it?" there's actually no implication that there's anything right about it, but it is a way to sort of nudge out the part that believes there is something right about it. And there is usually a part there. So we're really talking to the unconscious. We want the unconscious that's holding on to those beliefs to be exposed. So if you're looking at it in a rational way, it won't work. That's why I say with these questions, don't think about it. Don't think of words that someone else might answer. Say whatever comes to mind—it doesn't have to make any sense.

S: I tried that. Then toward the end, it felt like in my head there were shifting masses of stuff, but nothing came out. So I guess that's the resistance in me.

AH: We'll see. Maybe, maybe not. It may be something else.

S: I'd like to express the resistance that I'm feeling to sitting here and talking about this right now. Because I feel like I am on fire. I feel there's a big fire burning inside, and it's really hard to sit here and talk about this with anybody, even with you. I don't want to sit here and talk about it. I just want to be it and express it.

AH: Well, don't. That's fine. Just sit with it.

S: Well, it was a relief to be told that I didn't need to know what my inner Beloved is, to be reminded of that and to discover it again. When you talked about the image of the guest being a little more neutral, my partner came up with the fact that the guest is still an object; the use of the word makes it seem like that. But this image of the house, and that you serve the guest, and there's a certain humility in the guest... And when you talked about the heart as being the home of the Beloved, and even the throne... well, the image came to me that the house would have to be empty, like barren, for there to be room for the Beloved to enter. When I saw that, it was disturbing, but it felt true. There weren't thrones or anything, it was just barren to make room for it, without anything cluttering it up. I think this is what's going on in my life, that it's difficult to maintain the kind of lifestyle I have and still have the time to somehow be quiet enough for my heart to open, being attached to all the stuff in my house, the furniture, the artwork, and the books. So I'm bringing up that image of the barren house that the guest is invited to enter.

AH: Well, that is exactly the case. As I said, the house, the heart, has to be emptied completely of all the images, all the beliefs, all the knowledge, all the idols, just like the Kaaba had to be emptied, and swept clean completely. That's a necessity, a requirement for the Beloved to fully manifest. So the Sufis use it as a symbol. I don't know if Muhammad thought of it that way, but certainly in that religion, there are no images allowed, of God or any spiritual quality. No images, no pictures—that's why Islamic art is always designs, and you don't see pictures and images. That's where all that comes from. Because any image can become an idea in the mind, it can be reified and become some particular object.

S: I think I'm really struggling with how to live one's life with all these objects around us. It comes up on a lot of levels.

AH: I know. I understand. It's a bitch. It's true, it is difficult, and the pace of life, the crowding in our lives, is making it more and more difficult to have the time and space.

S: Over the past year or so I've found myself in love with the love. Is that something that I have to give up too?

AH: Anything that we can give a word to, we have to give up. Loving it as love is definitely a stage in nearness to the Beloved, but when the Beloved finally reveals itself completely, we cannot say what it is. Some people call the Beloved love, and it can be experienced that way, but the Beloved can still be more complete than that. So it's good to experience that, to cherish it and recognize the nearness in it. The point is not to give anything up. The point is not to hold on to anything, not to hold on to any image or any idea. So it's not really giving anything up. It's not like actively throwing something out.

S: Something I found out that I believe about the inner Beloved is that it's weak. How I know that it's weak is that it sends out weak signals that it's there or what its characteristics are. Sometimes it's mildly perceptible, and sometimes it's imperceptible. And I have memories of other experiences where it was unmistakable and my heart was flooded with joy, but those memories don't count from this point of view because I wasn't there for those experiences. And how I think this serves me to see the Beloved that way is . . . it makes me look pretty good, because I'm bigger and I seem pretty real to myself, having a physical manifestation and doing things. So it seems like I'm in competition there.

AH: So that can happen, and sometimes there's something real about it. We need to understand that we're realizing something real about ourselves. But at the same time we need to remember who we dedicate our work to: Who is it for? And in terms of the Beloved being weak, the way many traditions look at it, instead of saying it's very weak, they say it's very jealous. It won't appear strongly unless you're already completely committed. So the weakness means you're not seeing how your self is divided. Because if the self is divided, it's true, the messages are weak because the Beloved isn't trying to send any messages. It says, "Well, if you don't think about me, I'm not going to think about you." It sort of works like that. It's a way of seeing it.

FOUR

Fidelity of the Heart

We'll start with something from a book called *Divine Flashes*, by the Sufi Fakhruddīn 'Irāqī. The book is a mixture of prose and poetry, so first there's a short piece of prose and then a short poem. The term "spiritual resolve" is a translation of *himma*, the Arabic word we usually use, and when the poem talks about "meaning," it refers to what we usually call essence.

> When the sincere lover stamps his foot upon the neck of the world of forms, we know his spiritual resolve desires only a Beloved of transcendent attributes; and that he will not submit his own neck to any beloved chained with the fetters of shape and image, nor the tie of knowledge and union. No, all forms are now erased from his contemplation: he sees the Beloved directly, without the intermediary aid of form. As the Sufis say, "God can be seen clearly only when formal limitations dissolve."*

---

* Fakhruddīn 'Irāqī, *Divine Flashes* (Paulist Press, 1982), 90–91.

And the poem:

How can meaning be squeezed
into the box of form?
What business has the sultan
in this beggar's realm?
In the end, what can he know
who worships form, heedless of meaning?
Tell me: what business can he have
with the beauty of a hidden Beloved?*

So the true lover is not distracted by forms. And as our heart becomes less divided and more unified in its love, as its faithfulness to the inner Beloved becomes stronger and more sincere, the heart steadily divests itself of the various images and forms of its particular loves, both outer and inner. The more our heart lets go of these images and forms, the purer it becomes and the more devoted to the formless inner Beloved, which then begins to take precedence over all our other loves.

However, as the heart begins to leave these familiar forms and images behind, we can be assailed by many doubts and uncertainties—as we've seen in some of our explorations here. We may feel confused and conflicted about losing what we have relied on for so long for support. There is a sense of guilt at abandoning it, and a fear of reciprocal abandonment should we feel we need this support again. So a great deal of fear may arise as this all unfolds. There is also pain, a deep sense of loss, and a terror of even greater, unmanageable loss. In many ways, these are the difficulties and

---

* 'Irāqī, *Divine Flashes*, 90–91.

barriers that arise on the spiritual path generally when people are learning to let go of their attachments, but they have a particular flavor and meaning on the path of the heart.

It's only natural that as your heart becomes ever more focused on the inner Beloved, you fear losing everything that you love in the outside world. Even if I keep saying to you, "It's okay, this doesn't mean you really have to lose all your other beloveds," it doesn't help. That's because no matter what we might say about it conceptually, when this shift begins to happen, we *feel* as if we're going to lose something that's vitally important to us. The commitment and focus on the Beloved isn't just an abstract theoretical matter. It's real. You really feel it: "I love the Beloved, and that's all that really matters." It's becoming a reality for you that the Beloved is number one, your primary concern, and you're willing to lose whatever you may need to sacrifice to honor that commitment. So as your love homes in on the Beloved, it begins to shed all its other objects of love, which become fewer and fewer.

This doesn't necessarily mean that our relationship with the people we love changes much, because we've understood that the heart divesting itself of love objects is an inner experience, not a matter of what we do in our lives. So it's not something that has to be acted out physically, as if you're telling everyone, "Don't call or email me. I don't want to see anyone. I just want to go and meditate by myself for two years." Of course, it's not like that. People can be sending you emails and bothering you with phone calls and you'll be meeting up with them, but on some deep level you're not engaged with it all. Your real engagement is with the inner Beloved.

We're learning that ultimately, when we are able to see that our outer engagements are manifestations and expressions of this inner engagement, the relationship with our friends and beloveds actually becomes smoother and more harmonious. We need less and less from them, and since our heart is so full of love, we can be even more loving with them. It may seem paradoxical, but because we're not attached, we're even more deeply committed to them.

But when our love for the inner Beloved is first intensifying and deepening, we feel conflicted and concerned that our libido is being withdrawn from the external and focused inward. Our mind can interpret that in ways that make us think we might be betraying our other beloveds. We have to be willing to accept and experience this conflict and the fear of loss that comes with it. It arises because it feels like we are separating from all our external beloveds in some way, and that brings in the issues and feelings that tend to come with any kind of separation: a sense of loss, guilt, fear, and anxiety. The commitment we feel to the Beloved is pure and real, but the unconscious will temper it in all kinds of ways, depending on how we have experienced separation in the past. We might get caught up in replays of feelings we've had when we needed to separate from someone: guilt that we're possibly being cold, uncaring, and rejecting; anxiety that we're not being loving enough; fear of reprisal and hostility from the people we feel we're abandoning, and losing the care, support, and mirroring that we've needed from them.

This will also bring up from the unconscious the experience of separation from our earliest relationship, the original dual unity with our mothering person, and leaving behind the vital care, love, nourishment, pleasure, comfort, and security that it can provide. Stepping away from the world of forms now can evoke the deep insecurities and fears we felt as an infant about losing the support and moorings we needed.

These are all things that the mind tells us, but really all that's happening is the love is divesting itself of the mind. Mind is dissolving in the heart, and because our love is no longer being channeled by our mind, it flows naturally toward its true Beloved. The heart is just loving purely what it naturally loves, and all the relationships that have supported our sense of self until now are being dissolved. They're being melted. They're being burned.

As I will keep saying, it's because we don't yet have a clear understanding of the relationship between the inner Beloved and all our other loves that we experience this as a conflict. When we understand that relationship in the state of realization, the conflict disappears, but on the path it troubles us for a long time. That's partly because we don't understand how the two relate, and partly because of this triggering of our history with separation during our maturation and development.

As the heart continues to divest itself of all images, names, and forms, there is also a fear of losing what we have gained so far internally on the spiritual path. The most significant and meaningful experiences we've had of the Beloved have become enshrined in images, names, and forms, and now there is a fear of losing these familiar and precious ways of connecting with our true nature. We've developed a certain idea of the Beloved that gives us a feeling of knowing it in some way. If we let go of that, how can we trust that it's going to be replaced by a different knowing of the Beloved—one we cannot yet understand? We're afraid it's going to be replaced by nothing. So this fear of leaving behind and losing what we love and value is felt in both the inner and outer realm, and in both cases we don't know what, if anything, is going to take its place. It feels like a huge risk.

Nevertheless, because the heart knows what the Beloved is, it recognizes in some very deep intuitive and unconscious way that none of the things we fear losing are the true Beloved. It is therefore willing to take the risk of jumping into the abyss, saying, "None of those are my true Beloved, and because I love the true Beloved so much, so completely, so absolutely, so passionately, I don't want any of those beloveds. I just want the true Beloved, even if the true Beloved doesn't show up."

It's not a bargain, you see. It's not like, "Okay, I'll give these things up so that the true Beloved will love me." It doesn't work that way. If there's any bargaining going on, we're not true lovers yet. True lovers don't bargain as if they're in a business arrangement because, in truth, love and business don't go well together. They can be harmonized to some extent in the external world, but their nature is fundamentally different. In business, people are always thinking in terms of transactional relating—what am I going to get in return? With love you can't think that way. If you do, it's not love. It's not the heart, it's something else. The lover only gives.

The true lover is willing to sacrifice everything, willing to give it up without any promise of anything in return, because nothing else matters. It's like what you may have experienced if you've been strongly and deeply in love with somebody. If someone else comes up to you and says, "I really love you. I want to be with you," do you say, "Okay, fine," as if the one you love is easily replaceable? No, of course not. It's either the one you love or no one. It's the same with the Beloved, but a million times stronger, because the heart knows that the Beloved is completely irreplaceable—there is nothing else like it. Nothing will do what it can do. Nothing else will fit exactly in the heart. It's like the heart is designed in the way that the bezel on a ring is designed for a gemstone. It's designed for that particular stone, and only that stone will fit that ring. So you have to find the one love that will fit the heart, just as the ring has to find the only stone that will fit into it.

This need to shed all that we love, and our willingness to give up all that we have and sacrifice it at the altar of love for the Beloved, will lead us to what we call mystical poverty and the dark night of the soul. Going through mystical poverty, going through the dark night of the soul, ultimately means recognizing that we have to give up everything, until in the end we have absolutely nothing. At the stage we're looking at here, it's a question of renouncing all our objects of love—everything that we love, cherish, and value.

But remember, it's not that the love decides to say no to any of the objects, images, and forms. When it comes to the heart, it's not a calculated thing; it's not something we think through and decide. It's more that the heart is just flooded with love for the Beloved and the forms are dissolved and melted by the flood of love itself, by its sweetness, gentleness, and delicacy, and also by its passion and power. The images of our previous loves vanish the way little soap bubbles do. We can also experience the love as an all-consuming fire, whose flames incinerate all the forms. Whatever way we experience it, the heart wants only one thing, and the mind doesn't even know what that one thing is. The heart simply feels, "I just want to be near the Beloved, and nothing else will do. The nearer I am, the happier. The farther away, the sadder I am."

So in the fire of love for the Beloved, the heart is indeed like a shish kebab, turning one way and another as it's cooked. Turn it one way, a little farther away from the Beloved, and it's sad, filled with an ocean of tears. In the Kabir poem about the Guest,* the sadness was translated as "depressed," but that's not really the right word. When we say someone is depressed, it usually means empty and without feeling, and it's not like that. There's a great depth of feeling, a depth of sadness, a depth of tears, a depth of longing and yearning. So the heart isn't dead the way it often is in depression—it's fluttering and shaking and very much alive.

If the shish kebab turns the other way, closer to the Beloved, the sun of joy arises—you're just the happiest thing, and it's the happiest day. You only need to be a little bit closer, to feel a little more nearness, and the heart knows it. Sometimes you don't even realize you're getting nearer; you just find that you're feeling happy. "Why am I so happy?" you might wonder. You inquire into it, you look more closely and keep asking, "Why am I . . . ?" And then you see it and feel it: "Oh, it's because I feel nearer and closer!" If somebody asked you, "Nearer and closer to what?"—you'd say, "I don't know, and I don't care. I don't have a name for it. I just feel nearer. My Beloved doesn't have a shape, doesn't have a name, doesn't have a color. I don't know it with any of my senses because it's so intangible. But I know the Beloved, and I know when I'm near to it."

So we can go through times of love that bring joyfulness and celebration, and times of love that bring tears and sadness. As we go deeper, the pangs of love and the feelings of loss don't diminish. In fact they get deeper and stronger, because the closer we get to the Beloved and the more sensitive we become to its presence, to be moved farther away from it again becomes unbearably painful. Even the slightest distance feels like we're millions of miles away. Before, we were so numb that we couldn't tell how

---

* See page 40.

far away we were, but now we know the precious intimacy of its nearness, to be separated from it feels like a tremendous loss that makes our whole world feel empty and impoverished.

All these difficulties will arise—the conflict, the fear of loss, and the pain—but in some sense they can all just become fuel for the fire, wood for the fire of love to burn. Whether we see them as problems and barriers depends on how we look at them. If we identify with the feelings they arouse and take them too seriously, not seeing them in relationship to our love for the inner Beloved, that's when they take on an importance that they don't really deserve, and they become barriers.

So we need to understand these things for what they are—just associations that the mind makes to the path of love rather than barriers that exist in reality. As our love becomes deeper and purer, more distilled and unified, our growing fidelity to the Beloved is interpreted by the mind as something that will bring loss, abandonment, and separation. Letting go of the images of our beloveds and becoming faithful only to the inner Beloved will bring us the true aloneness of essential autonomy. But our mind can't help but associate that with the idea of losing the love and support of all the people and things we rely on. True aloneness then becomes confused with the prospect of painful loneliness. We're not actually losing anything, but it feels that way, so we just have to keep remembering that we're not really rejecting any of the people we love. Our love is simply recognizing its true Beloved and flowing there directly, more deeply, and more purely.

We also need to remember this when our history of loss is brought up, instead of taking all that to be real too: "I wasn't loved by my father, and I need to spend years working on that relationship. It's not something I can just let go of." Whether my father loves me or not is not really that significant now. If it arises that I feel my father didn't love me, I recognize it from the perspective that I'm loving the inner Beloved more deeply and purely. I take in the hurt of my father's abandonment and let it hurt even more deeply, so it burns through the images and memories of it and is subsumed in my burning love for the Beloved. We need to recognize all our hurts and then let them burn up in this way, so that we can let them go. We often talk about loving the truth for its own sake, and it's in that sense that we let go of all these images. That's why the love of truth is such a powerful motivation for inquiry—we don't inquire into these things because we're particularly interested in our history, our object relations, and our images. We do it because we're interested in liberating ourselves from them in order to get closer to the truth.

The fear of loss is an issue that always arises when we go deeper on the inner journey. And we've seen that we're not just afraid of losing things in our external life; we're also afraid of losing our essence, our inner connection to divinity in the way we've experienced it so far. This happens whenever we go from one dimension to another. That movement is always accompanied by a fear of losing everything in the previous dimension that has become of precious value to us, so it always brings up issues of separation, abandonment, guilt, conflict, and anxiety. Each time true nature is revealed to us in a new way, that becomes the Beloved, and to go beyond that feels as if we're abandoning that Beloved and losing it. But there's no way to go to the next way of beholding the Beloved without leaving behind the previous one.

The more we can recognize these fears and conflicts as associations of the mind to the process of getting nearer to and more intimate with the Beloved, the easier it is for us to let them go and let the heart deepen. The love then becomes more powerful, more immense, more burning. You can let the burning just burn and burn, so you feel completely on fire. Everything is burning—body, mind, heart, and soul. And sometimes everything is melting. Sometimes it's dissolving. Sometimes it's just disappearing. These are different ways the heart transforms.

So let's do an exercise now to explore the issues and barriers that may be arising for you personally.

PRACTICE SESSION: BARRIERS TO FIDELITY OF THE HEART

. . .

This will be a monologue, working with one or two other people if possible. Each person in the group will do a monologue for fifteen minutes. If you are alone, write out your exploration for fifteen minutes.

You want to explore the conflicts, issues, and distractions that arise as you feel your love for the inner Beloved taking you deeper and beyond your usual love objects. What doubts and uncertainties arise for you? Do you recognize any feelings of loss, separation, guilt, fear, and anxiety? Can you get a sense of where they are coming from?

. . . . .

Questions and Comments

Student: What strikes me most, and what's the scariest part right now, is that sometimes a very impersonal quality will arise that isn't loving per se. It isn't warm and huggy, and yet it's very powerful and sometimes absolutely silent. When that happens inside of me, I feel panic.

A. H. Almaas: It's normal to feel panic when that happens. But the Beloved does not always feel loving and huggy. Sometimes it does, but frequently it's just powerful and annihilating, and when it's annihilating, it's scary.

S: I feel like I'm gonna abandon my loved ones. I feel like I'm leaving them behind, and they won't understand. They'll feel hurt and abandoned by my impersonalness.

AH: So you're going to be impersonal with them, you mean?

S: Yeah.

AH: I see. So that's something that you're concerned about, and you need to see whether it's actually true. That's just what you believe is going to happen.

S: I see.

AH: The Beloved is impersonal and personal at the same time. It can be either or both, or neither. But the impersonal aspect of it obviously brings up that issue for you.

S: I did an exercise earlier with my sister, and in the middle of it I looked at her and she looked like a stranger to me. I looked at her and I did not recognize her. I didn't feel like I'd ever met her in my whole life.

AH: Well, that might be true.

S: I think you're right! Okay.

AH: That frequently happens when you go to a deep place and see people for who they are. It's a whole new thing. What we're used to, what we're familiar with, is an old thing. It's not necessarily who they truly are. And that can feel then like abandoning them. But in fact it's more that you're really knowing them then.

Fidelity of the Heart   77

S: I'm having trouble understanding who the Beloved is. It seems to me, my experience is that through knowing Nature, or another person, really seeing and perceiving them, that that is where the Beloved is found. It's found through form and actually through deep personalness. So I don't understand this whole notion of competition. It seems it's almost like the Beloved sort of calls to us through Nature, but you seem to be saying that we need to leave all forms in order to find it. So I'm confused.

AH: I think it is confusing. It's true that the Beloved appears through everything—through Nature, through people, all that. However, if you look at those things the way we usually perceive them, instead of looking through them, you will not see the Beloved.

S: So you're really talking about a *way* of being with . . .

AH: Exactly. Remember what I said when I talked about it being "inside." I explained that I meant the intangible, and that doesn't just mean inside you necessarily. It's inside of everything. That's why the poem kept talking about the meaning, instead of the form. The meaning, or essence, is the intangible nature of everything. So when we talk about idols, it means taking those forms of Nature—for example, taking a tree or a mountain and just seeing it as a tree or a mountain, the way we usually experience it, and taking that to be its reality and loving just that. If you do that, that's a reification, and that will block your perception from seeing its true nature.

S: I feel like I'm struggling with the same thing. My sense from what you're saying is that the Beloved is a quality, it's a quality of being that permeates everything. But you also speak about it almost as if it's a second person, so it's almost like the Beloved feels reified. And I'm wondering, if the Beloved is in everything and really everything is made of it, then doesn't it have compassion in it and acceptance to hold us with our sins and desires, so that the whole thing goes away?

AH: Yes, there is that. But that's not the way of the lover. The lover doesn't want anything from the Beloved. The lover wants the Beloved to take everything. The lover wants to give everything to the Beloved. That's what love means. Love is an overflow, it's a giving. When we say, "I want the Beloved to hold me, to be compassionate to me," we're not coming from love. We're coming from somewhere else, which is another and valid way. But when we are loving, we just want to give the Beloved everything.

S: Yes, I can experience it in that way, and in the brief moments that I experience myself as such, I experience myself as open, and things just move through me, and I'm accepting. And at that moment I accept myself with all those aspects of me that are there when I'm not a lover.

AH: Very true. That happens. The Beloved itself doesn't reject anything. And remember what I said: Love doesn't say no to anything. It isn't about saying no to one part of you or another. Love just loves its Beloved.

S: In looking at all the things we've been talking about, all the distractions, I can trace security, comfort, the need for romantic love, mirroring, community, any number of things. But if I go deeper than that, I find that it's almost as if in my heart there is really no room for the Beloved, because of my identity. There's almost like a usurpation of the seat of the Beloved. It could be my detachment or my status as a lover of God. It could be the new and improved ego identity that I have at this time, that takes the place and won't let go. Is it possible that that happens?

AH: All those are idols.

S: So how do you make that little kernel of yourself a lover? How do you teach it to be a lover?

AH: As I said, love, heart, gives away everything, including all that.

S: But you're talking about suicide!

AH: Well, giving, sacrifice—do you consider that suicide? We will get to these points that you're raising, the question of identity and the question of the lover and the question of suicide. We're going to spend time on each one of those. They're all relevant, all important things that come up. But, basically, the attitude of the heart is that whatever comes up—any question, any issue—it just melts it away with love. The solution is that as love intensifies and deepens, it becomes more powerful and just overwhelms all these things. As I've said, the love basically destroys boundaries, destroys limitations. So every time we see something like that, it's okay to see it, it's good to see it, but the way of the lover is that it just intensifies the love. So what does the lover feel? The lover says, "I don't know what this is about, and I don't know how it's going to work. I just recognize that it's love, and it's a longing for the Beloved." That way the love becomes purer and deeper and more unified. It's the same as the way we work with inquiry and loving the truth for its own sake. Whatever it is, whatever happens, it doesn't matter—we just want the truth. Here, we're calling the truth the Beloved. Or we can call the Beloved the truth. But they're both names, and in a way that's beyond that, the heart just has to have its Beloved.

S: There's part of the language being used that is deeply threatening to me. When you say love of truth, it's not as threatening as all these things you say about loving only the Beloved and giving everything else up. The language itself, it evokes a whole different part of my being that hasn't really been challenged yet, and it's being challenged here. It brings up much more fear and more of a sense of hopelessness and not knowing than I've experienced before.

AH: Very good. That's exactly what we're doing. We're challenging that part of us. We're opening up the heart, going deeper, and that will challenge those parts of us.

So as we see, there will be all these fears, all these insecurities, all these confusions and conflicts, anxieties and feelings of loss. We could say that all of this arises because our love is still divided, is still not completely faithful. But we could also say that it's because we don't understand that all these things are just associations to the deepening of our love. What's clear is that for the lover who really loves the inner Beloved, love is not just a matter of feeling sweet and comfortable and cozy. No, the path of love is actually sometimes more intense and more powerful than the path of the warrior. It's also tougher sometimes. And the range of experience, between the pain and the ecstasy, is much wider, because here we're dealing with the heart. So the lover needs to be more courageous than the warrior. The warrior knows fear and needs to be on guard and skillful in protecting itself from what it fears. But the lover has no guard at all. For the lover it's always surrender, always giving, and always giving in.

FIVE

Beyond Divinity

It's important to remember that this focus on the heart and the path of love is just one facet of the teaching of the Diamond Approach. True nature has many different facets, and so this teaching does as well—it presents many different ways of looking at things and working on oneself. The different facets reflect the various aspects of reality, and working on all of them brings a wholeness and completeness to the teaching that reflects the wholeness and completeness of reality. Our work actually contains all of the facets all of the time, but sometimes we emphasize one or more of them so that we can highlight certain things about true nature, certain things about reality, and certain things about the path and ourselves.

So although our work is about integrating the head, the heart, and the belly, at times we might emphasize the perspective of just one of those centers. Some people will resonate more with the way of awareness, some will resonate more with the way of love, while others will resonate more with the way of will. Some people will resonate with more than one facet, and a few people will resonate with all of them. This is all fine and natural—everybody has their own tendencies—but it's good to not get too settled in one way of working, just one perspective, for too long. If we get too comfortable in any particular perspective, it's easy for it to become solidified, objectified, and reified. The work then becomes a habit, and habit kills the work—it kills the living nature of our essence. As a result, true nature becomes a reified object, simply another piece of familiar content of the mind.

We might therefore do our work from the perspective of compassion sometimes, or from the perspective of expanded awareness and knowing, but at the moment we're emphasizing the heart and the devotional or bhakti approach of love. This gives rise to a particular manifestation of the truth that is traditionally called the Beloved. It's important to remember that the Beloved is nothing other than true nature. It's therefore our own nature, but because we're seeing it from the perspective of the heart, we're experiencing our alienation from it through the heart, and we feel that alienation then as a loss or separation.

Seeing true nature as the Beloved highlights an important dimension of true nature, and it brings to the foreground something important about what it means to be a human being—that a human being is characterized by heart. It's interesting that nowadays people think it's the mind that differentiates human beings from other beings, but in spiritual traditions, human beings have always been seen as different because of their heart. As I said when we looked at its orgiastic nature, the heart of a human being is what gives us such a wide range of experience, and it's through the heart that true nature comes into the conscious experience of the soul. The degree of discontent we feel in our heart is therefore the most direct measure of how intimate we are with our true nature, with its depth and completeness. The heart knows this so well it acts like a Geiger counter—the closer it gets to the truth, the faster and louder it ticks. The farther away it gets from the truth, the slower and quieter it becomes, until after a while you can barely hear it. The mind doesn't have that kind of sensitivity, nor do the instincts.

We're discovering that when we see truth as the Beloved, our attitude toward the Work is completely different—it's a whole other ballgame. All our concerns, fears, and conflicts become less important—just fodder for the journey, fuel for the love. It doesn't mean they're neglected or rejected or not attended to, but we see them as side effects of the journey rather than our main concern. Our main concern is the Beloved because, basically, the heart wants the Beloved and nothing else. Everything else is incidental—just a reflection, a reaction, or an association. The heart knows this and will not be fully contented with any of it.

So let's summarize what we've learned so far about this journey of the heart and get a basic outline of the path of love: The heart will not be satisfied and will not settle until it is united with its Beloved, and the inner Beloved is not going to show up unless the heart is completely faithful to it. There is therefore a process of emptying the heart of all its particular objects of love, and divesting our love of all that has form, image, shape, and quality. In that way the love is distilled, unified, and focused, which gives it a power that can have a melting quality, a dissolving quality, and also a burning, annihilating quality. The mere intensification and deepening of the love dissolves all barriers and obstacles to its fidelity. As the heart becomes increasingly faithful to the intangible, formless Beloved, it recognizes the transitory and particular for what it is, seeing beyond the forms of things to their essence and meaning. And with this increasing fidelity to the truth beyond forms, the heart ripens and the love deepens even further.

The journey of the heart tends to be tempestuous. We've seen the tempestuous quality of the love and yearning, with its intense ups and downs, and it is a characteristic of this path. However, it's not necessarily so intense all the time. At times the yearning can be gentle and delicate, and other things might dominate for a while—other facets of your process might be more predominant on the path, and the love more of an undercurrent. But then it can suddenly resurface and come to the foreground again, becoming once more the strongest, most powerful and influential force in our conscious experience. So when we talk about the journey of the heart, it doesn't necessarily mean that we're flooded with intense love and yearning every day. It depends on the person. Some people have it as a dominant thread in their journey, and for some people it's a thread that comes and goes periodically.

What's true for everyone is that the more we allow the heart to open up and orient itself toward the Beloved, the more that fuels the journey as a whole. It gives our spiritual unfolding a particular dimension of depth and intensity, and a particular kind of beauty—a kind of magic. I said at the beginning that the more love dominates our path, the more it becomes a love affair, and this is an important shift. It means that it's no longer all just hard work—it's not only a matter of being disciplined and dedicated in a way that's all about being responsible and earnest. We're now involved in an intoxicating love affair, and the way we feel has aspects to it that are best described as "drunken." That's partly what is meant by the term "ecstatic love"—that it has a drunken quality to it. It's not a rational, orderly, or reasonable quality, because it's not being restrained and regulated by the mind. So it might seem that we are irrational and drunk, but it's love that we are drunk on—it's a state of intoxication caused by passionate and ecstatic love.

We've been looking at how the deepening and intensification of this love gradually melts and burns away all the images and forms of our other beloveds, and we're going to look more deeply now into what we saw in the previous chapter—that this brings up a sense of loss and fear around what we hold as precious, not just externally but also internally. Generally the external objects of love are the first to be seen through and melted, and then the internal objects of love, which are closer to us and more representative of the Beloved. Ultimately we get to those manifestations of the Beloved that we have come to believe really are the Beloved—the states of essence and dimensions of true nature that for a long time have made us feel and believe we are seeing and experiencing the Beloved itself. Which we are in a way, but frequently not in the most pure or complete way.

We all develop images and concepts of the Beloved that are based on the different, partial ways we've seen and experienced various aspects and qualities of it—usually beautiful and wonderful experiences in their own right. But the culture we live in, the education we receive, and the stories we hear also provide us with images, forms, and names that we come to associate with the Beloved. Our cultural background and the cultural environment can solidify some of these images in a way that leaves us convinced we know what the Beloved is. However, we mustn't forget that these are all images in the mind, and if our love for the Beloved is sincere and our heart is mature and open, it's ultimately only the heart that will know whether something really is the Beloved or not. Because as we've learned, if it is not purely and completely the Beloved, the heart will not be completely contented—it will still feel a yearning and longing. That yearning and longing won't truly abate until the heart mirrors the ultimate Beloved in its absolute purity. Before that, the longing will continue to burn in the heart because there is still a sense of separation, even if the mind believes that what we are experiencing is the Beloved.

So the power of our cultural background—and all of us come from a particular culture, with its specific images, names, and concepts of divinity—is not to be underestimated. It's difficult for us not to develop some degree of fixation on our culture's notion of the Beloved. As children we are given a certain image of a divinity—that's what everybody says it is, and that's what all the literature tells us. And if you've been taught that the Beloved manifests in a certain way, and all the literature describes it that way, then naturally you'll come to experience it that way yourself. Your experience is then a confirmation of what you've been told, and so it's easy to believe that's what the Beloved is. But again, it's the mind that believes that, not the heart. If our heart is really sincere and its love is truly faithful to the Beloved, free of any mental image of it, then at some point we will be able to tell that whatever our culture and various teachings may have told us about the Beloved, that's not actually the way it is.

In our culture, which is by and large monotheistic, the most traditional name for the Beloved is God, and that's the name associated with the most traditional images of it. So when most people think of the Beloved, they equate it with this divine being called God. And if we give the Beloved the name of God, our histories provide us with all kinds of different associations with that word. If you have a Catholic or Jewish background, you'll have a certain way of experiencing God that will color the way you view divinity, and then also the way you think about the Beloved, even if you say that the notion of God that your culture gave you is not the kind of Beloved you're looking for.

Those with a different cultural background might have been encouraged to think of the Beloved as love, presence, or awareness. The various manifestations and dimensions of essence are commonly experienced by many people as a kind of inner God—the divinity within—especially when they experience in them the sense of universality, power, grace, love, and beauty. It's easy for us to then feel we are experiencing God in these essential qualities, and because it's an experience of a very lovable God, we can take it to be a manifestation of the Beloved. And we're not wrong in feeling that; it's just that the heart can go further, beyond that particular manifestation. If our love for the Beloved continues to intensify and expand, it will outgrow any of the concepts, names, images, and forms of the Beloved that our culture has taught us to accept as true, real, objective, final, or ultimate.

They are indeed just names and pictures, but a large part of the difficulty we have in approaching and being totally open to the inner Beloved lies in the influence of the names we've been taught to give it and our associations to them. Those influences can remain powerful at a deep level even when our rational mind no longer believes in them. So whether we have adopted the names of God or divinity that our culture gave us, or rejected those names because we were searching for something different, the fact that we grew up in an environment suffused by those names and concepts means they will continue to operate in our unconscious, along with all the other deep influences of our culture, schooling, and family.

When it becomes obvious to us that what we have learned and come to accept as our familiar experience of God or divinity does not fully satisfy the heart and give it contentment, and we then begin to go beyond it, it can give rise to a great deal of conflict and considerable anguish. If your heart is longing for something more, and you're feeling that there is something beyond that notion of God, your unconscious says, "What? Beyond God?!" Because of our cultural background, our unconscious rises up and says, "No way! This is blasphemy," or "Now you really are an infidel!" Our superego can become like one of the magistrates of the Inquisition of medieval times, threatening to damn and punish us for being a heretic.

So at this central juncture in the movement of the heart toward the Beloved, this feeling of conflict can lead to fear and trepidation, as well as guilt, mistrust, and anguish. Partly it's the fear and anguish that we're going to lose the most precious things in our experience of reality. Naturally, the experience we've had of God or the Beloved has become the cornerstone of our reality; it is our greatest support, our holding, and a nourishing source of grace, love, and goodness. Of course we're afraid of letting go of and abandoning that, because doing so will confront us with our inadequacy and leave us needing support again. And because of the guilt we feel, there is also another fear—of retaliation, especially if we're of a Catholic, Slavic, or Jewish background. There can be tremendous guilt and fear about effectively saying, "Right, I'm going to leave God behind." People have talked here about the fear and guilt they feel when it feels like they're leaving their other beloveds behind. And now God himself, this figure who plays such a powerful and central role in our inner world, is being seen as just another of the beloveds we must leave behind.

We've seen that withdrawing our focus from our other beloveds brings up all the conflicts and anxieties we have about any kind of separation, and what I'm stressing here is that there will be a particular component to these anxieties when it comes to "leaving God," determined by the religious culture we have grown up in and the influence it still has on our mind. We need to acknowledge the power of these earliest cultural influences, even if we think we no longer believe what they told us. Part of their unconscious power stems from the fact that when we are forming these early images of God, they tend to get mixed up with the images of our parents, who are in effect all-powerful deities to the very young and dependent child.

So whether we've grown up believing and experiencing that God has a particular form and quality or that the divinity is something more formless, some kind of intelligence or light, many of us may find that deep in the unconscious we still believe in a God who is more like the God of the Old Testament. Even if we now experience God and divinity as grace, power, love, harmony, and beauty, when it comes to the point of going beyond that, the belief in this biblical God can emerge. Because if it feels like we are leaving God, we also get the feeling that God isn't going to like it. And God knows what the all-powerful Old Testament God might send our way to punish us, be it plagues and diseases, floods and storms, or financial ruin—perhaps ultimately the loss of everything we value in life.

In my experience, it doesn't matter how agnostic or atheistic a person is—if those images of God existed in the environment in our childhood, they will manifest as part of the conflict arising at this point. I'm saying this so that you can be open to these feelings arising, instead of saying, "No, no, that couldn't happen to me because I've never believed in God." You don't have to believe in God to be afraid of God. One often hears nonreligious people saying that something "puts the fear of God" into them. And that fear can certainly arise when it comes to separating from whatever familiar notion of divinity we might have, along with a fear of the loss and retribution that might ensue.

On my own journey, I came to see divine being as a condition of the oneness and unity of all of existence—as one presence of abundance, fullness, love, and harmony. I experienced it as intelligence, as presence, as light, and as love, always dynamic and constantly creating and manifesting everything in the whole universe—the only doer, the only mover, the only thing that exists, with nothing outside of it, nothing excluded. So when I was experiencing that, which I generally called unity or oneness, and my heart started longing again, I couldn't understand why. How could there be a longing for something beyond that? I felt afraid of this seemingly insatiable longing and discontent. It was partly a fear of losing the condition I had arrived at, which seemed so complete and final, and partly some kind of guilt that I was being unfaithful to what I believed was the Beloved—that this was just another sign of my infidelity. There was also another fear that came when I found myself thinking, "What's left to discover? What else could there possibly be?" I couldn't imagine how the Beloved could be something else, so the notion of leaving this condition behind felt like jumping into the abyss.

To do that required basic trust—the trust that goes beyond the mind and is therefore prepared to go beyond any image, beyond any form, and beyond any concept that I'd known before, and take a leap into the dark. The heart that was still seeking something more needed to become courageous enough to say,

"Well, whatever reality is going to show up, let it show." It required great courage, sincerity, and as I said before, humility—a willingness to accept that I still didn't really know what the Beloved is. And here again, that can happen simply by the love itself intensifying and deepening and overcoming all these other concerns. Nevertheless, I remember this as a period of inner conflict, when I didn't understand what on earth was going on. Then finally I got it, and saw: "I didn't even know it was possible to see God that way." And that's when I discovered what it was that my heart had still been seeking.

We might not even see it as God, because this transition really does mean going beyond even the subtlest and most fundamental concepts of God, divinity, or the Beloved. You see, it doesn't matter whether we've been seeing the Beloved as some kind of form that can be imaged or named; as some kind of emptiness, presence, or awareness; or as boundless beingness, boundless love, or boundless intelligence—these are all ways of experiencing the Beloved in an object relation, and the crucial thing at this point is that we are leaving behind all ways of doing that.

This can bring up the most fundamental object relation from childhood—that we are a child relating to an adult. That confronts us with the child's need for support, love, holding, and guidance from something bigger, larger, and more powerful. It's usually a parent at the beginning, but in time it's easy for that to become God. So in this transition of going beyond God, we may encounter this fundamental object relation of being a child who is utterly dependent on adult support. To go beyond divinity means letting go of that object relation, which is fundamental in that it underlies all our various object relations as a child. And as we do that, we are moving into a final aloneness and complete autonomy.

This is extremely challenging, and of course it helps a great deal if we had parents who took care of us in a loving way, giving us the necessary holding, care, and guidance when we were children. The more we had that in childhood, the easier it is for us to let go of this fundamental object relation now. The less that object relation satisfied us, and the more we still believe we need it, the more difficult it is to let go of, and so it becomes more difficult to now let go of God, the divinity, or whatever notion of true nature we have seen as our support, our aid, and our holding.

So we need to see that the moment we conceptualize the Beloved, the moment we make an image of it, the moment we give a form or name to it, we make it an object with which we can have that fundamental object relation. This object relation can be conflictual, or we might get to the place of feeling the love in it, but no matter how you experience it, at the point when you feel you're going beyond it, some content of that object relation will arise to challenge you. It may be the fear and guilt around separation from the divine being, or it may be the feeling that you still need its love, care, and holding. It can feel like you're going to lose all the harmony you're seeking, and not only that, other people are going to have it and you might end up with nothing. You have this image of everyone else living in this wonderful, harmonious oneness, and you're striking out God knows where—to some place where there might be nothing there.

Of course, the intensity of the attachment to our notion of the Beloved, and the strength of our fixation on it, will depend on how long we have abided in that particular condition of intimate connection with oneness, divinity, or reality.

So it's time to do an exercise to explore this dilemma.

PRACTICE SESSION:
GOING BEYOND THE DIVINITY
YOU'VE KNOWN

• • •

We're going to do another monologue, so as before, work with one or two other people if possible. Each person in the group will do their monologue for fifteen minutes. If you are alone, write out your exploration for fifteen minutes.

Explore what arises for you as your love begins to move beyond the images or concepts you have of the Beloved as God, the divine being, or as the deepest state of true nature that you've known and come to see as the Beloved.

• • • • •

Questions and Comments

Student: I feel quite shaken from the exercise, and when I first started to explore the question, my heart got very excited. It felt like the question was in such support of my heart, and it felt like a real kind of movement, like "Let's just go! I wanna go home!" When I get into these groups of three, I usually experience fear, not excitement, and so it was a real shift for me. And when I followed my heart, one of the first things that came was this image of being very young. I had a very abusive childhood, and I saw myself when I was about three, turning away from my family in great desperation, and kind of turning away and up, and looking for something to help me or save me. The turning felt so huge, and there was so much emotion and trembling in it, and I felt this image suddenly being created in my mind of this God being my savior. The devotion that I feel this young person has is huge, and to feel the separation anxiety of going beyond that image feels very challenging.

A. H. Almaas: Yes, it is challenging. Especially in that kind of situation, it will be a difficult thing. So you don't try to do anything about it. You just recognize it and understand it. Be with it.

S: In looking at a recent event, I felt that I'd had a significant experience that touched on what you've been talking about, about the Beloved. I went through a process with someone who was going through a major ordeal in their life a few years ago, and I took the aim to listen to my heart, this unknown organ in my chest. I knew I had no training in doing it, so I was going blindly. But all went well, I think, and it was quite a lesson. Then I did the same when I found myself in a new relationship, and it seems that's easy to do when you're talking about personal relationships, but now I'm at a point in my life when I'm looking at things that aren't in that realm, like career, where I'm going to live—the rest of my life. That doesn't seem to lend itself so well to saying, "Okay, I'm gonna follow my heart," and just paying attention to it, doing it just as I'd done before when it all worked out so well. Because in giving myself over to following the dictates of my heart, the feeling now is that you can end up being like a mad monk. And even without the monk part, you can end up looking and behaving in ways that are crazy.

AH: When I listen to my heart, if I ask my heart about my career or other different interests, my heart tells me, "Don't bother me with these things. That's not my job. I only want the Beloved, that's all." So for me, to deal with those practical things, I use all my capacities—my heart is just one of them. It's like whatever I have—my intelligence, my heart, my knowledge—everything goes together. But when I go inside my heart and listen only to my heart, my heart is always taking me to the Beloved. The heart can guide us in terms of the affairs of the world if they are secondary in a way to the Beloved. We can then find guidance about how to deal with the affairs of the world in such a way that doesn't become a barrier to the Beloved.

S: I'm accustomed to courage and forbearance as qualities that have been supporting my unfoldment. The belief and images that arose in this exercise about what would be the consequences of going beyond my images of God, of true nature, remind me of the things that courage and forbearance, and other qualities, have supported me going into and going through. So my question is, is the love that is in the heart for what it truly wants—the passion, the yearning—is that complete? Does it make those other qualities not particularly germane in this particular pursuit?

AH: No, definitely the other qualities are important and necessary for the journey. Our love needs our will, our strength, and our courage—all these are needed to get us through. But let's say that those will become more available the more unified our heart is. It's like there are different ways of having those qualities available, and here we're discussing the way of the heart. The more we love, the more that those qualities will arise. So most of us don't have many of those qualities to start with, or we're not aware of them, but they come from the same place where love comes from. And the other thing is, all the qualities can be experienced as love.

S: Could you say more about that?

AH: Will as love, strength as love, truth as love—all those can be experienced as love. So love can have all these qualities. I mean, this is something we work on specifically in the Diamond Approach, certain dimensions where everything is love.

S: I find myself wanting to know, wanting to hear the word "the absolute," and wondering if the Beloved is the language of the heart as it relates to the absolute. Also knowing that that's a concept, and I don't pretend to know what that is, but I'm curious because that word hasn't come up yet.

AH: Sure. Well, sometimes we can call the Beloved that, the absolute. But we are working on going beyond words, beyond ideas, and beyond experiences.

SIX

Poverty of the Heart

We'll start with a poem by Rumi, "One Whisper of the Beloved," from the book *A Garden Beyond Paradise*:

Lovers share a sacred decree—
To seek the Beloved.
They roll head over heels,
Rushing toward the Beautiful One
Like a torrent of water.

In truth, everyone is a shadow of the Beloved—
Our seeking is His seeking,
Our words are His words.

At times we flow toward the Beloved
Like a dancing stream.
At times we are still water
Held in His pitcher.
At times we boil in a pot

Turning to vapor—
That is the job of the Beloved.

He breathes into my ear
Until my soul
Takes on His fragrance.
He is the soul of my soul—
How can I escape?
But why would any soul in this world
Want to escape from the Beloved?

He will melt your pride
Making you thin as a strand of hair,
Yet do not trade, even for both worlds,
One strand of His hair.

We search for Him here and there
While looking right at Him.
Sitting by His side we ask,
"O Beloved, where is the Beloved?"

Enough with such questions!
Let silence take you to the core of life.

All your talk is worthless
When compared to one whisper
Of the Beloved.[*]

---

[*] Jonathan Star and Shahram Shiva, trans., *A Garden Beyond Paradise: The Mystical Poetry of Rumi* (Bantam Books, 1992), 100.

Once we've truly seen how the various objects that fill our heart compete with our love for the Beloved, we're more willing to let go of our attachment to them—we stop holding on to them in our heart. So what happens as the love deepens and becomes more unified, liberating itself from all the idols—the images, forms, and ideas that it has taken to be its Beloved? How does it feel as our crowded heart is gradually emptied of all our desired love objects, to make more and more space for the Beloved? After all, the Beloved will only appear when the whole place is for Him and for Him only.

Now, it's not as if we empty our heart of all these objects, and then the next thing, we suddenly see the Beloved there. At least that's not what usually happens. As often occurs in our process, there is a transitional state, and in this case it is a mysterious state of limbo. This condition reflects the mysterious character of the Beloved, who only appears at night, when everything is asleep, still, and silent. It's a condition that can feel very uncomfortable, however, because as the heart becomes emptier and emptier and emptier, it will eventually reach the stage where it feels totally empty. By turning inward and becoming so concentrated in one place, our love has withdrawn from all the people and things it was focused on before, so it now feels like we don't have any love objects at all. Not only that, it feels like we don't even have love itself: "If I'm not loving anything, and I'm not loving anybody, where is my love?" We've associated love with our feelings for all the objects that have filled our heart—our concern for them, our preoccupation with them, and our reactions and responses to them. These feelings are what told us we have a heart that loves, so when we become completely detached from them, we're left with the sense that we no longer have any love, and not even a heart.

So when the Kaaba, the House of God that represents the heart, is finally emptied of all the idols, it feels uncomfortably empty at first. It's understandable that we can get scared at this point and think, "Oh no, I'm losing my heart!" We're dismayed, too, because this isn't at all what we expected—spiritual lovers assume that when their love for the Beloved becomes more focused, they'll experience a more intense kind of love. And yes, we do feel that sometimes, because our love for the inner Beloved is gradually expanding and deepening, but it's easy to be more preoccupied with how disconcerting this gradual emptying of our heart feels. As we become more and more detached from our habitual everyday loves, their absence in our heart is felt as the absence of love, and of the heart itself. This condition of "no heart" and "no love" is one of the most difficult stations on the path of love—and remember, it's not just the everyday external beloveds that our heart now feels empty of, but also the various inner beloveds that have sustained us on the spiritual path.

It can feel like we don't love anybody or anything, and we might worry that we're no longer even capable of giving and receiving love. That scares us, so we think, "Wait a minute. Let me call somebody and tell them how much I love them." Or we look for something that someone gave us, some romantic thing that will help us remember the love it came with: "Look, here's that lovely necklace my boyfriend gave me." Or perhaps you find yourself looking wistfully at the beautiful tie your wife gave you on your wedding anniversary. You're trying to bring back the feelings around these objects of love, and the loving relationships they reflect. However, if the redirection of our love has been accomplished well enough, we can't manage to do that. No matter how hard we try, it doesn't work because these things feel empty now—the heart has been emptied and is focused purely on getting ready for the Beloved. But we're conflicted because some part of us finds this difficult to tolerate—it wants to go back to having our normal heart and all its beloveds so it can get away from this troubling feeling of having no love at all.

So this condition can be very disconcerting, especially when it concerns someone who's been the central love in your life for many years. You wake up one day and it's like the love for them just isn't there. Perhaps your spouse is away on a long trip and you realize: "I don't miss them. What the hell's happened? Should I get a new one?" And it's hard when you think of your friends and realize you don't feel like seeing them. You don't even feel like calling them. You're not looking forward to seeing anybody or anything. You don't miss anyone, and you don't yearn for anyone or anything. So it really does feel like you don't love anything anymore.

Some of you may be approaching this condition already and feeling it to some extent. Some people have mentioned how they've looked for familiar feelings of love and found there's nothing there—just an emptiness, with no feelings of any kind. There seems to be a void where our heart should be, and naturally this can give rise to a tremendous sense of loss and the fear that we're never going to feel love again. We made a decision to give up all our other beloveds so we could know the true Beloved, but when they've all gone and there's nothing in their place, we get worried. There are moments when we doubt we've done the right thing—maybe we've abandoned all our other loves for nothing, because it seems like the Beloved has abandoned us. It reminds me of Jesus on the cross at the last moment, when he said, "Why have you forsaken me?" And for most of us, I'm sure, it's not something we're going to feel for just a moment. It might last hours, days, weeks.

The lover who has gotten to this point will have learned that whatever they are seeking, including the feeling of love, only comes from the Beloved, and it comes in its own time. But it's a challenging time when all our loves are gone and we still haven't completely seen or recognized the Beloved, even though he is staring us right in the face. He's actually pushing his face in our face when we're feeling the emptiness, but we don't get it. We think we have nothing. The Beloved is saying, "Look, look. See, it's me." We can only respond, "There's nothing here. It's all empty."

So there's a mystery here that we're still not able to penetrate at this point. And we don't need to try and penetrate it. All we have to do is just stay with this condition and not reject it. Even though we might not be experiencing heart, if our love is strong, we can just let this experience be, recognizing it to be one of the conditions of the path of love. Staying with it means we don't reject it, we don't accept it, we don't do anything to it. Even if we don't understand what's happening, simply letting it be is an important step toward the Beloved at this point.

If we let it be, we may be able to see that what's happened is a clearing of the heart—a letting go of all our attachments. But we see it as an absence of heart because we've been so accustomed to seeing heart as all the usual feelings, reactions, preoccupations, and responses that come with all the various kinds of love. We're used to having our heart be full of those objects that we love, so when we're no longer attached to them and they're not there, the heart is indeed empty. What we still haven't fully understood is that the heart is *supposed* to be empty for the Beloved to enter it. Sure, we may have grasped the concept of the Kaaba needing to be cleared so it can be the temple for the Beloved, but in practice we're finding this emptiness difficult to tolerate.

So it can seem like something terrible has happened when we feel we have no love and no heart, and we may want to reject this condition. But if we stay with it, we come to recognize that all the loves we've cleared from the heart never really belonged to us anyway. We can then see an important truth: This condition of emptiness that we want to reject is actually the natural condition of the heart that hasn't yet recognized its Beloved. And we can see that this fundamental emptiness has always been there—we've just been covering it up by filling the heart with all our objects of love. Though covered up, that emptiness continues to underlie the attachments to our many beloveds. So when we let go of those attachments and they dissolve, we become aware of the emptiness underneath—the emptiness that causes us to feel we have no heart and no love.

If we accept the emptiness of the heart, it expands, and we come to feel the emptiness of the whole person. We realize then that this person we've known ourselves to be throughout our life, the individual ego person, has always had this emptiness within it. Not surprisingly, we fight this awareness—we resist it and find all kinds of ways to defend ourselves against it. However, the reality is that this condition is what always underlies the ego self, because the ego self means that the soul is divorced from her Beloved.

This awareness of our emptiness is a stage on the spiritual journey that many traditions have called mystical poverty. It truly is a state of poverty because we see that our usual self has nothing of real value—it is devoid of Being and all its qualities and capacities. The feeling of emptiness and lovelessness is the mystical poverty of the heart, and it reveals the true condition of the soul that has been separated from her true nature, her Beloved. This emptiness is necessary if the Beloved is to appear. It's the beginning of what's called the dark night of the soul, when the Guest can arrive. And we've learned that the Guest only comes at night, which means everything's gone dark and there's nothing to see.

It's a challenging condition, but also an interesting one. It's like we're very close, we're almost there. We're on the verge of beholding the Beloved because we're not looking at anything else, but we don't see anything yet. We can't make out the Beloved in the darkness because we're still looking through the veil of the ego self, still identifying with the person we've always taken ourself to be. Because of that identification, we experience the emptiness as meaning we are deficient—we have nothing—and since we're experiencing this through the heart, we're left with the feeling that we have no love, and no care or concern for anyone or anything at all. This heartless feeling can make us feel so conflicted, guilty, worried, and scared that we hang on to our attachments. We take our various loves and quietly slip them back into the corners of a heart that otherwise feels too empty, without any juice, love, or nectar.

If we catch ourselves doing this, we need to keep remembering one of the key secrets of the Beloved—it is not going to show up unless there really is nothing else there. So here we are, well on the way toward nothing, which is good news, you see. But it's difficult for us to understand what this nothing is—we can only experience it as deficiency.

To the self, it is deficiency. To the soul on her journey, it is mystical poverty, one of the deep stations or stages of the path. In this stage, as Rumi describes in the poem, we are seeing the Beloved but not recognizing the Beloved—we only recognize our poverty. It means we experience our sense of self in all its nakedness, emptied of what usually fills it and without its defenses and protections. And we can experience our heart stripped bare of all its attachments, in an empty state that is its natural condition.

I'll read you a short passage from *Luminous Night's Journey*, describing my own process during the stage we're looking at, just to give you a personal flavor of it.

The next morning, I wake up with a crystal heart filling the chest. I feel it at this point as a hard, neutral presence. I feel an absence of love; this morning the crystal heart does not feel like love. In fact, I feel that I have no heart.*

The crystal heart is a dimension or level of the heart that brings about detachment from everything. So it's the heart of nonattachment, which makes it possible for us to love and have heart without attachment. But here, I wake up with this heart and feel it as hard, as a hard and neutral presence. It does not feel like love but like the absence of love and heart.

I cannot tell whether the crystal heart feels this way itself, or if it exposes an ego structure that feels empty of heart. By afternoon, it becomes clear that the absence of heart is not exactly related to the crystalline heart of presence, even though it's probably related to it in the sense that it's caused by it. The lack is revealed to be the reaction of the ego-self. I become aware of a deficient sense of personality.

As I contemplate this conditioned state of the soul, I notice that I slowly become it. I finally see myself as a person, an ego

---

* A. H. Almaas, *Luminous Night's Journey: An Autobiographical Fragment* (Shambhala Publications, 2000), 77.

person with feelings. This clarifies my confusion of the crystal heart with the absence of heart. This person of ego recognizes only familiar emotions and feelings as the presence of heart.

I experience myself now as a person who is not trying to defend or protect himself. The inner condition is naked, exposed. No defenses, no pretenses. There's vulnerability, helplessness, weakness, not knowing, innocence, and a very deep sadness. The person feels all these emotions. The sense of self, with its accompanying emotional state, appears simultaneously with the boundaries that I call the ego-line. There's a deep feeling of anguish in this condition.

I feel curious about this person whom I have known for most of my life, the person I have taken myself to be for many years.*

The important thing to notice here is that even though this condition can give rise to much fear and dismay, instead of rejecting it or reacting to it, what arises is a curiosity about it. We'll continue with this story later; for now what is important is the condition of mystical poverty and how it is a stage in approaching the Beloved. I'm discussing it in case something similar arises for you, so you'll see it as a normal experience on the path and not get as scared as I did. I'm sure you'll get scared anyway, but maybe not as much and not for as long. That's the thing, you see—sometimes something takes me several months to understand and process, but in somebody I'm working with, maybe it will only take a day or two.

So let's do an exercise to explore this process of letting go of our attachments to the many beloveds.

* Almaas, *Luminous Night's Journey*, 77–78.

Practice Session:
Staying Faithful to the Inner Beloved

...

We'll do the form of exercise called repeating question. If you have someone to do the exercise with, you will each take a turn for fifteen minutes, asking the other person the first question. When the fairly short response is complete, the person asking says, "Thank you" and then asks the question again until the fifteen minutes are up. It's then the turn of the other person to ask the question for fifteen minutes. If you don't have a partner to do this exercise with, you can answer in writing as many times as possible within the allotted time. Or you can record the question and have it spoken to you by your computer or device after you finish answering out loud.

The first question is:

What's right about having many beloveds?

Since we have many beloveds, in some place we must believe it's right. So we want to find out all the reasons and motives behind whatever we feel or believe about this. As I said before about this kind of question, when we ask, "What's right about . . . ?" you might think, "Well, I know by now that there's nothing right about it." But for you to say that is like repeating what you think my response would be, and I want you to respond personally and spontaneously, from your own unconscious. Find out what your own real reasons are for having and believing in so many beloveds. You need to remember, this is the path of love, and the lover is always orgiastically responsive. So no control. If you control what you feel and say, you can't allow your heart to be orgiastic and ecstatic.

You then both do the same with the second question, again for fifteen minutes each:

What would it be like for you to be faithful to the inner Beloved?

You want to contemplate that faithfulness and see: What does it mean to you? How does it make you feel? What do you think will happen if you fully commit to it?

· · · · ·

Questions and Comments

Student: I wondered how we can distinguish whether we're at this stage where the heart doesn't really feel anything and it's because we're moving really close to the Beloved, or whether the heart has just not yet opened.

A. H. Almaas: One of the ways you know it's the mystical poverty of the heart, and not just the heart not having opened yet, is that with the mystical poverty of the heart, you've already had the experience that the heart has opened intensely and strongly, for many years, and you've had all kinds of deep feelings of love and longing, hurt, fear and terror, and caring and attachment. And you've had to work very hard to give up those attachments, because of all the pain and suffering behind them, and you've gone through all that, and your heart has been shish-kebabbed. You know when it's been shish-kebabbed, so you know then that when this condition of feeling no love arises, it's not just a defense where the heart is closed. You see, when the heart is closed or we're being defensive—like in a schizoid condition, for instance— the reason the person isn't feeling anything is because they aren't *able* to feel anything. The feeling function hasn't woken up yet.

In the condition of poverty of the heart, the person isn't feeling anything because there's nothing to feel, even though the person is capable of feeling very deeply because the feeling function is developed and mature. So it's not like your heart can't feel anything; it is feeling, but there's nothing there for it to feel—the objects of feeling have left, so what you feel is an emptiness, a nothingness. That's why the person tends to associate that with deficiency. So it's a good thing to know the difference.

We can experience this nothingness in varying degrees too. Just as when the heart opens and we experience to different degrees the love and passion and all the heartache that people go through, especially lovers, we can also experience emptiness of various kinds and different depths. But this emptiness we're talking about here is more complete, and the feeling is that you've had a heart for a long time, a very deep and powerful juicy heart, and now it feels like it's gone, and that's why there's a feeling of loss to it.

So I'm glad you brought that up, because there are things that I say that can be misinterpreted. Just like when I said we want to go beyond the images and the names of the Beloved—I'm not saying that forms and names are inherently bad. For most conditions, names and forms are necessary, that's the context of our life, and when we want to understand each other, sometimes we point to things by naming them. But the naming needs to be a pointer rather than an enclosure around something. So as I said, even with the Beloved, if we take the names like God or divine being to be pointers to something that is nameless, that's okay, but if we take them to be definitions, that becomes a problem. So when I say we need to go beyond the names, some people might take it to mean we should never name our experience. But if you never name your experience, you'll never be able to inquire or understand anything. So if a name arises, let it arise, but then we want to go beyond it. By the name arising, we understand something, but the name should open up the door to another bigger and more subtle name, and that should open up to an even more subtle name, until after a while we arrive at the nameless.

S: My question revolves around the relationship between what we call "the flame" and the yearning for the Beloved. The flame, as I understand it, represents among other things the love of the truth, and it seems like it could help to hasten the arrival of the Beloved, or it could act as an impediment because of the attachments that come with identifying yourself as the lover, the one who loves.

AH: What we call the flame, which is a particular experience of the soul, represents the beginning of the conscious awareness that there is an inner path—that there's something we don't know, we don't realize—and we aspire toward it, long for it, love it, desire it, all that. So the flame is an awakening of the soul to that situation. The love of the Beloved includes the flame, but it comes before it and after it and is much bigger. The love for the truth can become like a flame, a big fire—I use that term often. So the flame is just one expression of the love for the Beloved, and usually when you feel the flame, it indicates that the person is aware that they need or yearn for something that they don't have and they don't know.

S: And that's not the yearning for the Beloved?

AH: It can be seen as a yearning for the Beloved, but the yearning might not always be felt in terms of the Beloved. It could be a yearning for enlightenment, a yearning for liberation—different people experience it differently.

S: My question is how it is that the Beloved is jealous when the Beloved is all that we could be jealous of—well, that I could be jealous of. How is it that the Beloved is jealous when it is, for me, everything? What is there to be jealous of?

AH: What I meant is that the Beloved is jealous of you having other lovers besides the Beloved. We say the Beloved is jealous as a way of pointing to the fact that the Beloved will not reveal itself completely when we want to share our love with others besides the Beloved. It's like if you have two beloveds, one of them will be jealous of the other. It's in that sense that the Beloved is jealous. Even when you experience the unity of everything, the divine being as I mentioned earlier, the Beloved is still deeper than that, which shows that the experience of unity has itself become one of the images, one of the forms. It is a manifestation of the Beloved, but it's not the most complete. Even the experience of the Beloved, if we have a memory of it, an idea or concept of it, that can then become an idol too. That's why the Arabic name that we use for the Beloved is Hu. In English, "Hu" sounds like "Who," as when we ask, "Who is it?" So it actually sounds like we don't know—it's like we're always chanting, "Who? Who?" The Sufis use that word, and it comes from the Arabic colloquial word that means "He." And that's why the reference is to "He" when we talk about God and all that. But etymologically it points to the nature and identity of who we are and everything else. So the Beloved becomes jealous if you separate one thing and you say, "I love this, and I love the Beloved," and so now there are two things. The Beloved is jealous only in the sense that it won't show up when something else is there in its place.

S: So where is the inner Beloved? I think of the Rumi line, "Is the one I love everywhere?" And in answering the first question, about what's right about loving many objects, sometimes it seemed, what's wrong with experiencing the inner Beloved everywhere, in everything? Is the Beloved not there in all the many love objects?

AH: Not for the one who does not love the Beloved completely. If you love the Beloved completely, the Beloved is everywhere. If you don't love the Beloved completely, no, the Beloved is not everywhere. What you see are idols, objects. So not everyone can say that the Beloved is everywhere. Rumi can say that because he sees that. But if you don't see it, you can't say it, because it's not true for you. If you see it, yes, it is true.

S: I'll remember that.

AH: It's always important to remember that. When we're reading mystical poetry that uses spiritual language and it says the Beloved is everywhere, some people might take it as, "So the Beloved is everywhere . . . Great! So I can just keep liking ice cream more and more." Or someone hears someone say, "Everyone has the Buddha in them" and thinks, "Okay, I've got the Buddha in me. So why meditate? I might as well continue my life goofing around and I've still got the Buddha inside me." That's not what is meant. That person doesn't know that the inner Buddha is inside, so for them the statement is not accurate, it's not valid.

S: I'd like some clarification. You say that the Beloved is a jealous lover and won't appear if there are other lovers, but I'm wondering if that means the Beloved won't appear fully and completely, or can the Beloved appear partially when there are other beloveds. Or will it not appear at all until there are no other Beloveds?

AH: That's what I've been saying—the more our love is unified and the more detached we are from the various beloveds, the more the Beloved will appear in various ways. It may appear in partial ways, it's true—in aspects, qualities, and various forms—but to appear completely and fully, and to appear to the heart, in the heart as its Beloved, the heart has to be completely empty of all other beloveds. So it's in that sense that we say the Beloved is jealous. In reality it doesn't make sense to say that the Beloved is jealous. It's just a human way of interpreting it, and people who are on the path of love tend to use that language. They use the human situation as a metaphor. That's why in much of the poetry, the Beloved is given human features like eyes and hair, and feet and toes, and stuff like that, to make it sound just like a human being. It's a way of talking about it that brings in the language of love that people are familiar with from being in love, because that's then an easy transition to make to the inner Beloved. In reality, the inner Beloved is formless, and these things don't truly apply. But some people get stuck on that and they think that's it. But if you see the inner Beloved with curly hair, then it's not going to be the inner Beloved. And some people do see the Beloved with curly hair, or black hair or blond hair, depending on what you like. And that will be a manifestation of the inner Beloved, but it's not really the essence of the inner Beloved. So it might appear also with straight hair, and maybe the Beloved appearing as bald is better for some people.

S: Would you say something more about the Beloved being deeper than the unity of all manifestation?
AH: Yes. As we get into the state of fullness and the unity of existence, the unity of being, the heart will still feel a longing, which means it's not yet the inner Beloved. The inner Beloved is

very specific. We'll find out that it's not separate from the unity, but it's not the unity itself. The unity itself, it's usual for it to be identified as Being. So the inner Beloved is quite mysterious. And we will find out more about that mystery.

SEVEN

Yearning for the Beloved

I'll start with another poem by Kabir.

> My body and my mind are in depression because you are
>   not with me.
> How much I love you and want you in my house!
> When I hear people describe me as your bride
> I look sideways ashamed,
> because I know that far inside us we have never met.
> Then what is this love of mine?
> I don't really care about food,
> I don't really care about sleep,
> I'm restless indoors and outdoors.
> The bride wants her lover as much as a thirsty man wants water.
> And how will I find someone who will take a message to
>   the Guest from me?
> How restless Kabir is all the time!
> How much he wants to see the Guest![*]

---

[*] Kabir, *The Kabir Book: Forty-Four of the Ecstatic Poems of Kabir*, ed. Robert Bly (Beacon Press, 1977), 20.

We can see that poetry tends to use the language of the heart, which is the language of love. It's an interesting and sometimes confusing language, because it combines and synthesizes the language of everyday duality and the language of nonduality. It's neither wholly one nor the other, and sometimes we can't tell which it is. So in the poetry of love that we're reading here, often one verse seems to be dual and then another verse seems to be nondual. The language of the heart constantly moves between the two, and this reflects the condition we humans find ourselves in. The ultimate truth is always nondual, all of the time, but most of the time we don't perceive it that way. We perceive it dualistically, and our experience is therefore a dual condition in which there is separation—we become separated because we create this experience of ourselves as separate entities.

So the language of the heart begins from where we are, our human condition, and it conveys our normal human experience of falling in love and loving, and all the yearning, hurt, and abandonment that comes with that. In this way it's a language that expresses the condition of separateness and duality, but at the same time, it's a language that can transcend it. That's why so many people get confused about what is being expressed by the language of love. If you try to be more accurate and clarify this confusion, you might end up saying something like, "From a nondual perspective, the lover is not completely seeing her total union with the Beloved because of the obscuration of believing in herself." Fine, that's all very precise, but it's no longer the language of love. If you bring in terms like "obscuration" and other abstract concepts, the heart says, "Forget it. You've lost me." As we've seen, the heart only knows in some very immediate and direct way whether we're separate or we're unified. That's it. We're entangled or we're not entangled. Bringing in subtle concepts somehow doesn't work very well with the heart because it's more primitive than that.

In other parts of our work, yes, we can get into subtle ways of looking at things and use more refined concepts in order to gain a precise understanding. But when it's a matter of experiencing our true nature as the Beloved through the heart, we need to use the appropriate language, and that's why we're reading a lot of poetry. Poetry works well here because it's a figurative language that uses metaphors and imagery to allude to things, without trying to define them and pin them down in a literal way. It's okay to leave things ambiguous in poetry, which means it can capture the fuzzy mixture of the dual and nondual that is natural to love and the heart.

The Kabir poem shows that when we are in love and the Beloved is not there, not with us, the love naturally turns into yearning. The yearning is evidence of both love and separation. If we did not love, we wouldn't yearn. If there was no separation, we wouldn't yearn. That's why the journey toward the Beloved involves a great deal of yearning and longing, because we begin from the condition of separation. We begin with the discontent of the heart that loves and wants to be totally intimate with its true Beloved but is aware of not having this intimacy—it knows that the Beloved is not even near.

The yearning can feel like grief, but it's slightly different. Grief has to do with loss, so that's more when you've had the connection and known intimacy with the Beloved but now it's lost. Yearning means you don't yet know what the intimacy is like, but you're aware of the separation from it nevertheless. So we feel grief when the intimacy has been disrupted and we can no longer feel it, and then after a while the grief also turns into yearning.

Whether it's grief or yearning, they both involve a lot of pain and sadness. It's a sad condition, this separation, full of hurt and tears, so when the translation of the Kabir poem talks about being depressed, it's not really accurate. "Sad" or "brokenhearted" would have been better than "depressed," because it's a deep and intense feeling, whereas in depression the feelings are often flat and deadened. The feelings are intense here because this sad condition of the heart is really an expression of love—it's the manifestation of our deep love for the Beloved when we are not in connection with it. So in our relationship with the inner Beloved, we sometimes feel the love and we sometimes feel the longing, and sometimes we feel them both in various combinations. It's just the same as we feel with a human beloved—it's not so different in that respect.

The yearning and the love are there from the beginning of the journey of the heart, as soon as we become aware of our discontent and separateness. They continue to be felt throughout the whole journey, and they actually become more intense the more our heart is unified. As the libido is clarified of the feelings for our everyday loves, it becomes deeper, more defined, and in some sense purified as it becomes more directed toward the inner Beloved. Every time we then behold a particular manifestation of the Beloved and feel its nearness, the love gets even stronger. But separation and loss always follow at some point, and after each experience of loss the yearning also becomes deeper, stronger, and more intense.

So this path of love is a passionate, intense, and often painful affair, but it's a necessary one for the heart. That's because the inner Beloved can manifest its fullness, luminosity, and mystery in many different ways while still not appearing in the heart, which means the heart will not be satisfied. You see, the heart doesn't just want the inner Beloved to appear—the heart wants the inner Beloved to appear *in the heart*, and it's only natural that it won't fully recognize it as the true Beloved of the heart until it appears there.

We know that this can't happen if the heart is filled with a multiplicity of beloveds, because there isn't enough space for the inner Beloved to appear there. And we've seen that through shedding our attachments to all these other objects of love, we arrive at the mystical poverty of the heart. We feel that the heart is completely empty at that point, and that we don't even have a heart or any love—there's just nothing. As I said, the inner Beloved is actually very close at this point, but we're not seeing it because the veil of self is still there, even if its many beloveds are gone. And we've recognized how challenging it is to just be with this emptiness of the heart—to stay in the empty valley of love without trying to fill it with new loves or return to our old ones.

You could say that the mystical poverty of the heart is the final stage of cleansing and purifying the love and longing so that it becomes more truly for the inner Beloved—free from the reactions and associations of our early history and the situations in which we reenact it. Until this happens, we will continue to project our parents onto the Beloved to some degree. We will also bring in all kinds of other projections, pretenses, defenses, and protections—all distractions that just get in the way and make our heart less open to what it truly seeks. So these all need to be seen, worked out, burned out, and melted away, and that's a large part of the function of the dark night of the heart, which comes about through our deepening and increasing fidelity to the inner Beloved.

The longing we then experience can feel similar to the longing we've had before, as it may still be somewhat mixed with the longing we've had for our other loves, but because it is now more truly for the inner Beloved, it has more purity, more directedness, and more power. And once we get to a place where all the other objects of love are gone and we're able to stay with the emptiness and poverty, the heart can now turn and begin to love and yearn purely for the inner Beloved. We still don't necessarily know what the inner Beloved is in a clear and direct way, but we feel it doesn't matter. We only know that we just want the Beloved and nothing else.

It's like what's left of the heart at this point, and of the self, is the barest minimum. There's a sense of just an outline, a boundary, with nothing to it—it really is empty. And then even this bare minimum of the heart or self can begin to melt. It begins to dissolve, and it dissolves into tears—tears of longing, yearning, and wanting. The tears can be as powerful as hard torrential rain, expressing a deep and passionately ecstatic longing that convulses the soul—it can feel like the whole soul is shaking. Or there might be a calm, deep ocean of tears that conveys a more delicate sense of longing and tender murmurings of the heart. When the yearning is felt with this gentle tenderness and loving sweetness, it's like the soul is trembling rather than shaking, and you feel exquisitely fragile and vulnerable. We can see that when the heart is unified and no longer busily preoccupied with its many love objects, it has a greater innocence and openness, and that's what makes it more vulnerable, more delicate, and tender.

When this happens, very deep and primitive feelings from early childhood can arise, a time when we felt delicate and defenseless in the same way. When we were little, our love and wanting were inseparable, and we had no defenses and protections against our feelings of longing. We just wanted union, which at that time meant union with the mother or mothering person, so there was a deep longing for the breast—for the mother and her love and caring. So when the newly unified heart now feels such innocent and completely undefended love and desire for the Beloved—which as we've seen can be both delicate and intensely passionate—it can be very reminiscent of the small child's experience. We need to recognize this association and use it as fuel, instead of being carried away by it. If we are carried away by it, that brings in all kinds of object relations and associations, and while it's important for us to see and not reject them, it's also important that we don't believe they have any bearing on our immediate experience now.

If we're not able to make this discrimination, it's easy for us to confuse the longing for unity with the inner Beloved with the desire for merging love with other human beings, because we can all feel that same delicacy and vulnerability in our longing for union with another. We might then go astray and return to thinking of the inner Beloved in the same way we think of human beings, and our love can get channeled externally again. It's a delicate time, and that's why it's important for us to know and experience that the longing for the Beloved is much deeper and more primordial than our longing for human love. It's more fundamental.

However, it's only natural that the longing and love for our everyday beloveds will keep getting mixed up with our love for the inner Beloved. At times the path of love actually uses that mixture in some ways—it uses the yearning and love we feel for another human as fuel for the journey toward the inner Beloved. There are many ways of working with that, and the main principle we've established is that when we're unable to keep our love directed purely toward the inner Beloved, we must at least make it primary and not betray it for any other beloved.

So the lover will continue to encounter the danger of the love becoming divided and externalized again, and that's why it's helpful if the person is already in a settled situation with regard to human love—it means there is less distraction from the exclusive focus on the inner Beloved. When that's not the case and the search for human love is ongoing, we are driven by two needs and tend to confuse them. It's important for us then to recognize the difference and see the association between the two. There's nothing we need to do about it other than just see how we associate the two and recognize the fundamental difference between them—namely, the Beloved is formless, while the earthly beloved always has form, and its form is an important factor for us. The forms and situations that our love is drawn to will reflect forms and situations from our history, and these can continue to usurp our love for the Beloved, using it for their earthly reenactments.

This discrimination is important, but it's no easy thing in an area as subtle as this. It may seem surprising that even when we're far along the path and our love has become intensely focused on the inner Beloved, we can still get distracted by confusing it with our human love, so I'll say a bit more about why that is and how it can actually become more challenging as we get ever closer to the inner Beloved.

When something draws our heart away from the Beloved, we need to understand how that is happening. It's basically because we are being pulled by a force, and I'm referring to something very simple that people experience in all situations and in all relationships—the power of attraction. All human beings know it, this pull that we feel toward someone or something. It can feel like a kind of magnetism when it's strong, and we recognize that it draws us to certain things and people and not to others. We accept this as part of life, a natural part of being human, but most of us don't stop to consider what this attraction is about, where it's coming from, and where it's taking us.

Clearly you can't make it happen—you can't work on being attracted. If you're attracted to somebody, you're attracted. If you're not attracted to them, there is nothing you can do about it. If somebody is attracted to you, you can't make them stop—there's no on or off switch for either of you. There's no volume control either, so we feel this attraction spontaneously in various degrees of power, intensity, and comprehensiveness. Sometimes we just feel interested and curious as we gravitate toward something or someone. Sometimes the attraction is strong and irresistible. Sometimes the attraction is fleeting and short-lived, and sometimes it is steadfast and persistent and won't go away. The difficulty we may encounter on the path toward complete fidelity to the Beloved is that sometimes it's not just persistent; it's overwhelming, and you can't hold yourself back from what it's pulling you toward.

So what drives this power of attraction? Well, we've already established that it's the power of love at work, an optimizing dynamism that seeks to overcome separation. We've seen that this is what drives our spiritual journey, because we feel it as a fundamental attraction toward the truth, a pull toward reality. And the pull is not just to know it but to overcome our separation and become completely one with it, all the way to full realization, full identity with the truth. So at the heart of the power of attraction is a force that ultimately seeks to draw us toward unity and enlightenment, and it is experienced most purely in the relationship between the soul and the divine, the Beloved. And when it's experienced in relation to the divine, it becomes clear that the attraction is from both sides. It's not just that the soul is being attracted to divine being; divine being is also attracted to the soul. The two are attracted to each other, and there are forces bringing them together.

When our love gets distracted from this true aim by external forms, it's helpful to see that it's still the same force of attraction at work and that it's simply being diverted outward toward a veiled form of the Beloved. We are attracted to certain people as friends, for example, and of course the power of attraction is felt most strongly when it happens in a romantic way. It's such a powerful force of attraction when people fall in love, which is why we say that they are falling, unable to withstand the gravitational pull even if they wanted to. That's why I tend to call that kind of love "magnetic love," because it has a powerful magnetic force that you can feel, just like the one that draws two magnets together. The opposite poles of two magnets can't help but come together because that is their nature, and people can be drawn together in the same way. And when they are together, what happens? What is the experience? The experience is of unity.

You see, even before we experience the true unity, it's already exerting a force in us. And when the unity is actually beginning to emerge in two people who are in some kind of dialectic or relationship, if they don't yet know that they are one but still experience themselves as two, the unity manifests itself as a very powerful attraction between them. There is a powerful gravitational pull between the two to go toward each other, to be with each other, to talk with each other, and possibly more. So the gravitational pull toward unity can be experienced through the inner Beloved or an external beloved, and when it comes to how this pull is felt in the heart, the two are not easily differentiated.

When we are experiencing the enlightenment drive seeking unity with the Beloved, it brings a wanting and desire that's different from a specific wanting based on deficiency or lack. It's a wanting that expresses the heart's true desire for the formless Beloved, and it is inseparable from love—the wanting and love are both functioning as the same force. So as we come very close to unity with the Beloved, the pure, luminous love that we feel is at the same time a pure, unadulterated desire and wanting. In spiritual circles, those two things are usually seen as separate, but when it comes to the unity as it impacts the heart, they are not differentiated.

But because the unity wants to bring *everything* together, its pull operates in the world of forms too, and as we get closer to the unity and the magnetic force intensifies, the powerful charge of it can also be felt toward another person. The magnetism is then felt as a wanting of a certain kind—it's a pull toward a certain form, a particular human being, for whom we feel the same luminous love and the same intense desire and wanting. In the later stages of our journey toward unity therefore, this pull toward another person can be felt more powerfully than we've experienced before in the sphere of human relationships.

So magnetic love is first felt as the call of the unity exerting its force in our consciousness and within our own soul, but when you begin to fully experience the unity, it can also become the expression of it. It either calls us back to inner unity or it expresses itself in our interaction with the outside world. Discriminating between these two modes is where skill is needed. This is an area that can become one of the most beautiful and most luminous in terms of how the heart relates to the unity, but it is also the most dangerous, where the most pitfalls and misinterpretations can happen.

I think it's possible that when people fall in love, they feel this magnetic love in its purest form for a while, as the unity acting through them. Falling in love is the expression of the unity that is already there, that wants to know itself and express itself through this glowing, beautiful, ecstatic lovingness. At its purest, this love is sacred because it is selfless—it has combined the selflessness of love with the gravitational pull of the unity. However, for most people, the magnetic love gets mixed up with self-centeredness and all kinds of object relations, desires, needs, and deficiencies. Because of that, it can create a lot of havoc, as many of us know. We can feel magnetic love toward another person without it being reciprocated, and that can lead to much grief and heartache if we don't understand what is happening. But again, if these feelings are allowed and understood, the force in them can help to power the journey toward unity with the Beloved, which is the only true satisfaction for the heart.

This magnetic force can be felt between a teacher and a student of this work, for example, which is a good thing—a good place for there to be a meeting of beings where the student can learn about the unity being felt in that way. But if one or both of the people involved don't understand it, then the student might interpret it to mean they are falling in love. They feel that they really have to be with that teacher because they are their real true partner and consort, and everybody else should disappear. That can create a difficult situation for the teacher, and sometimes it can happen the other way round—the teacher can feel that way. In situations like this, we are experiencing the unity but we're still experiencing the love for it dualistically. And we're better prepared to deal with the confusion this causes if we're aware that this dualistic manifestation of the magnetic force of unity can become more powerful the closer we are to the unity, which is where the pull is really coming from.

This magnetism is actually the very heart of love, and it explains why we gravitate toward what we love. We know that love can have many qualities—it can be appreciative and generous, for example—but what differentiates it from all the other manifestations of our spiritual nature is that implicit in its very nature, it has this gravitational force. It is not easy to experience this force of love in its purity. We have to go very deep in our heart, to the very essence of love, where we find loving and wanting become the same thing. This is not obvious in the other manifestations of spiritual love that we discussed in the previous two books of this series. The fact that magnetism is a fundamental characteristic of love only becomes apparent when our wanting comes not out of need but out of love. This kind of wanting is not longing or yearning but a very powerful desire—a desire of the heart. That's one reason why I see magnetic love as a distinct manifestation of love different from its other qualities. It reveals the inner secret of love—that love is a force, not just a presence.

Not everyone on the path of the heart gets to experience magnetic love. We have to go even beyond nonduality for this secret of love to reveal itself. It's one of the most deeply hidden secrets of the heart, one that manifests when we no longer feel the need to hold on to any particular view of reality, even the nondual one.

I've said that toward the end of our explorations here, we'll understand better how we can fully engage with our external loves without them becoming a confusion and a distraction. But until we've reached that stage and are able to really understand what this magnetic force is all about, we need to go through a period of minimizing the confusion of trying to interpret it within our conventional relationships. And that's what the emptying of the heart is about. It doesn't mean we can avoid this confusion altogether until we're enlightened enough to understand it—we just have to do our best to grapple with it and keep turning back toward the Beloved.

Again, what helps most with all this confusion is to simply recognize the association between our human loves and our love for the formless inner Beloved, and for our love to then become more powerfully directed toward the latter. The more we see the associations and are able to recognize them, the more our love can expand and deepen, and then it will just melt them and burn them as fuel for that love. The power of the passion we feel toward the inner Beloved will reveal how we're associating it with all these other things, and those things will then burn up and melt away.

So while the yearning for merging love with external beloveds can intensify with the poverty of the heart, we should remember that the yearning for the Beloved becomes more intense too. That yearning can become so total and complete that all we feel in our heart is: "Not only am I willing to forget all my other loves and all my other concerns, I also want to forget about myself. I want the inner Beloved to come and take me and make me completely disappear." That really melts the boundaries of the self, the boundaries of the heart, and turns into the flowing river of tears, yearning, and also sweetness.

The true longing and love for the Beloved is when the wish is for only the Beloved to be, and nothing else. It's not really "I want to have the Beloved"; it's more "I love the Beloved so much I want it to be there in a way that makes me irrelevant." That's not how you feel in a human love relationship. There can be moments of complete surrender when two people want to disappear into each other, and they may do this for a while. But when it comes to the inner Beloved, the feeling is: "No, I don't want the inner Beloved to disappear. *I* want to disappear." And that's not the same as with a human beloved. Perhaps at times there is a fantasy of you disappearing and the other person remaining there, but of course that doesn't work in reality.

So we can see now how this very deep yearning and total love for the Beloved is part of the reason why there have been so many fears and terrors along the way. Because it's not just a matter of losing the other beloveds, it's actually a matter of losing oneself, losing one's separateness.

Let's do an exercise now to help us see the associations we make between our human love and the love for the inner Beloved.

Practice Session: Confusing Love for the Beloved with Human Love
. . .

We'll do another monologue, working with one or two other people if possible. Each person in the group will do a monologue for fifteen minutes. If you are alone, write out your exploration for fifteen minutes.

We've looked at the question of the desire for merging love, the tender desire to be held by a beloved, whether it's a parent or another human being, and how that may arise at this juncture. As I said, we don't want to dismiss it, but we don't want to confuse it with our yearning to merge with our true Beloved. We've also looked at the question of mystical poverty and how the force of attraction in magnetic love can pull us back into seeking unity in external relationships.

So, inquire into your longing and desire for the inner Beloved and explore how it becomes associated and enmeshed with the desire for merging with a human love object. Of course, most deeply, if we go back far enough, this is usually the desire for the symbiotic merger with the mother. You want to inquire into this association until you can't differentiate the two loves—this symbiotic one and the primordial one for the Beloved. The primordial one can contain the symbiotic one, but it's larger, bigger, and deeper. And we want to see if we can see that in our own personal experience.

· · · · ·

Questions and Comments

Student: I wasn't sure how any of this was impacting me personally because it sounded very abstract, and then I had a dream last night that I was haphazardly buying a lot of jewelry, which isn't something I do normally. There was a feeling of a lot of anxiety, that it was very important to keep track of all these different pieces of jewelry, and I was putting them in a bag, and I was worried I was forgetting what they were or who they were for. And this anxiety started to come up now around having all these many beloveds, and it had a certain quality that felt familiar to me. And I'm wondering about—you haven't brought up anything yet about the ego structure, different ego structures as they relate to the many beloveds versus this devotion to the one. So I'm curious about that and particularly the frustration underneath that. I sense that underneath the anxiety I was feeling, which continued into this morning, was a sense of just complete emptiness, and blackness.

A. H. Almaas: So I think that's good. Just let yourself go into that complete emptiness and blackness. Just let it happen. It seems your inquiry, your work, is taking you there. So that's good.

S: I really appreciated the exercise. I really got to have a rich, felt sense of the difference between those two yearnings. I also have a question. You mentioned that we could use human love to fuel the process of connecting to the inner Beloved. And I fell kind of hard in human love about a week ago, so I'm still in the burning phase of that, and I wondered if you had any specific pointers for me on how to use this place that I'm in to facilitate my understanding of this.

AH: I get it. It's a good time to do it, actually. And one thing you could do is sense your love now and work on not forgetting the inner Beloved when you are with your love now. That'll be quite an exercise. See what happens.

S: Okay.

S: My question is like the flip of that last one. You're emphasizing that we don't have to completely give up on our human beloveds to be devoted to the inner Beloved, and you've also emphasized how having some kind of adequate fulfillment of human love can be an aid. So I'm wondering—it almost sounds like it's a method for people who've had sufficient human love, so what does one do if regular human love has been frustrating and difficult? I mean, I see the object relation with my mother played out almost infinitely.

AH: Yeah. So an important way of dealing with that is not to act on that frustration. Not to act on the deprivation. To experience the frustration, to experience the deprivation, and not act on it. Just feel it as fully as possible and understand everything that comes up in relation to it. Because if we act on that, then we try to fill that emptiness with whatever objects of love we can find, of one kind or another. While if we don't act on it and just let it be, then the heart will manifest whichever way it can. It can manifest by experiencing real love for another human being, or it may go deeper and begin to experience the love toward the inner Beloved, or the longing for the inner Beloved.

S: One thing I've noticed in the last few days is that I actually didn't have any idea about the inner Beloved until we started the retreat, and in the questions, what's happened is that I've actually remembered times when I felt like the guest had come, for hours or even a couple of days at a time, and then the sorrow of not having prepared a place for the guest, and not actually welcoming the guest. But in the practical sense, I'm also aware that at times when I become pearly and people are attracted to me, my heart leaps to want to have a connection with them.

AH: What's the problem with that?

S: That sort of recycles me into some of the frustration, so it's like, on one hand, I know that it's a natural human need to have that contact and the friendship and the love, but I also see with myself that the energetic quality is like having the desire for the Beloved but just shooting it to a human.

AH: So that can happen. As we've been seeing, it's natural for that to happen and in some sense it's unavoidable sometimes. The question is that you want to continue to be able to remember the Beloved and your love and longing for the Beloved. These other things will happen, that's fine, and that's how we have a life. Otherwise we won't have much of a life, we just become ascetics, living in a monastery or a cave. But since we live a life, we have relationships, we have families and friends, and much as we might focus on emptying the heart, when the heart love goes toward those, it can be expressed and there will be a degree of satisfaction. But we need to remember, that is not the same thing as fulfilling the longing for the inner Beloved. So we need to work on ourselves to be able to see the two and how they get confused, and that's what we did in the exercise. And practically speaking, as we've seen, it's not easy at all. The best approach when you're in love or you have a desire for something or somebody, is for a period of time not to act on it, and to follow that completely, one hundred percent. So you don't act on the desire, you don't act on the love, and you don't act on the frustration. If you can do that, that will naturally burn through all of the desire and turn it into real love, and then the love for the inner Beloved will dominate. But when I say that's the best thing to do, I'm not saying that it's easy—it's a very difficult thing for most people to do. Though in truth, you don't need to do it for very long—I'm not saying you should do it like for twenty years. If you could do that for a few months, that will create a transformation.

S: Would you distinguish what the difference is between the primordial relationship and the symbiotic relationship?
AH: By symbiotic I mean the earlier relationship with the mother or the mothering person, which has the quality of symbiosis in the sense that it's not differentiated. There's some kind of a merging in love when it is happening positively, but it can also be negative, depending on how much frustration there is. By primordial, I mean your unity with your true nature, which is primordially there. So if that is disrupted, there will be a longing for that union, for that connection, for that realization. And that is a longing for the primordial condition, not just for the earlier symbiotic condition.

S: I had an interesting experience of being with the primordial. I had no idea what that would feel like, but it wasn't like a longing that was reaching out, it was like receptive. It was totally undefended, totally open and vast and expecting. I mean, there was like no doubt, there was a total expectancy. And I was looking for yearning, and I only know yearning as an outreaching, and this did not feel like it. And yet, maybe it is yearning. And I guess that's my question.

AH: Well as I said, the range of the heart is infinite. There are so many ways we can experience love and yearning, and the heart has so many conditions when it's in a love relation oriented toward the Beloved. So sometimes being receptive, sometimes being active, sometimes intensely yearning, sometimes delicately loving. All these are possible. And the more open we are, the more things happen, the more different kinds of conditions, so that's one of the things that's arising for you—recognizing the ways that the heart can be.

S: I'm quite shaken and I'm trembling, and I feel like I got into contact with a fierce aspect of what I think is the Beloved. Looking into the differentiation, it was as if the merging love is more the love of a child that melts, and in a way that melting is also shielded from some of what the totality of life is. While in that contact here, I felt the Beloved coming with force like a black energy. And a friend of mine has just told me about an accident she'd seen in which a motorcyclist had his foot severed by a car. And when she told me a few days ago, I kind of shied away from that image, and now it was like saying, "Look at me! At all of me! And do you still love me? Do you still want me?" So there was this feeling like the demand of a great courage and a kind of unblinkingness.

AH: It's a demanding Beloved. It demands all, actually.

S: That's what it felt like. I mean, this is not for kids.

AH: Right. It's not for kids.

S: And it showed its absolute jealousy and demandingness, because yesterday night I felt that there was an urgent demand on a project that I'm working on, and I "had to" do something about it. And I was totally dissolved by the work we'd been doing here, and I got into my car and I somehow got home, and I drank a lot of coffee and I sat down at my computer and I did it. And I woke up early this morning and I came here, and I'm sitting here, and I'm totally shut off. I feel clear and present to a certain extent, and very functional, but I feel like the Beloved says, "Fine. You want to function in the world? Here, you have it. It's okay, you just go function in the world. But if you really want to be with me, don't mess around."

AH: Right. Very true. So basically it's probably the Beloved saying, "Okay then, find another way if you want to try. If working on computers is a priority for you, good, we'll see."

S: I have two questions The first is, could you say more about how to practice in a present relationship, with opening to this? It's like I feel so much love for my husband, and with that idea of not acting on something for a few months, what were you talking about? And the second question is a question I've been asking myself repeatedly recently: What keeps my heart from opening to life as it is? And so, the Beloved and life as it is, is that the same thing? Is any way we close our heart to life as it is, like with the previous question about trying to deny the reality of the motorcycle accident, is that also closing our heart to the Beloved?

AH: It's definitely the case, yes. Because if we close our heart to anything, we close our heart, basically. And how to practice when you are with your husband or your lover is, you continue loving your husband without forgetting the inner Beloved. That's the point. Meaning not forgetting your interest in the truth, in seeing the Beloved, in experiencing the Beloved. The Beloved might appear between the two of you. It might not. So you never forget in your love for the other person, or whatever you're doing, the bigger Beloved. And that can mean different things at different times in terms of what you do. And basically, in time it makes you more loving and more reasonable with the other person.

EIGHT

The Primal Cavity

We'll begin with another poem by Rumi from *A Garden Beyond Paradise*. This one's called "Don't Leave Me Unbaked."

> Be a lover for me, a cave for me,
> The sweet burn of love for me.
> O master, protect me!
>
> You are Noah, you are the soul,
> You are the slayer and the slain.
> You are the treasure of knowledge.
> O master, open your secret door for me!
>
> You are the light and celebration;
> The land rejoicing in victory.
> You are the great bird of Mount Sinai.
> O master, don't drop me from your beak!
>
> You are the ocean, and the shore;
> A kind word, and a heart

Filled with despair.
You are the sugar and the poison.
O master, more sugar and less poison!

You are the orb of the Sun,
And the house of Venus,
You are the light of hope
That touches the world.
O master, open up and let me see you!

You are the pain of hunger,
And the crumbs of every beggar.
You are the water overflowing.
O master, fill my empty cup!

You are the bait and the trap,
The wine and the glass.
You are the heat
And the bread in the oven.
O master, don't leave me unbaked!

This body is not fast enough
To reach the end
Of Love's path.
Let me enter that emptiness
O master, take away all these words of mine.*

---

* Jonathan Star and Shahram Shiva, trans., *A Garden Beyond Paradise: The Mystical Poetry of Rumi* (Bantam Books, 1992), 96.

The Primal Cavity

Here Rumi is describing how the Beloved appears and reveals itself in many different ways throughout our journey, and how the love and the yearning we feel are rekindled over and over again. As we alternate between union with and separation from the Beloved, we get cooked—or as Rumi puts it, baked. Over time, we are transformed as we burn and melt with all the love and yearning.

This process intensifies as our love becomes more faithful to the Beloved, which reveals itself more and more completely as our heart empties of its associations to our other beloveds. However, it can still be a process that takes many years, as our heart and love go through a series of peaks and valleys. The love divests itself of many different kinds of associations as we work through them, but as we know, they can still reappear at times, and late in the journey you might encounter an association that you hadn't even been aware of previously. It might take a long time for us to become aware of it as an association—to see that it's not a true yearning and love for the Beloved but for something else. At other times on the journey, associations might become apparent in rapid succession and get burned away quickly in the fire of our passion.

Each person's journey is different in this way, and the associations we meet depend partly on how the Beloved is appearing to us at any particular time—in what form or shape and with what quality it is manifesting. There are universals, however, and I want to work now with one of the associations that arises when the Beloved is beginning to appear in its very essence, its ultimate truth. At this point it begins to reveal its true characteristics, which some of the poems have already touched upon—the mystery, the darkness, the nonbeingness, and how it is actually the source and nature of everything.

So the journey of revelation has shown us many aspects and dimensions of the Beloved, but we now come to a point where it is revealed in its deepest dimension, which is the deepest dimension of true nature. It appears then as a luminosity that is deeply mysterious—it is beautiful and majestic while at the same time it is like an emptiness, a nonbeingness. Rumi talks of a cave, and it's like a cave that has no boundaries and can swallow the whole universe.

The mystery that we encounter here is indeterminable and unfathomable, and way beyond what the mind can grasp. Logically this makes little sense—why is this emptiness and nothingness such a big deal? But the heart knows and recognizes it, and for the heart, that's it—it's the biggest deal. So it's interesting to see how the heart responds as the mystery reveals itself, because even as we behold the mystery and find it unfathomable, this only makes the love more intense, more passionate, more focused, and more faithful.

Our yearning for the Beloved has had different qualities throughout our journey, and as we've already seen, at this stage it's felt as a longing to completely disappear into the Beloved. And that's because, even if the lover hasn't realized it yet, the Beloved is now manifesting its fundamental characteristic of nonbeingness. As the soul is touched by the Beloved deep within, she experiences this as a nearness that leads to the mystery of nonbeing, which she feels a profound love for. Yearning for union now means longing to disappear, to be gone.

So we discover that one of the main ways our yearning for the Beloved can appear is as a yearning for cessation, for complete annihilation. We seek annihilation into the Beloved—we sometimes feel we want the Beloved to overwhelm us, to come and take us and leave nothing behind. We want to be taken in, to be enfolded and completely absorbed, so that there's absolutely nothing left but the Beloved. This feels like a return to source—surrendering the soul form to go back to the formless, from being to nonbeing. The yearning for cessation, which can be felt as a gentle, delicate, and vulnerable kind of yearning to melt and disappear, or as a fierce and passionate wish for annihilation, is the desire to be taken in by the Beloved, by the mystery, such that we are gone. It feels like nothing could be sweeter than to simply vanish without a trace.

This yearning for cessation can take many forms, and one of them feels like a yearning to go back to where we came from, back to before we began, to be annihilated into nonbeing. And a particular association may arise here that we need to be aware of, because it can contaminate this love and distort our yearning for cessation. It relates to a wish that is similar to the one we are feeling with regard to the Beloved, but it's more psychodynamic in nature. It's a very early, primitive drive that we may have never acknowledged, and it could therefore be hidden from us now. Some of us may not have even felt it before, at least not in a way where we recognized and conceptualized it. Nevertheless, it can arise at this point in our process and it can easily be confused with the yearning and love for the Beloved that brings the wish for cessation.

What I'm referring to is the way we feel when we want to be completely relieved of existence, of life, because everything is just too much trouble. Sometimes it seems like there's only pain in life, and we feel we want to go back to where we came from, to disappear and dissolve so that there will be no more experience and therefore no more pain. That might sound the same as the yearning for cessation we're exploring here, but if we look more closely, we can see that it's not the desire of the lover who wants the Beloved. The longing is for the relief from pain, wanting to get away from a world that feels too hard, while the true lover wants to be annihilated and disappear out of love for the Beloved. That is a fundamental difference between these two drives, which in some respects can appear to have much in common.

Many of us will feel a mixture of both—wanting to dissolve out of love, but also wanting to dissolve in order to be free from problems, difficulties, pain, and suffering. The important thing to see is that the desire to dissolve out of love comes from a maturity of the heart, while the desire to leave the world of existence because of its conflicts and pain is more an infantile wish to escape. It's called a regressive wish, because it's a wish to regress backward, to go back, and back, and back, all the way back into the womb. This infantile desire is not driven by love, and yet the lover's yearning to disappear into the Beloved can be telescoped with this regressive desire and become so associated and confused with it that it's difficult to discriminate between them.

It's true that disappearing into the Beloved will bring peace and the end of suffering for the lover. That's partly why the association and telescoping of the two drives occurs, and it's why we need to look at what the lover is feeling in order to discriminate them. The lover doesn't really care about having a good time or not in this world, whether there is suffering or not. For the lover, the only thing that counts is being with the Beloved. "It doesn't matter what the Beloved does for me or to me as long as I am with the Beloved, as long as it's the Beloved that's doing it."

There is also the similarity in that both drives feel like a desire to return to the source of existence. Our body comes from the womb and our soul comes from the Beloved, and both seem to offer the prospect of going back to a peace before there was experience, which is what has brought all the strife and trouble. However, the regressive wish to go back to the source has a physical and temporal dimension to it—the fantasy is of going backward developmentally. The true wish for the Beloved, on the other hand, is going to the source primordially, not temporally. Because it's so easy to confuse with the regressive wish, it's important to recognize that the desire to disappear into the Beloved is an expression of our soul's development and maturation—it's not actually a desire to go backward.

It's only because of the confusion and telescoping that the desire to dissolve into the Beloved can be felt as the longing to go back into a dark primordial cavity. In depth psychology, this is what's called the regressive wish to return to the primal cavity. Primal cavity refers to the hole from which we physically emerged, and at times there is a natural wish to go back into the womb, where there was comfort and complete holding and no responsibility at all. Everything was provided for us 100 percent, and there wasn't even conscious experience most of the time. We can all experience a longing for that, depending upon what's going on in our life—the more difficulty there is, the more that longing will be activated and the more intense it will feel. And that wish can also be triggered and kindled when our desire for the Beloved manifests as a desire for cessation, as a wish to melt away into the Beloved. The fact that the Beloved is now manifesting more of its mysterious darkness only adds to the association we may have between wanting that, and wanting to go back into the dark primal cavity.

It was actually Freud who first came up with the idea, which I think was brilliant. In his explorations of unconscious processes, he recognized that there is this wish that he called the regressive wish to return to the primal cavity—to go back into the vagina and into the womb, into the darkness and unconsciousness that precedes life and existence. The way it's seen in depth psychology is that at some point, in dreams or in waking fantasy, the person envisions a dark black cavity and feels a longing to enter into it. With the longing come various conflicts, including the fear of the loss of life, of connection, and of autonomy. But despite that, there is still this deep pull to go back into that dark cavity and disappear.

In the images that arise and the fantasies and dreams that appear, this big, dark, mysterious hole feels like something comforting to return to and slither inside and just disappear. Small children sometimes have the experience of hiding under their mother's skirt when they feel very insecure and need shelter, and perhaps in the twilight they encounter there they may also have a fantasy of going even deeper into the shelter of her body, right back into the mysterious darkness of the womb, which they may have a prenatal memory of. It's common for child therapists to see this kind of material when working with very disturbed children, in drawings and paintings, and when it gets acted out by crawling inside a closet or cupboard that creates an enclosed womblike space. Hiding in the darkness seems appealing, as we may know ourselves if we've ever hidden under the covers when life is hard and getting out of bed feels like a trial—there's a desire to keep out the daylight that brings the light of consciousness and stay unconscious in a dark, womblike cavity. Of course, the dark space eventually becomes claustrophobic and disturbing, and our problems are not remedied by hiding away.

So we can see why this desire to get back inside the dark, mysterious womb can easily become confused with our yearning to disappear into the Beloved, because the Beloved is revealing a similar quality of dark mystery and blackness that will erase our conscious existence. Here, as always, it's important that in our movement toward union with the Beloved, our love is truly unified and our yearning is directed as precisely as possible toward the Beloved itself. And that means we need to be able to differentiate and recognize the regressive wish to go back to the primal cavity from the true yearning to disappear into the mystery of the Beloved.

As I said, one way to recognize the difference is to get a feel for where the movement is coming from. If it is truly toward the Beloved, it will be coming out of love, a flooding of love that you just can't help. The yearning to go back and disappear in order to leave this troublesome world doesn't feel like love—it's more like a withdrawal or a desire to escape. If we can see and feel the difference, that will help to liberate the true love and yearning from the association. If we don't, and we mistake the regressive wish for the true yearning, that won't take us to the Beloved—it will take us where that yearning wants to go, back into some kind of infantile fantasy of regression and merging with mother, right back into the womb. On the other hand, we might interpret everything we feel in the yearning for cessation to be just a regressive wish, and in that way, we won't recognize and follow the true longing to disappear into the Beloved.

Generally, psychoanalysts do the latter—they tend not to recognize the true longing to disappear into the Beloved and interpret it only as a regressive wish. That's why mystical longing is often seen as the expression of an infantile wish, and to be fair, it does often have an element of that in it. Spiritual people tend to do the former—they regard everything they feel as an expression of their desire for the Beloved, ignoring that fact that it will inevitably be mixed to some extent with the regressive infantile wish that's been there since they were a baby. But it's important to recognize this regressive kind of yearning and understand that it doesn't express maturity but a lack of maturity. It comes from the heart not being strong enough to handle the world.

When we are able to recognize and see the difference, that can intensify, deepen, and purify our true love, which will then melt and burn away the regressive wish. Just as we've seen with other associations, this regressive wish can then become an added fuel once it is subsumed into the true longing and directed more purely toward the Beloved. Along the way, we may realize that many of the issues that come up around the desire to disappear into the Beloved have to do with an association with the regressive wish. The infantile desire brings up all kinds of issues around prenatal experiences, being born, the separation from mother, and physical life and death. Disappearing into the Beloved has nothing to do with these things—it's simply about the inner journey back to our true source.

Being able to make that differentiation will make it easier for our heart to feel its love and yearning more purely and completely. As I said, however, many of us might never have experienced the wish to disappear into the primal cavity, or may not have been aware of it until it got activated around this stage of movement toward the Beloved. I myself had no idea about it until it was expressed in a dream, and from the dream I saw that it was no wonder that I had all these conflicts around the wish for cessation. I then became aware specifically of this wish to go back to the womb—a tender and passionate feeling of wanting to get smaller and smaller and kind of vanish into this welcoming, comfortable, and cozy hole or cavity. Seeing that clarified the real wish that comes from the love that floods the heart—the feeling that I just want this love to consume me so that nothing will be left but the Beloved and its mystery.

So this is another thing we can thank modern psychology for, that it has identified this regressive drive in a way that makes it possible for us to distinguish it from the true wish for cessation. And it's worth adding that when we look at the similarities between the two drives, we might consider what may be a genuine connection between them—we may well have experienced the Beloved in the womb, or even before that. That would make it even easier to confuse the two wishes, which are nevertheless fundamentally quite different in their motivation.

It's time now for you to explore this territory for yourself to uncover and distinguish these two different types of wish for cessation.

PRACTICE SESSION: THE WISH FOR CESSATION
. . .

You will work in pairs or groups of three if possible, and each person will do a monologue for fifteen minutes. If you are alone, write out your exploration for fifteen minutes.

You want to first look for and explore your wish for cessation, the desire to disappear, and see whether you can feel it or not. Is it something you're aware of sometimes, that you simply want to disappear or cease to exist? If you find the yearning for annihilation, explore if it feels like a manifestation of your love for the Beloved, or like a regressive wish. You also want to see if and how the love for the Beloved can get confounded and confused by association with the regressive wish to go back to the womb. You want to be able to feel and understand the regressive wish enough to be able to differentiate it from the true wish for cessation. I gave you some indications as to how you might do this, such as feeling into where the desire is coming from and what quality it has. You might find other ways of seeing the distinction that are more pertinent to you personally in your history. Regardless of the teaching, it is important to stay with what is true for you now and don't try to be somewhere you are not in your own process.

. . . . .

Questions and Comments

Student: This is an extraordinary topic, and it's opened up a lot of stuff. As I've been sitting with myself since the monologue, I'm having the experience that I didn't want to be here from day one. And how pervasive that has been in my life. In moments of conscious frustration, it takes the form of wanting to run away to a monastery, or frequently I just leave my body and I'm not even here. So this has been extremely helpful, and I just needed to say that.
A. H. Almaas: Good.

S: I'm either massively delusional or crystal clear, and I'm not quite sure where on that scale I am—maybe in some place in between. It seems to me that my own individual entry into my Beloved has actually been through objectification, through the creation of physical forms. And there have been many moments in various venues for me when I have gone beyond what I was working on to a different state. And yet it's been through the objectification process instead of the elimination of it. Now that seems to fly in the face of what you're talking about in terms of elimination, reduction.

AH: Exactly, right.

S: I think I tend to get stuck in whatever feeling I'm in at the moment, and this makes me aware of the continuous flow.

AH: So what do you mean, objectification process?

S: Working on a piece of sculpture, working on a design, working on a mechanism.

AH: Okay. So, by objectification I don't necessarily mean that. By objectification I mean the mental process of taking something and making it into a final object on its own, believing that it is what you just see. If you take that mental position, you take an object and say that that's all that it is, just that physical object the way your senses perceive it and there's nothing more to it—that's objectification. If you do that, you will not be able to see its nature, usually. However, if you don't do that, regardless of how much you work with it, if your mind doesn't take that position, if your mind is open to see that there's more to this object than that, then that can open it up.

S: Years ago I was told that I seem to see the essence beyond form. Is that what you're talking about?

AH: Right. Exactly. If you're seeing the essence beyond the form, you're not objectifying the form. Objectifying the form means to see it just as the form and nothing else, instead of seeing it as an expression of something else, by going beyond it or through it. But the person who doesn't believe there's anything else, that's it. They aren't open to going beyond it or through it. And that person is stuck with the objectification.

S: I have a question that's been with me for a while. I'm wondering what the difference is, if there is one, between the optimizing thrust and yearning for the Beloved.

AH: That's a subject we'll get to. The optimizing force is the force that comes from the Beloved and draws us nearer to it. And it is love, and the yearning is the expression of that love. So we don't experience the optimizing force directly, we experience it as our own love. As you see, many of the poems allude to that—that even our love, even our heart, comes from the Beloved. But I'm presenting it step by step, according to the stages of the path. I'm not looking at it from the final point of view. When we go further, you might look back at what was said earlier and say, "Oh, that's what that means." Things will be clearer. But I'm presenting all this in the way that we experience it as we go from one stage to the next. And as we go from one stage to the next, we don't know certain things yet. We don't know yet what the relationship is between the lover and the Beloved. So if I say right at the beginning that the lover and the Beloved are the same thing, well that's true, but for most people that would just be an intellectual concept. We need to go through the process so that that becomes a reality. That's the language of love. Remember I said that it crosses the dual and the nondual? So it starts where we are, which is a dual place, and gradually dissolves that.

S: As I went through the exercise, starting with the newness of me, I could differentiate between the symbiotic wishes and the desire for the Beloved. And as my inquiry led me deeper and deeper back into my past, when I got to a young child, the preverbal, it became confusing how to differentiate those. So my question is, does the young infant, before it starts its symbiotic phase, before it starts forming all these concepts, does it have a pure experience of the Beloved? And then the development of the ego comes in and implants itself in these symbiotic wishes, and so it takes over that pure experience of the Beloved with a need for the symbiosis to come back.

AH: I wouldn't say that the infant has a pure experience of the Beloved. It's like the infant or the young child early on is still not separated from true nature, but that's not the same thing as a clear experience of it. In some sense, as an infant I can be that pure nature without knowing it. I can be it and come from it, but it's too subtle for me to recognize it as an experience.

S: And all human beings are born with this possibility?

AH: The possibility to experience the Beloved?

S: Yes. I know it sounds like maybe a silly question, but . . .

AH: What do you think?

S: I don't know all human beings. I wonder about certain human beings.

AH: Like who? Who do you have in mind?

S: I won't mention names.

AH: That's alright.

S: Thank you.

S: When you talked this morning, I thought, "Well now you're off topic for me. I don't desire to dissolve into the Beloved and I don't wish to go back to the cavity, so I guess I'm just not there." And in the monologue I realized that because I had a painful time at the time of birth, I associate going back with going back to a place I don't want to go back to. And that, actually, the desire for dissolving into the Beloved is combined with a desire not to go there, so there were two "nots" that were telescoped rather than two desires. And seeing that has helped me feel, "Oh, there's a possibility," and like a curiosity or a flame toward wanting to find out about wanting to dissolve into the Beloved. Because they can be separated.

AH: That's a very good insight, I think. So the association happened in a negative way.

S: Yes.

S: I'd like to check if I've been understanding you. When you talked before and framed the inquiry, what I imagined was sort of a subtle difference between the desire to merge with the Beloved and the regressive desire. When I did the inquiry, to the extent I could find these things in my experience, they felt extremely different. I've had some experience particularly as we've worked with some yearning, some desire to step out of my personality, to just shed it like a suit of clothes and almost like a desire to let my molecules go free into the universe. That's at any rate what I was associating with the first desire. To the extent I have an experience of a regressive desire, it's very familiar, it's my response to being hurt, and it felt like a desire to go into a really dark, closed place and hold myself really tight, all alone. And what I've noticed of that is that it's a desire to hold on to the personality, or maybe to hold on to the self. It's like whatever else is happening, you can't take this away from me, this is who I am. That's what I experienced, and it felt really different from what I imagined you were saying. So I wanted to check with you.

AH: Yes. So the thing you're discussing is definitely different, and it's good that you're saying that, because everybody's different, how they experience these things; so the desire for cessation, for disappearing, can appear in many ways, like the way you describe it when you talk about the desire to sort of contract in order to disappear. This might be partly the regressive wish to go back to the womb—let's say it might be the beginning of it or part of it. The desire to go back to the womb will feel like going beyond the personality, because it's really going back to before you had a personality. And because of that, there are fears that you're going to lose your personality, so it will feel like dissolving or going back to nonbeing.

S: I feel vulnerable just standing up to talk. My question is—and I've been on this path a long time—what is it that's going to motivate me to stay on the path toward the Beloved and not be distracted by all of the other things that I love in the world? I haven't found it yet.

AH: It's like you need to recognize what your love is really for.

S: What my love is for?

AH: Yes. What is it that you really love? That's what you really need to find out. We all love the Beloved more than anything else, except we don't know it. We're not sure of it—we think we love this, and that, and that. We're looking for something, we're seeking something, we love something, we yearn for it. We need to find out what it is. So the distractions basically distract us from recognizing it. It's not like we're going to make ourselves love the Beloved more. It's already there, we just don't see it.

S: Okay. Thank you.

NINE

The Death Wish

I'll start with another poem by Kabir.

> Oh friend, I love you, think this over carefully!
> If you are in love, then why are you asleep?
> If you have found him, give yourself to him, take him.
>
> Why do you lose track of him again and again?
> If you are about to fall into heavy sleep anyway,
> Why waste time smoothing the bed and arranging the
>   pillows?
>
> Kabir will tell you the truth: this is what love is like:
> Suppose you had to cut your head off and give it to
>   someone else,
> What difference would that make?*

---

* Kabir, *The Kabir Book: Forty-Four of the Ecstatic Poems of Kabir*, ed. Robert Bly (Beacon Press, 1977), 3.

So at this point, giving our head for the Beloved is a price we're more than willing to pay. All that matters is the heart, and as our love and yearning for the Beloved becomes deeper and purer, it is increasingly free from the associations with our other concerns. The Beloved is getting nearer and nearer now, and it's beginning to touch the heart in a very deep place. And we've seen that the more the heart is touched by the Beloved, the more it is informed by its characteristics. The love and the longing begin to express the fundamental qualities of the Beloved itself, and so the yearning becomes a longing to disappear, to cease, to be extinguished, to be annihilated. Although this partly reflects the desire to give oneself completely to the Beloved, we've recognized that it goes deeper than that; the longing for disappearance and nonbeing is expressing something about the true nature of the Beloved.

We're so close to the Beloved now that what's happening is already an expression of the beginning of union. We're already tasting the Beloved, and as we taste it, the tongue disappears, because that's the inherent nature of the Beloved—it annihilates all forms. And we want more of that. We want to disappear completely because this quality of disappearing, of nonbeing, is a quality of the Beloved itself, and we want to partake of it.

We can see therefore that the desire for cessation is expressing a desire for the Beloved. Cessation and the Beloved are intimately connected, for the Beloved is the mystery that precedes all being, all existence—it is the nonbeing from which all being comes. So we long to disappear, and as we love the prospect of cessation and annihilation, we are actually loving the Beloved. It may feel different from the way we loved the Beloved before, but the Beloved has not changed—it's just that we now know more of its fundamental nature. I say we "know" more, but we've recognized that our mind can't really grasp all this yet. It's the heart that is perceiving the mysterious truth of the Beloved, and it's the heart that knows what it really loves. It loves the prospect of simply disappearing, melting away, and there being nothing there. The heart feels that would be just wonderful. The mind says, "What an odd thing to want!"

So it's in the language of love that the lover's desire for the Beloved expresses itself as a very deep and genuine yearning to just not be. And you know the famous question "To be or not to be?" Well, for the lover, the answer is simple! For the lover, not to be is for the Beloved to appear. It's not that the one is the cause of the other—it's not like the disappearance of the lover is necessary for the Beloved to appear. No, the disappearance of the lover and the appearance of the Beloved are one and the same thing, because the Beloved is the liberation of nonbeing and the majesty of absolute nonexistence.

This love for annihilation can therefore be seen as the heart's way of expressing the desire for enlightenment. It's what Buddhism calls *bodhichitta*, which means the idea, the thought of enlightenment, and also the desire for it. In the beginning there is a desire for enlightenment, but when that deepens and matures, it becomes the desire for cessation, usually called the desire for nirvana. So what is nirvana? Well, it's often understood to mean perfect bliss, but the literal translation of nirvana is "extinguished," or "blown out," like a candle. So it actually refers to the self and suffering being completely extinguished. It's the end of all that, and this cessation of the self and suffering is the appearance of nirvana.

For the lover, however, it's not that there's a yearning for enlightenment or nirvana—there's simply a desire for the Beloved.

The desire for the annihilation of the soul—for individual consciousness itself to just melt away—is an expression of very deep love for the Beloved and the yearning for intimacy and union with it. Annihilation and the Beloved are indistinguishable for the lover at this stage. In poetry and literature about this it often seems like there's a precondition—our extinction empties the space in which the Beloved will show itself, so the self needs to die for the Beloved to appear. That is true in some sense, but it's not the fundamental truth. The fundamental truth is that the cessation of the self and the appearance of the Beloved are the same thing, because the fundamental nature of the Beloved is extinction and nonbeing.

So we've reached the point where the Beloved is already touching the innermost depths of the heart and beginning to appear from within it, and that's when the heart starts to feel this love for annihilation. We want to be absolutely and completely gone so that we don't feel anything at all. We don't want to think of ourself any longer, and we don't want to remember anything or anybody. We don't just want no more loves; we want no more experience, no more awareness, and no more consciousness—we really do want absolute and complete nothingness. So it's not like we just want to leave existence; we don't even want to know that we ever existed in the first place. There is a wish to be so completely gone that nobody will ever remember us, so it will be as if there was never even anyone who left.

We could describe this desire to be completely gone as a kind of death wish, and it's not the first time on the path that we've experienced such a wish. If we use the language of movie franchises, this is *Death Wish III*. *Death Wish I* is usually the wish for the ego identity, what we call "the pea," to disappear.

We could more accurately call that just *Death Wish*, because we don't know at that point that there's going to be a sequel. Then there's the sequel, *Death Wish II*, which, as we saw in the second book in this series, *Nondual Love*, is the wish for the sense of separate individuality and boundaries to disappear. And *Death Wish III* is the wish for the soul, the whole individual and personal localized consciousness, to disappear.

Now, all this talk of death wishes could sound rather dark and destructive, but as we're seeing, the death wish that arises in seeking the Beloved is actually an expression of very sweet and pure thoughts and longings: "It'd be so nice to just forget everything and just stop being." But we still have mind, and the mind will have its associations, and we've seen how those associations can mix with the pure feeling of the heart and distort this wish for cessation. The association here isn't just about regressing into the primal cavity, but desiring death, the end of life. So the wish for cessation becomes an actual death wish—a wish for the death of the body—as if physical death is going to unite us with the Beloved. It won't. Only if we're already ready for the cessation of the soul herself at the time of death will it be followed by union.*

---

* This truth is expressed very clearly in another Kabir poem, "The Time Before Death":
> The idea that the soul will join with the ecstatic
> just because the body is rotten—that is all fantasy.
> What is found now is found then.
> If you find nothing now,
> you will simply end up with an apartment in the City of Death.

Kabir, *The Kabir Book: Forty-Four of the Ecstatic Poems of Kabir*, ed. Robert Bly (Beacon Press, 1977), 24.

When we're experiencing the death wish as the true desire for cessation of the soul, we don't feel like we want to physically die. Yes, we feel we want complete nonbeing, but we're not thinking specifically about body or mind or consciousness. And we're not harboring any destructive thoughts toward ourselves, because it's an expression of love. The contentment of the heart is finally getting very close, and it feels like it would be such a sweet thing to just not be. It feels like it would be so completely satisfying, especially as I wouldn't even be there to be able to contemplate whether I'm satisfied or not.

It's therefore a distortion of the yearning for cessation and nirvana that turns it into a wish for the death of the body, and this creates another syndrome that was also identified by Sigmund Freud. At some point he noticed that there were some difficult patients he'd worked with for many years who hadn't gotten any better and kept repeating the same problem in their lives over and over and over again. Freud called this "repetition compulsion," because there's a compulsion to repeat the same pattern regardless of how destructive it is. He wondered why these people were so self-destructive and didn't really seem to *want* to get better. After much speculation, he came to the conclusion that it was a death wish, and he connected it with the concept of extinction, actually calling it "the nirvana principle." He saw it as a force that was deeper even than the life force, leading people toward annihilation, cessation, and death. And he thought it was an inherent instinct in both the mind and body, which explained the self-destructiveness and repetition compulsion of neurosis.

Nowadays psychologists don't accept that. They interpret such destructive behavior and the repetition compulsion to be a consequence of early object relations and developmental issues, so they've pretty much thrown out the idea of an inherent death wish and the nirvana principle. However, I think that while Freud's account of the nirvana principle doesn't completely explain the death wish that many people experience, his ideas about it weren't completely wrong. He didn't see it exactly for what it is because he was looking mostly at neurotic illness. But despite there being some level of distortion in what Freud was seeing, if we look more deeply, we can see the same principle that he saw. We see that deep inside every human being there exists a desire for cessation. Every human being has in them the desire for nirvana, the love for cessation, and it's not neurotic when it comes out of the soul's love for her Beloved.

So we're able to recognize why this desire gets expressed explicitly as the death wish at this stage on the path, because we understand that the soul itself feels it would be good to completely disappear, and for everything to disappear, the whole universe. There would be nothing left then, just complete peace and stillness. That means there would be just the Beloved itself and nothing else, and our wish for that shows that it is really an expression of the fullness of love. It's only when there's neurosis or other negative dynamics in the personality—especially at times of great difficulty, pain, and suffering—that the death wish is experienced as a desire to end physical life. If someone feels that, it shows that the soul is not recognizing itself as a soul—it is still identifying with the physical body and interpreting the nirvana principle, or desire for cessation, from a physical perspective.

It's the same as we saw in the regressive wish to go back to the womb, which means we are interpreting the soul's desire to go back to her source as the physical body going back to its source. The same confusion and conflict between the body and the soul is expressed here in the death wish. It's the soul that wants to cease, but if we confuse that with thinking the physical body needs to die, then naturally that can bring a lot of fear and conflict—I mean, to be with the Beloved, do I really have to kill myself? And then Rumi is always talking about dying, drowning, and meeting the angel of death joyfully, so if someone has been depressed for years and the medication's stopped working, they might say, "Great, I'm going to end it all and go and be with the Beloved." But, of course, that's not the solution for depression, and it's not what Rumi's counsel is.

The kind of death we're talking about here is the consummation of a love affair, not the termination of it. If the desire for cessation becomes a desire for physical death, with suicidal thoughts or plans, then it's not an expression of love but of self-aggression and self-hatred. It's the opposite of love, because the body—and especially the human heart—is the house of the Beloved. The Beloved gave it to us so the Beloved can appear through it, so to annihilate the body would be an act of hatred and rejection toward ourselves, and ultimately toward the Beloved. Fortunately, it rarely goes as far as actual suicide, and even then it's generally in situations where people are already feeling inclined to take that course of action. But even when someone is feeling the true death wish as the desire for cessation of the soul, it can still feel scary and give rise to a sense of conflict and confusion. People often don't understand what they are feeling, and think, "That's weird. Why am I thinking that I want to die?"

I remember for me, there were months, and even years, when the thought of dying was pretty appealing. It seemed like a wonderful prospect, and yet it wasn't as if I hated life or was suffering and having a hard time. Quite the opposite—life was wonderful, but somehow death seemed sweeter and offered a much more absolute kind of contentment. It took me a while to recognize how this feeling was connected to the Beloved, and then I realized that it's not a matter of ending life but rather reaching complete union with the Beloved.

So we need to be clear that in yearning for cessation, we're simply yearning for the very essence of the Beloved, and that this yearning is a deepening of our love, informed by the Beloved's increasing nearness. Of course, we may have felt and expressed a deep love for the Beloved before that—"I love God above all else"—but our love doesn't appear as the desire for cessation until we go very deep indeed, and get so near to the Beloved that we're already being touched, and the melting is already happening from within. We then have a taste of delicacy going to its absolute extreme, love going to its absolute intensity, and softness going to its absolute limit. And then quite spontaneously we feel, "Ah yes, that's what will content the heart. Extinction."

Practice Session:
Yearning for the Beloved and the Wish for Cessation
• • •

It is time for you to explore how this death wish lands in you. You will do two repeating questions, so if you have someone to do the exercise with, you will each take a turn for fifteen minutes, asking the first question repeatedly and answering spontaneously. After that, you will each ask and answer the second question. If you don't have a partner to do it with, you can answer in writing as many times as possible within the allotted time, or you can record the question and have it spoken to you by your computer or device after you finish answering out loud.

The first question is:

Tell me a way you experience your yearning for the Beloved.

Trust what arises without a great deal of thought. Remember this is an invitation to the heart to express itself, regardless of whether your response makes sense or not.

The second question is:

Tell me a way you feel your wish for cessation.

This may feel like unfamiliar territory, which is fine. Just see what arises if you let yourself speak without thought or judgment.

. . . . .

Questions and Comments

Student: I had a lot of resistance to the second question in that I didn't want to lose myself, lose my soul to . . . eternity, I guess. So my question would be, in the context of having many lives, of having a reincarnated life, does that fit with what we're exploring here, or are we absorbed back into a collective?

A. H. Almaas: Being absorbed, becoming completely indistinguishable, so you can't tell yourself from other people and it's all chaotic and messed up—that's the fear, right? That you'll completely disappear and that's it, forever and ever. So these are the fears that arise, and it's understandable, because we don't really know what it's like. And there are many such fears that the lover encounters on the path of love. Now when we finally go through the journey of realization, we recognize at some point that there isn't really any cessation. That's because the soul never ceases—all that happens is the soul knows her nature. However, on the path toward that, we don't know that yet, and so it will feel to us like there's going to be a cessation, as if we're going to end, and we don't know what's going to happen after that. But as we keep seeing, it's love that makes it possible to allow it. When we feel how deep and strong that love can be, and when we really connect with it, we don't care anymore. We love the Beloved so much, the feeling is that "I simply don't want to exist, because I want only the Beloved to exist. It doesn't matter what happens after that. If I vanish into the Beloved and only the Beloved is there, I don't care what's happened to me." That's the natural consummation of this love affair, and that's what can bring about the complete union with the Beloved. At some later point it will be revealed to us that the soul actually continues as a manifestation of the Beloved, but even if we think we know that at this point, it's just a theoretical thing. So when the experience comes, the fear is still going to be there, and the only thing that can help us go through it—or the best thing that can help us go through it—is the love itself. Love, of its very nature, is giving, and it gives of itself. So the more loving we are, the more we are willing to give of ourself. There's a selflessness that happens. And there's an overflow of love that can bring such generosity that we want to give unconditionally. It's a problem if we try to do that with another human being. It's not appropriate, because no single human being can handle that—what are they going to do with you? But with the inner Beloved it's different.

S: My heart is alive and pumping right now after being kind of heavy, and I didn't think it had something to share. And with the last question, there was absolutely no wish of mine to have anything to do with cessation. And I just stayed with that, and that's what I gave as the answer. And then I realized my mind was the one answering the question, and it controls, and it makes all the decisions, and it makes everything into a nice little package all the time and doesn't really consult the heart very often. So when I saw that, it was as if my belly, my heart, and my mind were on this island, and the belly and the heart decided to vote the mind off the island. And they ganged up, and when they did that, all of a sudden the heart started speaking. I checked in with the belly and it didn't have a whole lot to say, so my heart started speaking, and just as it did, it wanted to dissolve into like a pool. And then my mind started thinking, "Oh, that doesn't make sense, I'm not up for that," and my belly took its hand and put it over the mouth of my mind to shut it up. This is what I was seeing. and the heart was able to keep speaking and just say, "Yes, I want to dissolve, I want tenderness and gentleness and to just disappear and feel like there isn't constant activity in the mind." So it was a very powerful exercise. It began with difficulty, but I was grateful for what I got from it.

AH: That's wonderful. So that's why it's important to stay with our truth, with our experience, and not try to impose anything on it ourselves. Let our experience speak, and at some point the heart will speak, and the heart is always different. And that is something we find out. We don't make it happen.

S: This retreat seems almost revolutionary to me. Seeing everything from the way of the heart is so simple, and so direct, and confounding, but it's like I can go back and look at everything I've been exposed to in the work with a switch, and it's the heart.

And that came to me in this last exercise in a way that was dramatic, in that question of, "What do I wish for in terms of a wish for cessation?" And there were a number of things that arose that didn't surprise me, wishes for kind of an annihilation. And then something arose, like a jolt, and it was so obvious that I'd never considered it from the heart, and that is: I don't want to decide anymore. I'm not good at it—most of my decisions are bad, and I either regret them or I want to hold on to them; I want to fight somebody about it. And the actual heart feeling that I want that to stop is profound.

AH: That's why people talk about the knowledge of the heart. There is a particular knowingness that comes directly through the heart.

S: I saw something that was quite surprising, that I've believed since I've been a child, that I could extinguish myself with enough self-hatred. That with the hatred, I've been kind of doing this in reverse—if I could hate myself enough, I'd go away. It made me quite sad to see that.

AH: Yes, hatred is some kind of imitation of annihilation. But the true annihilation is love. The thing that will extinguish you completely is love. With hatred, it will feel as if you're reducing yourself, but you're still there—the hate itself is a self.

TEN

Stupa Love

First, another poem by Rumi, from *Divan-i Shams-i Tabrizi*, translated by R. A. Nicholson. It's a poem I've used before in other contexts, including the first volume of this series on love, *Love Unveiled*.*

> This is Love: to fly heavenward.
> To rend, every instant, a hundred veils.
> The first moment, to renounce life;
> The last step, to fare without feet.
> To regard this world as invisible,
> Not to see what appears to one's self.
> "O heart," I said, "may it bless thee
> To have entered the circle of lovers,
> To look beyond the range of the eye,
> To penetrate the windings of the bosom!"
> Whence did this breath come to thee, O my soul,
> Whence this throbbing, O my heart?†

---

* See *Love Unveiled*, pp. 10–15, for a detailed interpretation of this poem.
† Jalal al-Din Rumi, "XL," in *Divani Shamsi Tabriz*, ed. and trans. Reynold A. Nicholson (San Francisco: Rainbow Bridge, 1973), 96.

So rending the veils that obscure the Beloved, going through these veils, is inseparable from love. At least that's how love operates in the work we're doing here.

To get some sense of why this rending is important, we need to remember that from early childhood through to adulthood, our souls become structured. What we then experience as a sense of self is this structured part of the soul. The whole soul doesn't get structured, just the part that we end up identifying with as this person that is the self. That structure tends to keep the rest of the soul outside of its boundaries and constrain our experience within them.

Generally speaking, then, our experience happens from within that structure. Occasionally the structure becomes somewhat relaxed and other parts of the soul emerge, and we then have a different, expanded experience of ourselves—what people often call a peak experience. Such experiences occur spontaneously once in a while, but they don't change us. That's because when this happens, the structure isn't penetrated, so it isn't dissolved; the veils remain in place because they are not rent in any fundamental way. As a result, these experiences don't really challenge our structure and our beliefs about who and what we are.

When it comes to doing inner work on ourselves, there are basically two ways of experiencing more of what we are outside of this structure. The most common way is to work on specific practices that are directed in some way. There are many such practices that seek to activate or embody one particular spiritual experience or another—practices of meditation, concentration, visualization, or embodiment, for example. These practices work on opening up parts of the soul that haven't been rigidified within the structure. As those parts begin to develop through these practices, the soul develops an openness to certain kinds of experience that are outside of the usual structure of the self.

However, this still doesn't usually challenge and transform the structure, and that's because focusing on particular practices doesn't deal directly with the structure of the personality, exploring its history, identifications, and issues. If transformation of the personality does happen in these traditions, it's either through interaction with the teacher or through trying to embody and integrate a realization into one's life after it has occurred. That can then become a further aspect of the work if the person seeks to become more aware of how their structure operates in everyday life. But people who work in these essentially transcendent traditions normally develop another part of themselves while the usual part remains intact. It might recede into the background as a result of their work, but when a challenging life situation arises, it tends to be the habitual self that comes through, not the more developed one.

I've seen this often with people who've done a lot of concentrated work on themselves using a specific practice that's oriented toward opening the soul in a particular way. I can see that the person is developed and has access to deep and subtle experiences. They may therefore have a great deal of knowledge and spiritual insight, but when it comes to their personality, I realize that it's just the way it was when the person started their practice. A whole lot of other work still needs to be done if the personality is to be metabolized and transformed.

The other way of working is to work directly with the personality itself, focusing on the structure of identification with the self, and the positions, issues, and barriers that arise from it. If we observe and inquire into the habitual structure of the personality as we experience it, it becomes more transparent. That kind of work opens up the personality, and the increased openness we feel isn't just a result of developing parts of the soul that circumvent the structure and are separate from it. In other words, expanded experience becomes available through penetrating the veils of the personality, which is thereby transformed rather than transcended.

Obviously the work we do in the Diamond Approach is primarily of the second kind, although we employ some practices similar to those that are central to the first way of working. So we don't just focus on particular ways of developing other parts of the soul—we work more on the self itself, on the personality, so that it becomes transparent and its veils are rent. As the personality begins to open up, the openness arises *within* our habitual sense of self, and it's this identity that is transformed and becomes transparent.

That's how we work generally, and we're doing the same thing here on the path of the heart, working through our usual experience of the heart. That's why we didn't start out by just loving and yearning for the Beloved—we began by looking at the divided and fickle nature of the heart in our everyday lives. By inquiring into and challenging the love and yearning we feel for our external beloveds, we've become aware of the difficulties that arise from making associations between that and the true, focused love and yearning for the inner Beloved. We've explored the many different kinds of confusion this conflation can create, and how it can result in our love for the Beloved becoming somewhat tangential rather than pure and directed.

As we uncovered various associations from our history, more and more of the soul's pure yearning for the Beloved arose, until we finally reached the yearning for cessation. We've seen that this yearning for cessation arises as we recognize the true poverty of the soul, and that even the heart and the love is not ours—we don't own it, and we're actually empty of it. And we saw that this yearning to disappear leads us to a mysterious paradox—that the cessation of the self is the same thing as the beholding of the Beloved.

If we continue with humility and sincerity and manage to not get sidetracked and distracted by our external objects of love, as well as all the names, concepts, and forms that we've developed around the inner Beloved, and if we manage to see through all the associations we make in relation to our body and our history, we become more steadfast in our love. At some point our yearning then reveals what underlies and prompts it—the true, pure selfless love for the Beloved.

It's actually quite simple when we see it clearly—the yearning, the longing, and the pain of separation are all just symptoms of the fact that we are in love. We love the Beloved completely and can't bear to be separated from it. So now we're feeling the Beloved—but this has been happening all along as we've felt the love come and go. The interesting thing to consider here is *who* has been loving the Beloved. The process we've been following takes place in the usual personal heart of the usual person we take ourselves to be. As we go through the confusions and associations with our true love for the Beloved, we recognize and understand them, and we can let them go. The usual person that we've known ourselves to be thus becomes empty, as the heart of that person is emptied.

This is an example of what I pointed out earlier: we're working with the person we've always known ourselves to be—the structured part of the soul, not a different part of the soul outside of it. We've observed and penetrated our familiar historical self, the one we know ourselves as, and we experience that person now, without defenses, without protection, without pretense, and with all its weaknesses, insufficiencies, and vulnerability. And here we discover a profound and unexpected secret—this person, this part of the soul structured by the ego, is the one who experiences the love for the Beloved.

It's a surprise, because this person, this self, has always been interested in external things only, so we had to rend the veils all the way through to the real essential heart of that person to find this truth. We penetrated the habitual identity in the soul, all the way to its true heart, and that's where we find that this person, who's been distracted from the truth for whatever reason—be it feeling deficient, weak, or scared—has been a deeply mystic lover all along. It is that person who loves the mystery of reality.

This is a very significant and radical thing to recognize, because usually we experience love and appreciation for the Beloved when the person is gone. This reflects the fact that it's the essential part of us outside the structured soul that has access to the Beloved, and when the familiar person comes back, it acts once more as a barrier with its focus on other things. Here, however, the person has let go of all its attachments, illusions, associations, and history, and has become so transparent that it finally recognizes for itself what or who it truly loves—the inner Beloved and the mystery of the truth. We realize that the soul loves the Beloved inherently, whether it is structured or not.

That's quite an awakening for many of us, and also quite a healing. It means that no part of us is alienated any longer. We don't have to keep sidestepping ourselves to fully love the Beloved and feel the true fidelity and commitment that this requires. We may have struggled to do this before because the self was unloved or wounded in various ways, but this has all been burned through, melted by the love that's coming from within. Finally, the love manifests through that person, the structure itself, and that's when we recognize that *as this person* we've always been in love with the truth, with the inner Beloved—we just didn't know it consciously.

So it's the true personal heart that is completely and intimately in love—not something we developed through a practice but the heart we've always felt as ours. And as we begin to feel the Beloved appearing in that heart, in its inscrutable mystery and luminosity, its majesty and beauty, we feel the love more directly. It may be felt first as a very gentle, soft, delicate, and sweet appreciation, which can then deepen into an unfathomable, oceanic kind of sweetness.

Our love now has this personal quality, but at the same time it's pure—free from the confusion with our mother and all the other object relations and associations. As a result, the love is not only pure and uncontaminated, it's also precise. We don't just feel it as a flooding now—there's more of a sense of stability and solidity in its presence and its depth of intense, completely pure sweetness. And because we've gone through and shed the veils of our heart, there's no longer any conflict in the love. There's no misunderstanding about what the love is about, so there's no guilt in it, no holding back, no dissociation, no splitting. It is a wholehearted and complete love that has a sense of holy divinity because of its purity. And it is precise because we know exactly who and what it is for.

As the heart shows its capacity to feel this intensely, deliciously sweet and heavenly kind of love, which also has a sense of realness, substantiality, and exact truth to it, it has become what we call in our work the Stupa—the body of love. The Stupa is one of the diamond vehicles,* and in it all the essential qualities arising as various flavors of love are integrated into one thing in the heart. So the heart is now the presence of essence itself with all its qualities, felt as the purity of love that is also personal. The Stupa is faceted, but it is precise, clear, and unoccluded. That's why it has such a sense of amazing purity and wholeness to it, and a sense of grace and surrender that is sublime.

As we feel the true, complete, selfless love for the Beloved, the heart comes into its fullness in loving its source—ultimate nature, ultimate truth. We now see the mystery that underlies all of reality and is the source of everything—the mystery of Being. Its mysterious beauty dazzles and enchants us, and intensifies the love we feel. You may have noticed that when you're in love, there's always a sense of mystery. If someone feels they know everything about their beloved, that limits the love, because love always seeks to know more—it thrives on penetrating deeper and finding out more and being more intimate with more parts and more qualities of the beloved. That's why there's so much excitement, so much thrill, in the early stages of being in love, before the love has been consummated. Your heart is racing, you're sweating and shaking, and you feel awkward. Why is that? It's because of the mystery—you don't know what's going to happen!

* Diamond vehicles, also known as wisdom vehicles, are whole bodies of essential knowledge that relate to a particular phase of the soul's journey toward the truth. In response to the soul's need for and openness to guidance, the specific details of the objective knowledge needed are provided by each diamond of the vehicle.

It's the same with the inner Beloved, but even more so. You can never tell what's going to happen there because the inner Beloved is a complete and everlasting mystery that we can never know. No matter how much we feel we know, and how much we love the beauty it has already revealed, there's always the sense of a greater mystery and a beauty that will keep revealing more and more of itself. And this fuels our passion and intensifies and deepens our love.

So the love is pure and complete, precise, clear, and clean. It also has a limitless range of depth and intensity. It can be gentle, delicate, sweet, and melting; it can be appreciative and valuing; it can be steadfast and strong; it can also be ecstatic and passionate. And the more intense, passionate, and consuming the love becomes, the more we experience how the passionate love itself begins to annihilate. Eventually we can't distinguish the love in our heart from the mystery itself, as the Beloved comes through the soul as annihilation from within. We feel the force of annihilation as an all-consuming, passionate, and ecstatic love, and we drown into the mystery of it.

It's interesting that this all comes from the recognition that at its depth, I—the person I've known myself to be all this time—loves this mystery. That is when the love develops and appears in its fullness as the Stupa, the body of love itself. The Stupa can manifest love in a variety of qualities and colors, which become deeper and darker as they are penetrated by the darkness and mystery, and more passionate and ecstatic. Then at some point you can no longer tell what's what—there's no distinction between I, the soul, the love, the heart, the mystery, or the Beloved.

So we've talked a lot about the yearning and longing, but now we've fully uncovered the love that underlies it and is the cause and reason for it. And it's this love—which in its very nature is melting, dissolving, consuming, and annihilating—that brings about the union, annihilating the perception of separateness between the lover and the Beloved. This can happen in a different way for each person, and in many ways for the same person. And for each person it is a very private matter. In the deep encounter with the true Beloved—the Absolute dimension of our true nature and the actual mystery of Being—there's always a sense of privacy, as it happens in the innermost chamber of the heart. That's where we meet the Beloved, and it engages the deepest, most private part of us. That's one reason why the Beloved is called "the secret," because we meet the Beloved in this secret, dark place, deep inside. Secrecy, darkness, and mystery all go together, and the combination has its own deliciousness, its own sense of ecstasy and thrill that burns, sears, and annihilates.

The meeting with the Beloved isn't only inner and private because it takes place in a hidden chamber, but also because its inner depth is so difficult to put into words, to communicate, or to share. You might try to express some part of the experience to someone, but in its fullness the experience is so inner and so deep that it will always remain secret and private. It is sacred. The sense of privacy, secrecy, innerness, and mystery evokes the sacred, as this is all happening in an inner place that feels dark and secluded. This love therefore has an ecstasy of a specific kind, an ecstasy of innerness, of mystery, and of secrecy, and sacredness that is like a rare wine with its own kind of delicious intoxication.

So because of all the work on rending the veils, our heart can now manifest in its completeness and fullness. And remember, it's not that we need to direct the heart in order to make it love the Beloved—it's something already there that we discover once the veils are gone. When our normal heart is cleared of all the idols and distractions and we get to the very depth of it, we see what it innately loves and wants. It's the inner Beloved.

I'll read you more from *Luminous Night's Journey* to illustrate what I discovered in myself in connection with this love. It's a continuation from the passage I read before about mystical poverty, where I found the person experiencing the emptiness of the heart. Seeing that person in its complete nakedness, I wondered what this person wants—if anything.

I feel curious about this person I have known for most of my life, the person I've taken myself to be for many years. I wonder whether this person wants something.

To my surprise, a longing arises, a longing for the absolute Beloved. I see the mysterious blackness of the absolute, and as this empty and helpless person, I feel a definite longing to annihilate into it. The longing arises first as a sad and gentle yearning. Then it gradually transforms into a deep and intense love for the absolute.

The love appears after the longing, as if the longing has been hiding it. The love first manifests as an exquisitely faceted form of presence, a form that combines all aspects of essence in one manifestation. I feel it as an intense, pure and selfless love, of various flavors and colors. The sweetness is heavenly, and the appreciation feels so pure it has a sense of divinity.

I realize that many things have been preventing me from recognizing and feeling this longing, and from fully becoming the person I have been, with all of its feelings and emotions. The heart has been slowly turning, directing its love and yearning towards the absolute. This turning of the heart has produced guilt—guilt for not loving or longing for anything or anyone. I have unconsciously interpreted the shift of libido towards the absolute as a turning away from what I have loved before. This explains the subtle guilt I have been experiencing lately for not feeling that I miss my wife, or my friends, when I'm away from them. At the same time there has also been guilt for not feeling enough love and longing for the divine being, the unity of being, which I have loved since I recognized it some years ago. I did not realize that my heart was turning inexorably toward this greater truth.

There has also been jealousy and insecurity, relating to unconscious fears that others will enjoy the love of the divine being, and that perhaps I will miss out through not staying faithful to it. I recognize this jealousy and insecurity as a reflection of my early experience, when younger siblings enjoyed merging love with my mother and I felt alone and empty. I believed then that the loneliness was a consequence of my moving toward autonomy. This anguished feeling of the ego mind results in this negative relationship, full of frustration, hurt, insecurity, and guilt.

I realize that this person now feels the same as I often felt before Being began revealing its nature: insecure, helpless, lonely and alone, very sad, weak, and without love or connection. But at this point of the unfoldment, it is surprising to see that this person longs for and loves only the absolute. This is amazing; the person of ego, when denuded of all defense and pretense, turns out to be a true lover of the Truth. It is a healing surprise.[*]

---

[*] A. H. Almaas, *Luminous Night's Journey: An Autobiographical Fragment* (Shambhala Publications, 1995), 78–79.

It's time to do an exercise to investigate your own situation in terms of loving the Beloved.

Practice Session:
Your Love for the Beloved

• • •

You will do two repeating questions. If you have someone to do the exercise with, you each take a turn for fifteen minutes, asking the first question repeatedly, and then take the same time for the second one. If you don't have a partner to do the exercise with, you can answer in writing, or you can record the question and have it spoken to you by your computer or device after you finish answering out loud. The first question is:

Tell me something that makes you limit your love for the inner Beloved.

I've talked about my own history around this, but everybody's got their own history, their own fears, conflicts, and associations that make it difficult for them to recognize the love and to feel and embody it completely.

The second question is:

Tell me a way you feel your love toward the inner Beloved.

• • • • •

Questions and Comments

Student: I feel kind of disoriented. During that second question I was having the experience of my heart as this primary sensory space that was becoming just space, with a real fine, shimmery, effervescent . . . I was going to say porous, but it's not even porous because it's not that dense to begin with, but just completely penetrable. And I had this realization that part of what keeps me from being turned toward the inner Beloved is some idea of limitation in containing this in my body. And as I was noticing all that, something even deeper in that space was appearing that felt really dense and invisible, and this is where I was feeling, "This is so mysterious I can't keep going with this; it's just impenetrable but empty at the same time, and within the space of my heart." It was a magnificent experience, and so when I came back, I just felt kind of shaky. I'm feeling more grounded now.

A. H. Almaas: There's nothing wrong with being shaky. But what you're sharing, it sounds great. And the heart of course, it has no limits in terms of size. It can hold the whole universe. And when it is empty, all kinds of things can appear within it that we don't expect.

S: I've heard you say before that the animal soul is never quite transformed, but always remains driven. So I might have misunderstood you, but it feels like you're also saying that the personality can feel purified all the way through into this love, which I do feel like never before, in a way. It's kind of an ongoing experience, and it's not always very strong and passionate, but it's just there, this feeling that everything is aligning itself, and everything wants this. But even if I don't feel it, I sense that my animal soul is wanting something that is different from the heart.

AH: So you remembered one thing I said, but you didn't remember another thing I said, about conversion. The animal soul gets converted by true nature arising within it, which is one of the steps toward the movement that we're talking about here.

S: So finally there is an alignment of all.

AH: Yes. When true nature appears within the animal soul and touches it from within, it doesn't get changed through understanding or anything else but through being touched by the exact quality that the animal soul wants.

S: And that is the merging love?

AH: Exactly.

S: So the merging love transforms the animal soul, but it isn't the merging love that takes us to the Beloved. That's then the next step?

AH: Yes. It's a further process, and that's what we're doing here. And the animal soul never loses the fact that it has an animal quality to it, but definitely there is more alignment.

S: When this retreat started, the whole idea of the Beloved was not something I could really connect with. And then in one of the exercises, I suddenly realized, "Oh, I know the Beloved by its absence." So I saw that something in myself must have known it at one point. And as we went on, I saw that something really very moving is happening in my soul. There is actually a turning toward the Beloved, and actually I'm experiencing being touched by it. And it's very different from having essential experiences—it's something different altogether. I'm just very grateful.

AH: That's wonderful.

S: Before the exercise you said that it's the ego, that part of who we take ourselves to be, that also loves the Beloved. And when you said that, something clicked in me and I had this sense of . . . it felt first like a sense of relief, and a truth that I felt this love for the truth of what you were saying. And that love, I felt it in a falling away, in that that understanding somehow aligned all of my loves. What fell away was this idea that only a part of me—the pure, developed part—loves the Beloved, and the undeveloped parts of me are all entangled and confused . . . I had the sense of everything coming together, and a unification, and the more you spoke, the less I heard. I don't really know what you said after that, but there was this pure, sort of bigger devotion and love, and then I felt such love for you. And as I stayed with it . . . I don't know if I can really describe how it felt. I also had this sense of this part of me all of a sudden falling in love with you, and also sensing something behind you. So thank you.

AH: My pleasure. And it's okay not to remember, because I don't remember much of what I said.

S: I don't know if I can talk! But I feel like I really want to. What I feel is incredible gratification. I'm a classic enneagram nine in the sense of separation. In the Gurdjieff work, you take snapshots of yourself and then the concept is that you get a history of your life. And the feeling I've had in the last year and a half is, it has to do with life, it has to do with birth and death. And last night it felt like I was slipping into a depression, but what I realized today is that I was recalling or being with all the issues of my life, just coming up and being there. And when you said it is that ego self that loves, it was an "Aha!" for me, because it was like all my life there was no love. My separation from my parents meant I couldn't get love from outside because they were so far away, but in reality, there was no love inside, and so when you said that it is that ego self that loves the Beloved, it's just like all the pain of my life came up, and it was like life and death compressed into this one moment. And I was almost overwhelmed. It was just beautiful, so I want to say thanks.

AH: Okay.

ELEVEN

Luminous Night

We'll begin with two poems from *Divine Flashes*, by Fakhruddīn 'Irāqī. The first one:

> Other than that Essence
> Not one atom existed;
> When It manifested Itself
> These "others" came to life.
> O Thou Whose Outward is "lover,"
> Whose Inward is "Beloved"!
> Who has ever seen
> Sought become seeker?*

And the second poem:

> And when Its ray of loveliness appeared
> At once the world came into being
> At once the world borrowed sight

---

* Fakhruddīn 'Irāqī, *Divine Flashes* (Paulist Press, 1982), 73.

> From Love's Beauty, saw the loveliness of Its Face
> At once went raving mad;
> Borrowed sugar from Love's lips
> And tasting it at once began to speak.
> One needs Thy Light
> To see Thee.*

I've been presenting and discussing some of the stages on the path of the lover encountering and uniting with the Beloved. I've highlighted some of the transitions and some of the places of confusion, and I've been presenting it all as if it happens in some kind of sequence. However, the process is not linear in that way, and we shouldn't assume that we'll go through these experiences in the same sequence and in the same way as I've described them here.

One reason we might not recognize the process as it's been presented here is that most of us go through these things over a very long time span—years and decades. When it's happening over that long a time, we may not be able to see the stages and the overall progression, even though it's there. Someone may have already gone through some of these stages, these peaks and valleys, some time ago, and then, because of an intensification of the love and the unfolding, they might go through the whole process again. It can then seem as if some of the stages don't appear, but that may be because they've already been through them, and go through them so fast now that they don't register as a particular stage this time.

So the process is rich, alive, and complex, and each person may experience it somewhat differently—each heart has its own

---

* 'Irāqī, *Divine Flashes*, 75.

character, its own history, and its own inclinations. Nevertheless, there is the common general outline that we've observed—the heart's discontent becomes yearning, the yearning becomes love, and the love becomes union. The union is attained by the unification of the heart, through which the heart finds its true love and liberates that love from all the other associations to it. It can then naturally redirect itself inward toward the true Beloved, the only beloved that can truly, completely, satisfy the heart.

Our fidelity continues to deepen until it becomes unwavering and absolute, and our love for the inner Beloved then supersedes all of our other loves and subsumes them into itself. The love matures and purifies itself, and as that happens, we can say that in some sense the love brings us closer to the Beloved. But at the same time, we experience the intensification of the love as an expression of the Beloved coming nearer to us. This leads us to a pivotal realization—the lover and the Beloved are actually two sides of the same truth.

We've seen that as the Beloved draws ever nearer in our experience, we feel an all-consuming love that has an annihilating quality. It annihilates the heart and annihilates the lover into the Beloved. But remember, what's really happening is that the Beloved is manifesting itself in the heart through this love, consuming the heart and annihilating it from within. So the experience of annihilation and the experience of this intensification of passion and sweetness are also two sides of the same thing.

We can now begin to behold the Beloved as it truly is. The Beloved begins to reveal itself not just partially, through its aspects, but in its very essence. This can still happen in many different ways, however. We might find one particular way the Beloved appears to us and settle on that, but the Beloved can appear to us in infinite ways, and each way the Beloved reveals itself shows us something slightly different about it, how we are connected to it, and how the Beloved is related to everything else.

We know that one common way the Beloved appears is when we experience the emptiness of the heart—the emptiness of inner mystical poverty. As the last barriers of self and boundary disappear, melted by the love and the Beloved, the emptiness reveals itself to be nothing but the vast nonbeingness of the Beloved. It becomes obvious then that although we've been seeing the Beloved to a certain degree, we've never seen it completely—it's always been through some kind of veil. As the veil is parted and dissolved, we recognize, "It's just emptiness. But oh, how wonderful! I've never experienced an emptiness like this before." We thought we were poor because we've got nothing, but the poverty turns out to be this exquisite nonbeingness that is the source of all being. It's the source of all light, all existence, all knowing, all experience, all awareness, and all consciousness.

So we're beginning to have direct experience of the mysterious nature of the Beloved. We become fully aware that although it appears everywhere and fills all consciousness, it is truly intangible—it's the essence of intangible. Of course we cannot touch it, because *there's nothing there*. It's obvious to us now why we cannot possess it—it's so formless, so light, so empty, and so free. That's why we cannot make it into an object—if we try to, we're just erecting an idol for it.

We're witnessing the paradoxical heart of the mystery now: the Beloved is an empty nothing, yet at the same time, we experience it as a mysterious night that has a luminous vastness. There is a spaciousness that is vast, empty, and dark, but in its pure, pure darkness, in its silence and utter stillness, it illuminates and scintillates. It has a sense of majesty, a sense of beauty, and a kind of sparkle that appears out of nowhere. And there we have it, the ultimate enigma: it is a nothing that sparkles.

This is so mysterious, it bedazzles the mind and completely shatters it. It defies all logical analysis, so no wonder the mind can't grasp it. How could the mind possibly comprehend something that doesn't make any sense at all? There's absolutely nothing there, and yet it's the most powerful force possible. It's completely empty, but there's nothing that can exist without it.

And that's the dilemma we're in here—it's so difficult to talk about it. To talk about it, even to simply call it "the Beloved," means that our mind starts to think of it as an object, as something circumscribed that exists someplace. But the ineffable truth is, it isn't anything. So we can refer to it as "the absolute," but that's not really describing it in any meaningful way. I mean, to call it "the absolute," what does that actually say? And we've seen that giving it any name just gets in the way of us knowing it.

Part of the difficulty we have in conceiving of this nothing is that we generally underestimate the power of a vacuum. We think mass is powerful, while a vacuum can't be. In fact, a true vacuum—true emptiness with absolutely nothing there, so true nonbeingness—has an incredible and shatteringly magnificent power. And its magnificence and power derives from the very fact that there's absolutely nothing there. This confounds our logic because we think for something to be powerful, it has to be there as something. But the fact that it's absolutely nothing is what gives it the power to penetrate everything. It penetrates the inside and the outside, all the layers in between, and beyond. There's nowhere where nothing cannot go, so nothing can escape it. As 'Irāqī says in the first poem, not one atom exists outside of it.

So we're reaching the inner of the inner, the secret of everything. We may have already experienced the Beloved revealing its mystery as this luminous night that is the absolute truth of reality, but without recognizing it as the Beloved of the heart. We've recognized that the heart isn't ready to do that when it's full of other distractions—it needs to be free and empty, which is why it had to go through the process of regaining its complete fidelity and faithfulness to the Beloved. So while the heart may have known before that there's something there, and felt attracted to it, there wasn't the certainty that this is precisely what it always wanted, one hundred percent. So the heart has to cook, it has to bake, and then one day the mystery just appears and we recognize, "Oh God, that's it, exactly. I didn't even realize that I knew it that precisely." And that's when we are completely overpowered, completely overwhelmed with the passionate love and the passionate melting. As that passion flares up from within, there is a desire to completely melt and incinerate and disappear into this mystery.

We couldn't recognize how much we wanted the Beloved before because of all the projections and object relations from our history that got in the way, and might even have made us afraid of it. So one way it can become manifest is by penetrating all the boundaries and reification that we've put around everything in the world. As that all becomes transparent, the mystery is revealed. The Beloved appears then, not just within me, but within everything, as the depth of everything, as the center of everything, as the inner essence of everything. It is the essence of the nature of the soul, the essence of the nature of the body, and the essence of the nature of the heart. It is the essence of the nature of the world, and we now begin to see that it is in fact the essence of the nature of all our other beloveds.

I said before that the lover and the Beloved are just two sides of the same truth—or as the poem puts it: Thou whose outward is "lover," whose inward is "Beloved." But in reality, there aren't any sides or different directions. The whole notion of lover and Beloved is just some kind of make-believe, an imaginary story that makes it possible to engage in the love affair that takes us toward the Beloved.

I'll finish with another passage from *Luminous Night's Journey*. It pertains to this stage after the pure love for the Beloved arises within the individual soul. We saw how important it is for the journey that what matures is the usual personal heart, so that it's the usual person we've been who recognizes its love of the Beloved. And to be clear, I don't mean the structure of that person, with all its ideas; I mean the part of the soul that has been structured by our history. That part becomes more and more liberated from the history, but there is still a recognition that that's who I am, and it's that person who feels this pure love now. That means the love is completely personal on all levels and in all ways, and that's what brings in the Stupa love, because the Stupa is personal love—the very intimate personal expression of your soul's heart. So here, as I get to that place, the person of ego, denuded of all defense and pretense, turns out to be a true lover of the Truth.

> Contemplating my inner state, I experience myself as a thin film of a gooey substance of the personality, stretched over the tremendous presence of the absolute. Then I become aware of the world as a harmonious unity of all appearance, a oneness.

The experience of the person as a "gooey substance" reflects the fact that it is almost like a boundary, but a very fluid one, which then gets transformed into the oneness of existence.

I see all of existence as beauty beyond words, full of love and grace. But even this is only a thin skin; its substance, its inner nature is the vast, completely black absolute. So through my turning toward the absolute, and loving it exclusively, risking the loss of the divine being and the unity of existence, the absolute reveals itself as the inner nature of this unity. The immense silence discloses itself as the self of the divine being. I recognize that what I love most is the essence of the divine, the very self of God. It is the divine ipseity, the self of everything: absolute blackness, complete annihilation, beyond being and nonbeing.

The absolute is majesty; when it manifests its crystal brilliancy, it also has beauty. The beauty evokes passionate love; the crystal form of love attains a deep pomegranate color. The feeling is more than love; it is more like bedazzlement. The beauty bedazzles and enchants. I feel a deep devotional and passionate love, and desire for it to take me and completely annihilate me. That is what I have always wanted.[*]

When we discover the absolute and recognize that it is the inner nature of everything, it evokes this passionate love to dissolve into it—to be nothing but it, so we are completely inseparable from it. This desire to annihilate into the Beloved is simply a way of saying, "I am an expression of the Beloved, and the Beloved is my nature." And because it is my nature and essence, when I'm not feeling it one hundred percent and there isn't absolute union, it means there's only nearness, with some degree of distance. That

---

[*] A. H. Almaas, *Luminous Night's Journey: An Autobiographical Fragment* (Boston: Shambhala Publications, 1995), 79–80.

experience of only nearness will manifest as a passionate, sweet, melting, and annihilating love—a love that is basically saying, "No, you're not separate. You're me." So who is saying that? Well, it's the love speaking, and it's therefore both the lover and the Beloved. That's the message of love—it reveals the unity between the one who loves and the one who is loved.

So the intriguing thing we discover is that all we have given up, all that we have sacrificed at the altar of the Beloved, reappears now as an expression of the Beloved, as we now see that the Beloved is the inner secret nature of everything. Ultimately we had to let go of even our concept of God—whatever form or notion of divinity or divine being we had—in order to discover the formless Beloved. And now the Beloved reveals itself to be the inner essence of that and any notion of divine being. That's why when some traditions talk about God, they describe it as having two aspects—the divine being and the divine essence. The divine essence is the essence of the Beloved. The divine being is the external appearance of the divine essence, just as everything we behold is the external appearance of the Beloved. It's like the whole universe is the body of the Beloved, and the Beloved is the essence of that body.

As we approach the condition of complete union, the distinctions between love and heart, between love and lover, between lover and Beloved, between love and Beloved, all disappear and merge into one thing. We know that this kind of union can be arrived at in different ways, but through the heart it happens in this particular way, through the melting, ecstatic, dissolving action of love. We've described it as the love liberating itself from its distractions and dispersions, and becoming more concentrated, focused, and unified so that it flows naturally toward its Beloved.

But that is where the heart then finds itself turning and looking at itself, and the self it sees has no end. As we look through that endlessness, we look through everything.

So as the individual human being, we can now look through things and see the Beloved. In the ultimate station of union, however, we look from the vantage point of the Beloved. We're not looking through things from the outside then, but from the inside, because the Beloved is the inside of everything. It's like witnessing the Big Bang from the center of it—everything is there before it has dispersed.

We can see that the farther we go on this journey, the more things get turned upside down and the less logical we sound. But that is part of the nature and the way of love—it keeps confounding, bedazzling, and enchanting the mind. We know that the mind will often fight this along the way, but when it finally surrenders, it actually loves to be bedazzled. In the end, there's nothing the mind loves more than to be taken to its limits so it can't think anymore, and it ends up so bedazzled and awed that all it can say is, "Wow!"

There are many ways the Beloved can arise and many things that prevent us from seeing it fully, so let's explore this in an exercise now.

Practice Session: Beholding the Beloved
...

You will do two repeating questions with a partner, with each person taking fifteen minutes to answer each question. The first question is:

Tell me something preventing you from beholding the Beloved.

And the second question is:

Tell me a way the Beloved is revealing himself to you.

So with the first question, you want to see what's left; what else might still be veiling the Beloved from you and limiting your perception of it. It might be holding on to your sense of self, your identity, your boundaries, your other beloveds, or some other concerns, fears, and confusions. The more you see through these things, the more clearly the Beloved will reveal himself. With the second question, just explore whatever ways the Beloved shows himself to you.

. . . . .

Questions and Comments

Student: I have a comment and then I'd like some help on something. During the exercise I asked my partner to say how the Beloved is revealing *her*self to you, not himself. And that was key for me. I mean, I wanted to joke about it and recommend it to the other women, you know, "Hey girls, you should try this, it's really powerful!" Because it opened something, it was more direct for me, it opened something in my body to let the guest in, not as something that's outside of me but something that's inside. But what's happening to me now is that to feel so powerful, I am terrified. I feel cold, and it's okay; I mean, I don't mind it, but I wanted to bring it up with you and ask you to talk about it with me.

A. H. Almaas: Talk about what?

S: The terror.

AH: What are you terrified of?

S: I don't know. Would you tell me?!

AH: I thought you were the one who was powerful!

S: Well that's what feels . . . I don't know if this is a reaction against being powerful, I'm not sure, I just . . .

AH: It might be. To be powerful can be scary. So that's what you need to investigate. What is it about being powerful that's scary?

S: Okay.

AH: And the Beloved is traditionally referred to in literature as "He" but I don't think the Beloved has a gender. It's not a question of gender, which is why most of the time here we're referring to the Beloved as "it."

S: Okay, what I want to say to you about that is that I think we all know that inside, but when you're not realized yet or you're not realizing yourself in that moment, as a woman, I think I speak for a lot of us that it's hard for us to think of ourselves as the Beloved when we're not. The image of God is male, and I know once you get there you go, "Oh, that was silly, that gender business," but on the way there, I think that deserves like a whole . . .

AH: I thought that as a woman it would be easier to think of the Beloved as male.

S: I thought of that, too.

AH: Usually with Christian mystics it's the females who make the Beloved more male and use more of a sexual and love terminology.

S: Okay. Then what I'd like to suggest to you is that you use both in your languaging of it, so that we get a chance to . . .

AH: I never call the absolute "she" myself because it's not my experience. Other people do experience it that way, so that's fine, but I usually talk from my own experience. For me the soul is a "she," so I always refer to the soul as a "she." The soul is feminine, and the absolute is masculine—that's my experience. Sometimes I could see myself and other people seeing the absolute in relation to father and mother. They make the absolute into masculine and feminine that way. But in terms of the actual qualities between the states, it makes more sense that the soul is the feminine, in my experience.

S: Okay, I accept that that's your experience, but...

AH: That's what I'm saying, yeah?

S: I hear you, man.

AH: Okay. So by objectification I don't necessarily mean that. By objectification I mean the mental process

S: I hear you, man. But you just said that the absolute didn't have any gender, but yet you experience it as masculine.

AH: Yeah, it doesn't have a gender in the sense of woman or man, in that sense. But in terms of qualitatively—you know, feminine or masculine, not in terms of man or woman—all of us, men and women, have feminine and masculine qualities. Right? So some of our qualities, some of our manifestations are feminine, some of them are masculine. In that way I mean it.

S: Okay, but it didn't...

AH: So I invite you to explore that. How about that? Find out, and maybe your experience will be different. And when I invite you, I mean I invite everybody.

S: Okay, so I just want it registered that it was easier for me to feel the Beloved when I imagined her as female today.

AH: Sounds good. And some other people might also experience it in that way.

S: Thanks.

S: I had a rather interesting response to the first question, which was, "Thou shalt have no internal Beloved other than thy mother." Which caught me totally unaware, and I started laughing.

AH: That's usually the case!

S: There seems to be arising this black vastness that absorbs everything, even the Beloved. Can you speak to that?

AH: The black vastness *is* the essence of the Beloved. That's the true Beloved. All other beloveds are images or forms. The true Beloved absorbs everything else. It consumes everything else. There's nothing there, but it's vast and it consumes everything. That's the amazing mystery.

TWELVE

Secrets of the Heart

First another piece from *Divine Flashes*. This enigmatic stanza points to a particularly deep secret of the heart that we'll be looking at in this chapter.

> O Thou Who art my very sight and hearing,
> Occupy me so
> With Thy Love
> That in such Love I no more
> Busy myself with Thee.*

Basically what we're working on here is the realization of the Absolute dimension of our true nature. We know that this can be approached in different ways, each revealing different facets of the truth, but all approaches address the central fact that we're not whole; we're not completely unified and we are therefore alienated from our fundamental nature. So whichever path we take, the process is one of reunification, of healing the rupture.

---

* Fakhruddīn 'Irāqī, *Divine Flashes* (Paulist Press, 1982), 118.

And ultimately that means healing the duality we're caught up in and recognizing the true nondual nature of experience.

Our approach here is through the heart, which really means love, and the primary element of this path of love is the realization of the Beloved as the innermost truth of all reality. On the path of love, the duality and alienation is recognized as a separation between the lover and the Beloved. The lover is the soul, the individual being who is separated from the Beloved, which ultimately turns out to be the essence of the soul.

The way of love is the human way, and it begins where human beings find themselves naturally—feeling the discontent of the separation that arises out of the dual condition. Recognizing the discontent as separateness opens up all the yearning and longing.

We've seen how love by its very nature unites—it seeks to overcome the separation between things and bring them together. We established at the beginning that everybody loves in some way, and love is something that all human beings know to some degree, so love is something the dual mind understands readily. For most of us therefore, love appears to be an inherently dual kind of engagement: I love someone or something.

However, if you look more closely, there's more to love than that. Yes, love arises in a dual condition, but at the same time the love appears in the heart as nonduality. If we learn to truly love, the dualism and sense of separation melt away, giving rise to an experience of true unity that is a mystical kind of merging. Love is therefore extraordinary in the way it allows the nonduality of the truth to appear directly in the dual world.

Because love has this capacity to bridge the dual and nondual worlds, the teaching on love encompasses the knowledge of both and mixes them together in a kind of recipe that cooks the heart and cooks the soul. It does this in such a way that simply by following her love and longing for her Beloved, the soul arrives naturally at the nondual realization of reality. That's very different from thinking and talking about nonduality, which doesn't really make sense to most human beings. For some people, nonduality is a fascinating notion for the mind to explore, but that doesn't do anything for the heart. The heart just loves and wants to be close to what it loves—concepts like duality and nonduality are too much of an abstraction. That's why most traditions that take the path of love don't even talk about duality and nonduality—it's not really their concern. In our work, however, since we include other approaches as well as the path of love, using these terms to explain and explore the path can help us discover the deepest secrets of the heart.

So love can always bring us nearer to the truth, no matter where we are on the path and how we happen to be experiencing it. We saw earlier that some languages have different words for the many different kinds of love—the love of the mother for her child, for example, or the child for the mother; the love between siblings; the love of a man and woman; the love between the individual and God. In all these contexts, love is fundamentally operating as a kind of inherent gravitational pull toward nondual reality. There's actually a word for love as a gravitational pull in some languages, describing the kind of love that I've referred to as magnetic love.

When Sufis talk about the way of love, they don't use the general Arabic word for love, *hubb*, which people would use for the love between a child and parent, for example. They use the word *ashk*, which doesn't really have an equivalent in English. We would have to translate it as something like "ecstatic, passionate love that's continually focused on the Beloved and is unable to forget it." That's really what we're working with here, and we feel it increasingly as we begin to behold the Beloved's inner nature and recognize that it's our deepest heart's desire.

This ecstatic, passionate love is what I call the pomegranate love.* Pomegranate love has a deep dark red quality, and a zesty, searing kind of sweetness and passion. The passion implies that the Beloved is already being felt from within the heart and the soul is already beginning to dissolve. We experience the intensity of this annihilation from within as this ecstatic and sweet passionate love, because that's how the annihilation feels—it's delicious. We can therefore experience a passionate abandon that allows us to let go and give ourselves over to the annihilation. This love can also bring the necessary strength and courage to let go of everything that has supported and been dear to us, so that we can open our hearts fully to the Beloved. In the beginning, we can often experience frustration, anger, or rage in our struggle to make this expansive movement, but this is just another manifestation of the passionate desire to incinerate the forms our love is shackled by, and to break out and free the heart.

Because love combines the dual and nondual worlds, it gives rise to many paradoxes, and we need to be aware that some of them can become barriers that we need to penetrate and dissolve. There's one particularly problematic barrier that is inherent to the way of love, and that's the fact that we're so used to knowing and experiencing love from a dual perspective. For human beings, love always means a relationship between lovers, which means it is fundamentally a condition of separation. There's an

---

* See *Love Unveiled*, part three, "Pomegranate," pp. 199–233.

inherent understanding in the mind that love implies somebody loving a separate other, and love is always about trying to end the separation.

The very language of love—"I love you. Do you love me?"—implies this barrier of a dual perspective and separation, and naturally we transfer this to the context of loving the Beloved. On our journey so far, it's been intrinsic to the path of love that there's a relationship with the Beloved. Because it's so deeply ingrained in us that love is something felt by one being relating to another, the path of love incorporates this and uses it from the beginning. The love we feel toward the Beloved is what gives us liftoff on the journey we're embarking on—without it we would never get off the ground. The downside is that if we continue to feel we are relating to the Beloved, the journey will remain trapped in a gravity-bound orbit that keeps us separate from the Beloved. We'll never be able to escape that orbit unless our love goes beyond the duality of lover and Beloved.

So just as love draws us nearer to the Beloved, the familiar human experience of love as a relationship continues to separate us from it. As long as we love the Beloved in this relational way, it means there's still a mental component in it—the position that there is the Beloved, and there's me, this individual soul loving it. Our love may have intensified and deepened to the point where we are now completely denuded, undefended, and vulnerable, and we therefore feel a longing to love nothing but the truth, but we're still holding on to the position of being the lover who is in love with the Beloved. That means we're continuing to anthropomorphize the Beloved and think of it in human terms, and we're still making the Beloved into an object. The Beloved therefore remains just one object among the many other objects we have loved.

We can see the paradox of love in all the poetry we've been reading. It talks about burning through and emerging from duality, and yet so much of it expresses the duality of the lover yearning for the Beloved. And that's because it's so implicit for human beings that the condition of love is something that happens between two.

So this is a veil that still obscures the heart. It obscures us from recognizing and beholding the Beloved in all its glory, beauty, and majesty, and it prevents us experiencing the completeness and wholeness of the mystery. It's a veil that may operate in subtle ways, but it's ultimately a barrier that makes realization of the Beloved and union impossible. While it's in place, the Beloved is unable to appear completely and occupy its rightful place.

This position of being a lover isn't easy to relinquish—we have a strong attachment to it. That's because we think that letting go of the position of the lover means letting go of the love situation altogether. It feels as if it means giving up the love itself, because the mind can't conceive of love without there being a lover loving its Beloved. And naturally, if we think we're being asked to give up our love for the Beloved, it seems too big a sacrifice to make.

We can see now why love is such a paradox. When we feel love for something or somebody, we want to be closer—we want to be as close as possible. And when we love passionately, we want to eliminate all distance and all boundaries—in effect, we don't want there to be two any longer. So love is trying to eliminate the twoness, and yet we continue to view love as something that happens between two. This view persists because of the mental component that's lodged in the heart. It's a part of the mind that still sees love inherently as an object relation—a relationship between the self that loves and the object of the love.

Now, you may remember what was said in the very first poem we read: "Annihilate mind in heart." When it comes to the path of love, the deepest practice is to abandon all relationships and then simply love. That's what 'Irāqī means when he says: "Occupy me so with thy love, that in such love I no more busy myself with thee." In other words, let the love increase so much that I stop thinking of wanting a you that is separate from me. I want there to be just love, without there being any lovers. He's pointing to the secret of the heart that is the way out—there's a force inherent in love that can eliminate the mental component still residing in the heart.

So it's a paradoxical situation that contains both the dilemma and solution. It contains the dilemma because love manifests in duality. It contains the solution because love comes from and leads back to nonduality. And that's the beauty of the paradox of love—anyone can relate to it, no matter where they are in terms of duality or nonduality.

We can see then that even as we behold the Beloved up close, and we feel a passionate love and yearning for the annihilation of the distance between, we become aware of a subtle distance that remains. There's a subtle veil over the Beloved and still some sense of separation, so the heart isn't completely one hundred percent content. If we inquire, we'll find out that as usual the problem is that we are still in the way. The very thing that has brought us to this point of deep, passionate longing is what has always been frustrating it—the fact that we are lovers. So we have to give up what has brought us all the way here. We have to give up the condition that maintains there is a lover and a Beloved, and that there is a relationship.

Recognizing and understanding this can help a great deal, but as we've seen before, the path of love has its own approach to solving the dilemmas it encounters. And here, when I as the lover see this subtle distance, this subtle veil that still separates me from the Beloved, I don't need to think about veils and duality or nonduality. There'll still be separation if I bring the mind in like that. Instead I just feel the separation, and because I love the Beloved so much, simply feeling that separation increases and deepens the yearning and intensifies the love. The love then intensifies to such a degree, and the fire of passion burns so strongly, that it incinerates whatever is left of the mind—which at this point is the notion that I'm a lover who is engaged in a relationship with the Beloved.

So through love's own deepening, through its own passion and burning, the melting happens. The love itself obliterates the condition of duality. It eliminates the lover and it eliminates the Beloved. It eliminates everything. The feeling is, "I love the Beloved so much that eventually I just can't think any more." I forget who is feeling the love and who or what it's for—I'm just completely drunk with love and completely gone. And this is the deepest secret of the heart: The heart's love can become so deep, so vast, so powerful, so overwhelming that no veil can withstand its annihilating power. Anything that stands in its way will just melt, incinerate, and disappear.

Again, this intensity of love is actually nothing but the Beloved drawing nearer and nearer, touching us ever more closely, more intimately, and incinerating us from the inside, melting us with its fire and passion. The way we've described it before is that it's not just the lover loving the Beloved; it's also the Beloved loving the lover. But now we can't tell who's loving who. We become so bedazzled and intoxicated that we're literally out of our mind at this point. We're really not sure who loves who because we can't actually tell if it's one or it's two. All we can feel is the love.

And love needs to get that powerful, that strong, that overwhelming, if this is to happen. It can bring in fear, of course, and even terror. As I've said, there's the fear of losing the love situation and therefore the love itself. That's what the mind thinks automatically—if there's no lover loving the Beloved, there isn't going to be a Beloved, and no love. So it's another jump that's needed here, into an even bigger abyss. In a sense, this abyss removes the fundamental basis of how the mind works, which is always through making some kind of relationship between one thing and another—that's how duality manifests and clouds the heart.

So recognizing this last barrier helps us to see the separation it causes, and that allows the love to get even stronger, deeper, and more passionate. And it's that intensity of passion that melts and burns away this last veil—the position of being the lover—which is the last idol that's filling the heart. If we're still holding on to that position, then we are in some sense loving ourselves—we're in love with and still attached to being the lover instead of one hundred percent loving the Beloved. To one hundred percent love the Beloved, the lover disappears, because it's not important anymore. And eventually there's no Beloved either. There's just the love that burns through and consumes everything, dissolves everything, revealing itself to be the heart of the Beloved. That takes us beyond the question of relationship with the Beloved, and it clears and empties the heart completely. This is the secret of the heart, giving it the power of realization through love.

So here's another segment from *Luminous Night's Journey*, relating to this junction of truly beholding the Beloved.

A subtle understanding further illuminates my situation. I see that when I feel increasing longing, devotion, and love I become more identified as the person, the one who longs. As the longing person I am only a shell over the mystery, veiling it even while longing for it. In other words, even by loving the absolute, I assert myself as the individual, and thus become a veil over what I love. To completely have the Beloved, my love must annihilate me totally.

I can have the Beloved when only the Beloved is.

This understanding reveals the loving person as a film over the heart. It is the personality showing its bare condition as a somewhat opaque, somewhat soft, layer of soul substance covering the area of the heart. Through the transparency of this personality trace I see a dark emptiness in the heart area, which I recognize as the feeling of absence of heart, or more exactly, of an empty heart. Understanding of this situation of the soul as lover affects this structure by beginning to dissolve it.

As I feel my very substance melting and disappearing, I first experience the state of poverty. The emptiness of the heart reveals itself as the state of poverty, in which I feel I have nothing. The love, however, is too overwhelming to allow me to remain in any limited state, even that of mystical poverty. The intensification of love melts away even the state of poverty, where now the emptiness in the heart transforms into the dazzling majesty of the absolute. The love becomes so intense, so passionately deep red, that after a while I cannot tell who loves whom. Do I love the absolute, or does the absolute love me? The passionate love is the intensity of the annihilating power of the absolute as it erases all but itself.[*]

---

[*] A. H. Almaas, *Luminous Night's Journey: An Autobiographical Fragment* (Boston: Shambhala Publications, 1995), 80.

It's time for an exercise, so you can explore how you understand your relationship with the Beloved.

Practice Session: Identifying as the Lover of the Beloved

. . .

We'll do another monologue in pairs or groups of three, each person taking fifteen minutes for their monologue. If you are alone, write out your exploration for fifteen minutes.

Inquire into your experience of being a lover of the truth, a lover of the Beloved. Explore your love to see the identification with the person who is a lover, and the underlying concept of a relationship implicit in that. Explore what happens to the love and the lover as you see this identification.

. . . . .

Questions and Comments

Student: I have a comment and a question. The comment is, I'm finding how important and valuable it is to be in the body to do this work, and although that sounds simple, it's a huge thing for me. The question is, when I hear you say that the mind, or the ego mind, is the last outpost, the last veil before annihilation into the Beloved, what is the use of the mind? What is its function?

A. H. Almaas: Well, that's a big question. But definitely the mind has its uses, has its place, has its function. The mind transgresses its function when it tries to define the Beloved or tries to define us. As long as the mind does not define you or the Beloved, it is doing its function fine.

S: I never thought in my wildest dreams I'd ever see the Beloved as dark, black, blackness, but I've come to see that and it's been absolutely lovely. I have two questions. One is that in this exercise I experienced myself letting go of the duality that I started to see, except to the point of my consciousness. And I got to this precipice where it felt like consciousness was the next thing to let go of, and it was like, how in the world can I make that next step? And be conscious of it. It felt like it's not possible to do that and . . .

AH: That's true! You can do it, without being conscious of it.

S: Well, it was a strange sense of, how do I let go? And I also realized that if I do let go, I'm not going to know it.

AH: There is that fear.

S: I wonder if you could comment on this.

AH: Obviously there is a yearning for that kind of complete disappearing, for the consciousness to go. That's where the question comes from, I imagine. That yearning indicates a love for that disappearing, and the love for that, as it happens, will extinguish itself at some point. It's like the love, and the consciousness of the love, will burn itself out.

S: Yeah, that feels really right.

AH: That's how it feels. And it's true, you won't know it. You'll know it as it is happening, but when it's completely happened, you won't know it. And that is one reason why it is said that the Beloved is unknowable. Because to know the Beloved in its completeness, without consciousness, is not possible.

S: And now as you say that, I see the difference between, in my experience I was trying to do it, instead of loving it. And that's huge. And the second question may seem sort of frivolous, but it has come up quite a bit for me lately, and that is whether the astronomers and their black hole are touching on the black hole of God. I mean, there are so many similarities with the voraciousness of the black hole of the Beloved, and frequently I see it as a tornado, just wanting to suck me into this black hole. And it sounds like the black hole that the astronomers are talking about, it just eats up everything that's around, and it seems like the same thing. You can use the same language to describe both.

AH: Yes, I think we can use the language of science these days to describe the journey of the lover. And the black hole is now connected to the Big Bang, right? And the Big Bang is the beginning, so the black hole is somehow similar to going to the beginning, the beginning before everything happens. And before everything happens there was nothing in particular. So in some sense the black hole and the space before the Big Bang are physical ways of seeing what the Beloved is in relationship to everything else. Whether it is going to be the same will be interesting. I don't really know, it might turn out to be the same. But I agree with you, it's curious that the Beloved turns out to be black. Most people think it's going to be white, because people hear about the white light and all these things. Or they think that it's colorless. I myself didn't know, so for me it was quite a surprise. And that's why I say it is best to give up all images and forms and ideas about what the Beloved is. And that's one reason why in this work we talk about a love for truth, without giving the truth an image or form or idea. Truth can reveal itself on so many levels, in so many ways, until it finally reveals the ultimate truth, which turns out to be the Beloved of the heart. So truth is a neutral way of referring to the same thing as the Beloved, but our heart needs to be somewhat developed to really connect to it. That's not the case when we refer to it as the Beloved, as the language already engages normal consciousness—in loving relationships.

S: When I started doing this monologue, I noticed a couple of things. One is that I could feel my heart open and expansive, and I could feel the rest of myself as a certain presence, but I did not identify with the heart. It's like I was a presence having a heart but I wasn't my heart—there seemed to be a duality right there.

AH: A duality between your heart and yourself?

S: Yes. It's like I'm here and I'm feeling my heart, although somehow it wasn't quite me the way the rest of me was.

AH: When you say "you," what do you mean by "you" in this case?

S: This felt sense of the rest of my body.

AH: Okay. That's how it happens a lot. That you experience the self and the self has a heart and the heart opens and expands or whatever. As the experience opens up deeper and deeper, the sense of the self will get less. It will melt away and be just like a heart, or the heart and the self are not separate, which is the same thing. And even that at some point disappears.

S: I was able to also get inside the heart and look through the eyes of the heart.

AH: How was that?

S: It was great. When I looked through the eyes of the heart, everything looked different. And there was no one doing the looking. Like with my regular self, there's me doing the looking. With the eyes of the heart there's no one looking, it's just perception.

AH: Right. Well, that's the eyes of the Beloved. Remember what we keep saying about the Beloved—there's nothing there. So when the Beloved looks, there's nothing, no one looking. We're used to there always being somebody there looking, but you can have looking, perception, seeing, witnessing, all of it, with nobody there.

S: It felt like a nondual space to that extent.

AH: Sounds good.

S: I went into that exercise as I often do—I didn't have anything to say. And so I went first. Occasionally I'll do that, and I've found it really makes it fresh. At first I didn't have anything to say, and I just started exploring my experience. And I suddenly found myself, like, there, where there was nothing. And the intriguing thing for me is, one of the reasons why I push that away is because I can't imagine having any interest in nothing. But it was like the most exquisite fascination that I had for this, and one of the other people working with me called me a bliss ninny. I don't know what that is, but it was really like I was gone. There was nothing there, just sounds, and I feel really grateful for a taste of what you were talking about, and how far my mind is off in terms of judging how far I am from the truth. It's like my mind often says, "You are so far away." But it's not true, because a slight shift that I take, and I can be right there. That just amazes me.

AH: Right. Sometimes you could also listen to yourself when you say, "I have nothing to say." It was true. That's how it works sometimes.

S: I had difficulties relating to the exercise, and I think it's because my heart continually closes down again, and I'm much more in touch with the pain of this relentless closing down.

AH: What kind of pain?

S: It's just pain. It's tears, and it feels like I could cry over that forever, that this happens. And it seems to be hardest for me to tolerate the pain—that's why I'm closing it down in the first place.

AH: Ah, I see. Because when you're feeling the pain, your heart is not closing down, it's just feeling pain. And the pain is what you need to attend to.

S: But it feels like I'm more in touch with the separation than with...

AH: Okay, yeah. So the heart is feeling the separation. Sure. The heart feels the separation and is sad. That's natural. I've been saying that that's how love manifests itself.

S: I must have not been hearing that.

AH: It's good to feel the sadness of separation.

S: This is the part of Christ on the cross I didn't want to hear about.

AH: It's a profound condition, the sadness of separation. It's what most of the poetry and songs are about if you notice.

THIRTEEN

The Beloved

First another piece from *Divine Flashes*, by Fakhruddīn 'Irāqī.

> Without cease
> gazing into the purity
> of the Friend's face, he sees the universe
> imaged in his own reality
> and if he once looks back
> into the chamber of his heart
> he finds there like a blazing sun
> the sweet face of his heart-thief.*

We're more or less in the middle stage of the journey of love. The last idol has been dissolved and the heart is completely empty. The space is clear. This means the love is unrestrained now; it's wide and open and it flows freely. It has a passionate sweetness that is self-dissolving—as the heart loves, it dissolves into its own love. And then the love dissolves, annihilating into the Beloved. We're at

---

* Fakhruddīn 'Irāqī, *Divine Flashes* (New York: Paulist Press, 1982), 83.

the stage where we can't tell who's loving who, because the nearness is so overwhelming, the intimacy so intensely palpable. So there's very little that separates lover and Beloved now, and while it sometimes feels like mutual love, it can also feel like there's just the love itself, beyond any notion of relationship. This love is ecstatically self-erasing, erasing its own existence, and this is what makes it possible for us to truly behold the Beloved.

We may have experienced various partial manifestations of the Beloved before, many of its aspects, qualities, and dimensions. We might even have experienced it in its essence as the absolute, in its mystery and vastness, its depth and beauty. But experiencing the absolute as the ultimate nature of everything, the essence of reality, and even realizing it and being it—this is still not the same thing as beholding the Beloved. The Beloved is a very specific way of experiencing the absolute in the heart.

You see, the heart isn't really looking for the nature of reality. It's not searching for the mystery of being and the essence of things. The heart is simply looking for its own Beloved, the Beloved of the heart. It's been primed to recognize it, and the heart knows that it's the only thing that will completely satisfy it. When we experience manifestations of the absolute in its vastness and mystery, the heart may feel it's getting close to what it's searching for. But for the heart, close isn't enough. It wants to experience this mystery directly, within the heart, and that's why it's had to be completely emptied and then have its poverty incinerated and annihilated from within. Only then will the absolute appear as the Beloved, as the bedazzling luminous night in the cave of the heart.

When the Beloved does arise within the heart, it's so clear and so obvious: "Ah, that's what's supposed to be there. That fits exactly. That completely hits the spot." We know that this is the Beloved we've been wanting all these years. Every lover we've ever had, everything we've ever loved, all the yearning and loving we've ever experienced—in reality it's always been about this secret Beloved. It seemed such a difficult challenge to empty our heart of all those other loves so that this one could take their place, but now it's finally happened, it feels just right. And the love just loses itself at this point—the meeting with the true Beloved really ignites the passion, and this igniting of the passion is the same thing as the dissolving and annihilation, which is the same thing as the union, which is the same thing as the Beloved taking its place. We now see clearly that the heart is its throne and its chamber, the place the Beloved made for itself to appear in.

So it's a very interesting and very distinct phenomenon, the way the absolute appears within the soul as the Beloved. It means that the absolute can be experienced within the self, through the usual heart of the individual soul, appearing within it not only as its essence and nature, but as its Beloved that has been missing all along. Only when this station is reached does the heart feel fulfilled, with a contentment it's never known before. The heart feels, "Yes, now I can rest, now I can relax completely. There's nothing to go after anymore, nowhere to go."

There is a holy saying that many Sufi lovers consider to be central to the path of love, and I think it refers to this station. It's the divine or the Beloved saying, "If you're going to seek for me, don't look for me in mosques, churches, synagogues, or temples. Don't look for me anywhere in the manifest world. To find me, look into the heart of my faithful lovers." This holy saying confirms that the heart is the specific locus of the Beloved's full revelation.

Now, it's true that the Beloved appears through absolutely everything, because it is the inner nature and the heart of everything. But as the specific Beloved of the heart, naturally the heart is where it needs to manifest. And when it occupies the heart, it feels very different from all the previous occupants. Yes, they often felt wonderful and beautiful, but there was always a feeling of something not fitting exactly, of something missing, and so a vague sense of dissonance. Here, there's no dissonance.

So although we may have recognized the Beloved before in ways that were magical, loving, tender, and beautiful, the heart wasn't completely involved yet and wasn't fully penetrated by the Beloved. The heart has to be totally empty for that to happen, so it becomes the clear window through which we behold the Beloved in a much fuller and more complete way. Only then can the heart recognize and know that the Beloved needs to take his place on the throne he has made for himself there. That's what 'Irāqī means when he says that if you look into the chamber of the heart, you'll find the heart-thief—the Beloved that has stolen the heart.

I think it's a very beautiful thing that when our heart truly loves—when its love is perfect, complete, and whole—it turns out that what it loves is the Beloved, the absolute truth of reality. I mean, what more guidance do we need than that? How could we be any more fortunate? How could it be any more miraculous, that the only thing that will truly satisfy the heart is the condition of absolute freedom, absolute truth, absolute reality?

So we may have felt troubled and frustrated on the path of love, and complained when our experiences of love have brought us so much hurt and heartache, but it's actually all a good thing. If it wasn't that way, we would be satisfied with our imperfect loves, and we'd never come to know the true freedom of the ultimate truth. That's why true lovers don't mind feeling heartbroken—they know it's good they feel that way, because it's useful guidance, an indication that the true revelation hasn't happened yet. And if the heart is broken, at least it means it's not dead, because the heart is pretty much dead when it's numb enough to be satisfied with something that isn't the real thing. So the options are to have your heart dead, broken, or fulfilled. If it's broken, at least it's alive and still sensitive enough to tell you that it's not fulfilled yet.

We can say then that it's the compassion, mercy, and love of the Beloved that gave us a heart that is only for the Beloved itself. We could also say it makes the Beloved completely narcissistic, wanting nothing but itself to exist there, but it's a kind of narcissism we love. The fact that it wants us all for itself and doesn't want us to want anything or anybody else, that's what ultimately leads to our liberation. So the Beloved made us to serve as a mirror. The heart becomes a mirror in which we recognize the Beloved, and that's how the Beloved is revealed and known.

So for the transformation of the self, for the soul to transform and become an organ of perception and experience for the Beloved, it's clear that we need to go through this journey of the heart, where the absolute truth comes through the personal heart of the usual individual we've known ourselves to be. We know it's *our* Beloved then. Nobody has to tell us that—we're completely and personally convinced of it.

For some, this might mean waking up to the fact that for a long time they've had a secret love without even realizing it. Others may have known all along that they were in love, but didn't really know who the Beloved was and what it was like. We've all been seeing the Beloved in many different forms—in other people, objects, and situations, and in all kinds of inner forms too. Some of us see the Beloved in a combination of the two, as some kind of divinity with a human form and shape.

We've tried to feel satisfied with these other loves that we confuse with the Beloved, but when at some point the Beloved throws off all its disguises, all the shapes and forms that it has assumed, we realize that no other beloved could ever be as perfect as this one. None of our other loves has been as beautiful, as sublime, as exquisite, and as complete. And though we might make such comparisons as our appreciation for the Beloved grows, they don't really mean much, because the heart doesn't care. The fact is, this is the Beloved and it's here in the heart. That's all that matters, not what it looks and feels like. The heart is one hundred percent faithful in its love for the Beloved now, so there's no comparison to be made and no question of infidelity. And we see how the completeness of this love and the arising of the Beloved are the same thing—the Beloved arises when our love is complete, and our love is complete when the Beloved arises.

When we experience this unrestricted love, we recognize that it's all come from the Beloved really. Everything—all our experience, all the opportunities that arose within it, all the realizations, all the joy, and all the love—it's all come from the Beloved. The state of inner poverty was just the beginning of the recognition that as the individual, we haven't been the source of any of it—the Beloved has been the source of everything. And now the Beloved itself, the very essence of the Beloved, appears in full glory, in its brilliance, radiance, and exquisiteness. It's so delicate, so faceted, and so scintillating, and at its core lies the ultimate mystery—it's as if it is something while at the same time it's actually nothing.

This scintillating Beloved expands to fill the heart, and then it expands to fill everything, the whole universe. It reveals that the whole universe is its love, its universal heart. So we begin to see the truth: It's not just our love that comes from the Beloved—the whole universe appears as love that is emerging out from this mysterious beauty.

As always, there may be different ways the Beloved will appear within the heart to claim the heart. But however it happens, the crucial point is that the dazzling, luminous night that bedazzles the consciousness of the mind appears *in the heart* and *through the heart*.

I'll continue with my personal experience of this stage, taken from *Luminous Night's Journey*. This passage begins with the lines that ended the previous extract:

> The love becomes so intense, so passionately deep red, after a while I cannot tell who loves whom. Do I love the absolute, or does the absolute love me? The passionate love is the intensity of the annihilating power of the absolute as it erases all but itself.
>
> I, as the soul, behold the absolute appearing in the heart, occupying it as its rightful resident. The heart beholds the absolute as the most beautiful thing my eyes have ever beheld. It is dazzling and intoxicating, so black it is brilliant with blackness. It is nothing, but it shimmers and shines in such a dazzling way that I can see it has a crystalline quality. It is an infinite black crystal absence, brilliantly shimmering. The radiance is so bright it illuminates the cave of the heart the way a lightning storm illuminates the night. The lightning illumination ricochets in the cavern of the heart with such power that I can hear it thundering and exploding.

The Beloved now claims the heart fully. It has taken full possession of it, as its own throne. The Beloved is not an other. It is the true dweller of the heart, my source, my ultimate self, and the ultimate essence of everything.

I am struck by the realization that in this experience I perceive the absolute for the first time in the heart, by the heart. The absolute is perceived inside the soul, by the soul. The heart reveals itself to be the abode of the absolute. More exactly, the heart is the window to the absolute. I have experienced the absolute many times before, almost continuously, but not in the heart, and not through the individual soul.

A new feeling arises, a completely welcome feeling that expresses a deep realization. I feel I am finally arriving home. This mystery, this majesty, is my home, my original place. It is what my heart longs for and loves more than anything else. I realize I have always loved this mystery and always longed to melt into it, even though I did not know consciously what I loved and longed for. I knew I loved the truth, but I was not aware that the truth is ultimately this inexplicable reality. I see that I have always felt exiled, that I have always been seeking to return home. As I recognize the home of the soul, I recognize the totality of her search and its true meaning.*

It's interesting to see how the heart has its own mode of experience, its own way of perceiving. It's as if it is sensing, feeling,

---

* A. H. Almaas, *Luminous Night's Journey: An Autobiographical Fragment* (Boston: Shambhala Publications, 1995), 80–81.

hearing, seeing all of it happening, and at that point it might appear to be taking place in the actual heart, the physical heart. But then that opens up, and it appears to be a cave, a cavernous space. And after a while, we lose all sense of size and location. So it's not only about finding and recognizing the Beloved with absolute certainty, but also about seeing what the heart truly is—the abode of absolute reality. It's where our subtle autonomy is designed to become the place of residence for the Beloved, the absolute.

It's no wonder then that various traditions talk about true nature residing in the chamber of the heart, in many different manifestations. In our work, we can see the Pearl being born there. We can see the Point, the manifestation of essential identity, residing there. And there are many other ways we can experience true nature arising within the heart, all the way to the absolute Beloved. This shows that when we really love, it is the absolute that is loving, because the Beloved is the true dweller of the heart and the source of all its love.

And again, remember what we said at the beginning, that all humans love. That means that in all human beings, regardless of how blind they are to it, the absolute as the Beloved is still managing to come through. That's what makes us human, and why traditionally the heart is seen as what characterizes humanity and sets it aside from all other beings.

So, by this point our heart is not only stolen but willingly sold—sold to the Beloved. This initiates further developments, but it's time now for an exercise to explore your own heart and your beholding of the Beloved.

Practice Session:
The Heart and the Beloved

• • •

You'll do two repeating questions with a partner, each person taking fifteen minutes to ask each question repeatedly. If you don't have a partner to do it with, you can answer in writing.

The first question is:

Tell me what you experience occupying your heart.

It doesn't matter what it is. You just want to see: Is it hatred? Is it love? Is it fear? Is it rubber? Iron? Your mother's image? Your wife's image? You just want to say whatever it is that's occupying your heart. Remember, in our love for the Beloved, we don't have to see the absolute, especially at the beginning, and we don't want to try to make ourself see it. We want to see whatever way the truth is manifesting to us. And it's only by recognizing the truth and following it that the truth reveals itself more deeply and completely, until it is finally revealed as the Beloved. So it's not a matter of forcing; it's a matter of really finding out.

And the second question is:

Tell me a way you recognize the Beloved.

Say whatever way you have known and recognized the Beloved, even if it's just a partial manifestation.

• • • • •

Questions and Comments

Student: I'm really surprised by that exercise. I feel really ignited. In the first question, about what was occupying my heart, it was just a lot of pain, sadness, brokenness, all my insecurities

and fears. It felt so full of all that stuff, all my stuff, but it was okay. And then with the second question, I was recognizing the Beloved, and it was like I got ignited by recognizing that all of that stuff is just the fuel. And I feel like I'm burning up right now, and it's like the Beloved was in all that stuff; it was in all of it, and it just feels so big. And then when I came back in the room, the flowers looked different, everything looked different, and it was just like, ah . . . And it's not a controlled burn, you know! So I could probably work for the forestry department. So I just wanted to share that. The burning just feels sensational right now.
A. H. Almaas: Great. Beautiful. You always need to cook, always a little more.

S: One thing that keeps coming up in various forms is what becomes more and more like a continuum. There's this incredibly hot burning lavalike feeling—it's so red-hot, the passion, that it's black. And it has a lot to do with the horror of the world, and why it is like this, and there is this fear. It's like I've never fully allowed myself to really be touched by either that darkness inside myself or in the world, and it's like I want to shower in it and see in it the love. I mean, recognize the lover or the Beloved fully in all this darkness. And then on the other side of the continuum there is the experience of this different manifestation of, I think, living daylight. It's so human, but in a way where it's like ultimately healing, just as if the holy spirit, whatever it touched totally transformed into light and healing. And I noticed that you didn't really address living daylight in this retreat, even though it's the dimension of love, and so I wondered about that.
AH: Living daylight is just one big manifestation of love. It's the boundless love, and it's definitely part of the love for the Beloved.

That's the grace of the Beloved. So it seems in your case there is a need for healing, and that's what's happening. The quality that's needed for that specific healing is arising as that kind of grace.

S: I'm curious. You haven't mentioned the holy spirit in this aspect of absorption, and I had an experience in the last exercise in which I felt there was this absorption, but then there was this witness outside. It's like I saw an entering into the chamber, and then there was a witness. Is that the holy spirit? What is that?

AH: How are you experiencing the witness? Like, were you the witness or was something else witnessing you, or what?

S: I was the witness.

AH: You were the witness. And the witness was witnessing what's happening?

S: Yes.

AH: And was it within what's happening or outside of it?

S: Outside of it.

AH: Okay. So there's a dissolving happening, there's a witness witnessing the dissolving?

S: Yes.

AH: I would say the holy spirit is more the dissolving agent. It is the love that is dissolving the soul. And the witness is the manifestation of the Beloved.

S: When the absorption happens totally, is there a witness?

AH: What happens when it's total is that there is no witness, of course. No consciousness, no awareness. But that's a stage, and then there can be a witnessing happening from this condition of oneness or unity.

S: Thank you.

S: I'm seeing how I'm into images, and they always used to be out there, so I was seeing this image of this black screen, a black curtain, and there was this person sitting in a chair in front of it, you, and this quality of unpretentiousness, and this ordinary guy there. And the awesome emptiness of what I'm seeing out there, and with this burning and this new absorption and letting things in to feel them, I'm seeing part of myself. And it's almost very frightening, but also, in this process I'm just saying things and I don't know where they're coming from. It seems like there's just this outflowing from an emptiness, and it's extraordinary.

AH: Sounds good. I don't think you need to say more.

S: I'm curious if it was your intention that one of the questions could be heard in two different ways.

AH: So what are the ways you saw?

S: Well, the normal way was to think of what occupies my heart in terms of what I love. But I feel like I've just had a whack on the head and I began to hear the question completely differently. What would I experience if I occupied the heart? And my world just turned upside down. And my question is, am I going to black out?

AH: It might happen. Sure, you might black out for a few seconds while you're meditating. I mean, that's why they call it cessation or extinction. But that's not really what happens. It seems like there is a fear around that, some concern.

S: Well, you know, the fear is dissolving, but it's kind of somewhere I've... I'm curious about...

AH: That's what I mean, when we sometimes desire to disappear, what does that mean? It will feel like a blackout at some point.

I want to finish with a poem by Rumi, about the station we're working with.

> O my soul, who is this, stationed in the house of the heart?
> Who may occupy the royal seat save the King and the Prince?
> He beckoned with his hand: 'Say, what do you desire of me?'
> What does a drunken man desire except sweetmeats and a cup of wine?
> Sweetmeats derived from the soul, a cup of the Absolute Light,
> An eternal banquet laid in the privacy of "*He is the Truth.*"
> How many deceivers are there at the wine-drinkers' feast!
> Take heed lest thou fall, O easy simple man!
> Beware! Do not keep, in a circle of reprobates,
> Thine eye shut like a bud, thy mouth open like the rose.
> The world resembles a mirror: thy Love is the perfect image;
> O people, who has ever seen a part greater than the whole?
> Go on foot, like the grass, because in this garden
> The Beloved, like the rose, is riding, all the rest are on foot.
> He is both the sword and the swordsman, both the slain and the slayer,
> He is at once all Reason and brings Reason to naught.*

---

* Jalaluddin Rumi, "XL" in *Divan-i Shams-i Tabrizi*, trans. Reynold A. Nicholson (Cambridge University Press, 1898), 96.

FOURTEEN

Bedazzlement

We'll begin with another poem by Kabir, from *The Kabir Book*.

The Guest is inside you, and also inside me;
you know the sprout is hidden inside the seed.
We are all struggling; none of us has gone far.
Let your arrogance go, and look around inside.

The blue sky opens out farther and farther,
the daily sense of failure goes away,
the damage I have done to myself fades,
a million suns come forward with light,
when I sit firmly in that world.

I hear bells ringing that no one has shaken,
inside "love" there is more joy than we know of,
rain pours down, although the sky is clear of clouds,
there are whole rivers of light.

The universe is shot through in all parts by a single sort
of love.
How hard it is to feel that joy in all our four bodies!

Those who hope to be reasonable about it fail.
The arrogance of reason has separated us from that love.
With the word "reason" you already feel miles away.

How lucky Kabir is, that surrounded by all this joy
he sings inside his own little boat.
His poems amount to one soul meeting another.
These songs are about forgetting dying and loss.
They rise above both coming in and going out.*

    Many of the poems we've looked at talk about going beyond reason—leaving the mind, dissolving the mind, annihilating the mind in heart, or throwing the mind away. After a while, we begin to wonder what this is all about and whether it's some kind of mistake, because the mind is something we're aware of all the time, and it seems an indispensable part of being human.

    So what is the role of the mind on our journey? Where does our capacity for reason fit into the picture? And how is the mind related to the heart, and to love? I'm going to spend some time exploring this now, to get a better understanding of why it's said that the mind is a barrier and what this means for us in practice. Because simply throwing away such a major part of our functioning seems questionable—surely it would mean we were no longer whole?

---

* Kabir, *The Kabir Book: Forty-Four of the Ecstatic Poems of Kabir*, ed. Robert Bly (Beacon Press, 1977), 57.

We've seen throughout the journey of the heart that the mind obstructs or obscures our love for the Beloved. It takes the direct experience of the heart and creates images and concepts of it. It then labels these images and concepts by giving them names and categorizing them, and it fleshes them out with all kinds of associations and memories. This is the usual function of the mind as we know it—what we can call the usual mind.

When poems, and many teachings, talk about the mind, they usually mean that mind. They rarely go as far as exploring the real mind, although some poems do allude to the nature of that sometimes. So it's the usual mind that's being addressed, and it's that mind that tends to take precedence over the heart in our normal experience, impeding its natural flow. With its reflective capacity for reasoning, the mind becomes the main guide for most people in their lives and their main way of navigating their experience. The result is a more disembodied and less direct kind of knowing than that afforded by the heart.

So basically we can say that the heart gives us more direct experience, while the mind's tendency to use memory and association makes it an indirect way of discriminating and knowing our experience. The images, memories, and associations that our mind creates become our conceptualized version of the truth, which replaces the truth of pure, direct experience and disconnects us from it. This is how we lose touch with and become alienated from the direct, intimate experience and taste of the Beloved.

Of course, this doesn't mean that the mind's way of functioning isn't useful sometimes—we need to discriminate and use reason in our everyday lives, in areas where these things are necessary. The question is where it's appropriate to apply this way of operating, and when we apply it to the question of love, and specifically to the love of the Beloved, it certainly becomes an obstruction. That's not just because of the nature of the mind but also because of the nature of the Beloved. The only way to truly behold the Beloved is directly, and as we've seen, that ultimately means nondualistically—without the duality of subject and object, and all the images, inferences, memories, and associations that come with that. That's why in the end we have to give up all the mental images we've made of the Beloved, because they've become things that define and confine it. And the Beloved cannot be defined and confined.

Kabir tells us that even using the word "reason" means we're already miles away from the truth. Again, this is not to say that reason is always a bad thing. As long as the mind is operating in the right context, we can achieve great things by applying reason. But reason relies on logic, and logic is based on particular rules, categories, and conceptual dichotomies—big and small, old and new, for example. That's how reason works—it's basically a question of whether something is *A* or *not A*. Without the proposition of it being either *A* or *not A*, logic and reason cannot work, because logically *A* cannot be the same thing as *not A*. Reason is based on such logical propositions, and it's an important and necessary tool in our practical lives.

When we try to apply the mind to the ultimate truth, however, it doesn't work. As I said, that's mainly because we can only truly behold and know the Beloved—the true essence and nature of everything—in a direct and immediate way. Any concepts or images that replace that direct experience are always going to be partial, somewhat empty, and incomplete. They're always missing the immediacy, and the immediacy of the Beloved is the most important thing about it.

Another reason why using the mind doesn't work is that the Beloved is formless in an absolute way. This makes it impossible to apprehend using reason, because the conceptual categories, ideas, and dichotomies that reason relies on are all forms. Reason uses these forms to delineate and define separate elements of reality, which it can then compare and contrast—because X is such and such, then it must or can't be Y, which is so and so. When it comes to the Beloved, however, basic categories, concepts, and fundamental dichotomies just don't hold, and contrasts disappear.

So the Beloved is beyond form, beyond image, beyond name, and beyond concept in general. That means it is completely nonconceptual, and not just in the usual sense of that word. What most people understand by nonconceptual is that something exists without it being a creation and content of thought. And it's true, the Beloved isn't a content of thought because it's beyond anything the mind can create and define. But the Beloved is also nonconceptual in the sense that no conceptual category can apply to it. We cannot say the Beloved is big, and we cannot say it's small. We cannot say it's old, and we cannot say it's new. Ultimately we cannot even say that it exists, or that it doesn't exist, and that is clearly the most fundamental conceptual dichotomy possible.

That's why we've approached the Beloved through the path of the heart, not the mind that relies on concepts. And as the heart has been emptied of all its objects, forms, and concepts, we've recognized the poverty of the heart. We experience the heart as completely empty—there's nothing there—and this is when we begin to experience the Beloved directly, because the Beloved is empty of everything. It is the absolute emptiness, having no form or content.

The emptiness of the Beloved is radical, because when the heart is emptied of everything, and all the objects, idols, and forms are gone, nothing arises to take their place. No thing. So when we've talked about the absolute, or the Beloved, arising and appearing as nothingness, that isn't actually true. It doesn't arise and appear, it's simply what's there when everything is gone. The nothingness is already there and always has been, but we haven't seen it because we've been looking at all this other stuff.

Initially we don't recognize the truth of this radical emptiness and nothingness. We automatically see it as some kind of deficiency in which something is missing. We view it the same way we view a container that's had all the contents taken out, so only the empty container remains. We feel we need to remedy the emptiness and put something back in to fill it up—especially the jewels and diamonds of our nature! But the Beloved is not like an empty container. The Beloved is the absence of everything, including the container.

This is why we need to throw away the images, throw away the idols, and throw away the memories. Unless we remove all forms and concepts entirely, without replacing them, we can't see the radical emptiness of the Beloved. We'll still be experiencing it through some of the more subtle veils, such as the dual concept of being a lover in relation to something we call the Beloved. It's only when these last veils are finally cast away that we see the Beloved just as it is. And there's absolutely nothing to see because absolutely nothing remains.

We realize then that although we feel we've been experiencing many things ceasing, disappearing, and annihilating, in reality none of this has happened. The self has not annihilated and consciousness has not ceased. All that's happened is we've recognized that the nature of our consciousness—our essential nature—is that there's nothing there. We've just been obstructing and obscuring the complete, total emptiness with all kinds of mental objects. We've experienced something being there, when in reality, underlying it all there's nothing. This doesn't mean that all the forms we see in the world aren't there—it's more that the inherent nature of those forms, the essence of those forms, is nonbeing.

This is simply impenetrable by the mind—the mind just doesn't know what to do with it. The mind needs content, things that it can discriminate, analyze, isolate, conceptualize, and think about. Here there's only the absence of content. As the mind is being confronted by all this and trying to grapple with it, the presence of the mind is being annihilated in the process. But again, all that's actually happening is a recognition that the cessation, annihilation, absence, and emptiness is the actual nature of things. There's no way the mind can know that, because the mind can't possibly comprehend absolute absence. It can use the words but it can't really grasp what they mean. If you genuinely think about what absolute absence is and try to know it, you will simply disappear—and then you won't know it! That's quite a paradox, and the mind just gets entangled in it.

So while we've been talking all this time about focusing purely on the Beloved, the mind has inevitably created some kind of concept of this "thing" called the Beloved that we need to focus on. And now that we are finally focusing on the Beloved and nothing else, the mind finds that there's nothing there. It's quite a surprise, though it shouldn't be: How can the Beloved exist when the Beloved is the nonexistence of things? Still, our mind thinks that even this nonexistence must be something in particular:

"Okay, now I've found the nonexistence thing. What can I learn about it? There must be something there to love." But no, there really is nothing there, and it's the same nothingness that is the true nature of the heart, which we first began to recognize in the poverty of the heart.

But the mind will keep trying to think about all this emptiness and nothingness and make something of it. And the trouble is, the mind can conceptualize it—it thinks, "I know what empty is, it's the opposite of full" and "I know that nothing is the opposite of something and nonbeing is the opposite of being." So the mind can play with all these terms and mental images, and get tangled up in them, but it's actually all very simple. It can't possibly be complicated because there's nothing there to complicate. The mind tries to compare this nonexistence to something it knows, but there's nothing there to compare with anything. The mind tries to analyze it, which means dividing it into some kind of constituent parts, but there's nothing there to divide. The Beloved is an emptiness that is absolutely indivisible, which is another reason why the analytical mind can't deal with its complete emptiness.

For the heart, however, it's not just complete emptiness—it's complete spaciousness, which means complete openness. The heart knows and recognizes this emptiness and nothingness and is absolutely open to it. The nothingness means there's no thing standing in the way of its love for the Beloved, no obstruction, nothing held back, nothing to protect, nothing to defend, and so its love is complete. The heart has no difficulty experiencing the Beloved's absolute emptiness and absence because, at the same time, to the heart it is absolute love. So experiencing the Beloved is really the same as experiencing the secret and essence of the heart.

It's clear now why we had to eliminate everything to finally get to the mystery of complete nonbeing. But there's still a deeper mystery beyond that, namely that nonbeingness itself is not the absolute, the Beloved—it's still just a conceptual facet of it. We can't confine the Beloved solely to the category of nonbeing because its nonbeingness is absolutely inseparable from being. So we could say that it is both being and nonbeing, but the true Beloved is also neither, because it is beyond being and nonbeing. This is a mystery that is way beyond what the mind can cope with, and it can no longer even conceptualize it. It can mouth the words still, and say, "Ah yes, the Beloved is beyond being and nonbeing," but the mind doesn't have a clue what it's talking about. Again, it's the perception of the heart that's needed, because the heart can feel a direct intimacy and connection with this truth.

The truth the heart perceives and recognizes is that the nothingness and nonbeingness of the Beloved is at the same time an immense presence that is the essence and nature of everything. It's what makes everything appear and everything be. It's the source of everything, which means it's also the very essence of our love. The Beloved that is empty of things is the center of all reality, so paradoxically it's the inherent nature of all form, and all perception.

The mind will always try to play a role in our perception, however, and we can't get rid of it completely because it's intrinsic to the operation of our soul consciousness. But as we begin to behold the true reality of the Beloved, we eventually reach a point where the mind is done with saying that it doesn't understand. "I don't understand" usually suggests that there's a potential for understanding that is proving elusive, but here it's like the mind finally accepts: "I will *never* understand this—it's simply not possible." It knows it's not even about being confused, because confusion means there's content, with different elements that are difficult to discriminate, so you can't tell which is which. This is beyond confusion. And the mind itself isn't overwhelmed in the way its reasoning and logic have been overwhelmed. It's more that on this journey, the mind has grown up; it has been expanded to its maximum.

So what's present now is a sense of being dumbfounded, completely flabbergasted, and what arises is a sense of awe. In moving beyond reason and the attempt to know, the mind is confounded as it is taken over by the mystery of the Beloved, which it beholds freely without any understanding of it. It's ironic that once the mind gives up any prospect of knowing, it is completely illuminated, full of a brilliance and radiance it can't conceive of. It's the radiant brilliance of this dark mystery, and the mind is dazzled by it. Bedazzled!

We're stuck in a bind discussing this here because we're having to use words to try to describe what's beyond description. So we can say this dark luminous mystery is black, but it's not really black—not in the way we think of black as a color. We're dealing with the mystery that is before light and before color. So before there's light, what is there to see? There's nothing to see, and we might call that blackness, but it isn't really. It's the complete and fundamental absence of light or color, and describing it as blackness or darkness is the best we can do to convey a mystery that goes beyond all differentiations and concepts—it's beyond knowing, beyond awareness, and even beyond consciousness. So as ever, it's the heart that's able to fully experience the mystery of the nature of things before there is knowledge, discrimination, conceptualization, and reason.

It's similar to when people speculate about how things were at the beginning of the Big Bang. You can't talk about that in terms of time and space because time and space came after the Big Bang. So if you're trying to describe the inception of the universe, you can't say anything was small or large, or how long it took for something to happen. You can't actually say anything about it at all, because it's before form and activity became manifest—space and time are needed for that to happen. So all theories and logic break down. That's not because there's something wrong with the theories or logic. It's just that before there's any manifestation of separation and duality, there's only nondual reality, which is total intimacy and total immediacy.

The heart knows and recognizes that immediacy and intimacy as the Beloved. And for the mind now, there's this bedazzlement, a drunkenness of sorts, full of radiance and explosions of brilliance. It's like intergalactic space, with momentary flashes of lightning that induce a sense of mystery and magic, and delicious, blissful ecstasy. It's an ecstasy of release for both mind and heart, because whenever we think or feel anything about what's being experienced, it's instantly annihilated in a shower of stars.

Everything we see is constantly revealing itself to be absolutely nothing—nonbeing—and at the same time, there is brilliance and radiance because that is the appearance of things, the being of things. We can now see that the Beloved is both being and nonbeing, and neither and beyond that. We find being and we find nonbeing, and we can't separate them from each other. The fundamental conceptual dichotomy between existence and nonexistence, presence and absence, being and nonbeing, is gone. Reason can't possibly penetrate this, and nobody ever said it should or could—it's not the job of reason. Here, reason might take you all the way to the edge of knowing, but beyond that point, the intimate knowledge of the Beloved is the heart's business.

The heart has always had the inherent capacity to know this mystery, but only in complete nothingness and unobstructedness can the heart finally experience its essence, without any obscuration. And the heart can't help but love that, because the very essence of the heart is an unobstructed openness that makes it possible for us to experience, feel, and sense absolutely anything. When that happens, it's said that the heart dweller, the guest, has become the rightful owner of the heart and taken its place as its king.

The delicate exquisiteness of this is indescribable because it's absolute. Whenever something reaches the absolute, you can't describe it. Still, the poets keep trying, don't they? And poetry is just the mind trying to describe what the heart is experiencing. If there were no mind, there would be no poets. Poets can use the mind to create images and metaphors, and if it's good poetry, the metaphors will become pointers, windows into the experience beyond the metaphors. If poetry uses a metaphor to trap you in the metaphor, it's not good poetry—a good poet creates images and metaphors that have the capacity to self-destruct. That's the power of Rumi's imagery—he's always using unusual images that take us out of our usual mind. They're not pointing to themselves but to something else—talking about the king of reality, the Beloved, riding on a horse while everybody else is walking on foot. That's an image that uses things we know in our everyday world, but we know it's just a way of evoking an essential truth that is shattering and brilliant.

So all the poets can do is try to say something about this ultimate reality, while knowing that they'll never manage it. All the same, they can't help but say these things because even the saying of them, the uttering of poetry, is some kind of invocation of the radiance and brilliance that comes with the shattering annihilation of the self and consciousness. The usual way of using the mind tends to obstruct the heart, but for people like Rumi, the mind only serves the heart.

So let's do an exercise to find out which of those is happening with our own heart.

Practice Session:
The Mind Obstructing the Heart

. . .

You'll do a fifteen-minute monologue, in groups of two or three if possible, or you can write out your exploration for fifteen minutes if you're alone.

In your monologue you want to explore how your mind tends to obstruct your heart, in general, and how it's doing that in the present moment. You might begin with how it happens in general, but you want to get more and more into the present and see what's happening now. Is the mind obstructing your heart now? And if so, how?

. . . . .

Questions and Comments

Student: I wanted to ask you about an experience. Normally my mind tries to control things and tries to compare my process to what's happened before, and this time I was able to let go of that, and I gave my mind the role of poet in residence. I would just sit there and describe what was going on in the heart, and I would feel something in the heart and an image would arise, and then my mind would describe that image and communicate it to my partners. And the process seemed to go quite freely, and the mind didn't seem to get in the way. So I was wondering if you could comment on that and if you do something similar.

A. H. Almaas: So that sounds good to me. It sounds like one way the mind can harmonize with the heart, definitely, by following the experience of the heart instead of coming up with its own ideas. At least for the inner journey, that seems a good way for it to work. And that's in fact the way it can work.

S: So my constant mantra is, "I have no true nature, I don't have any interior." And as a child it was demanded of me that I abandon my own experience, and I was shamed if my experience didn't mirror my parents'. So it's extremely hard for me to stay with myself and not have the superego. I've been wondering if the superego is an idol in my temple, because I don't seem to be able to wrestle loose from it. And then, after inquiries, I hear everyone saying, "Oh God!"—you know, fireworks and all that stuff—while I don't have any of that. But the other day we had a repeating question and I had the most wonderful guide as my partner, and she kept saying, "How do you feel as . . ." I don't even remember the question, but all I know is, my mind couldn't wrestle with anything and there wasn't any . . . I mean I was perfectly aware that I was sitting in the room and I could hear all the noise, but my mind just couldn't do anything. So it's like I don't know, but this morning I wrote down, "I don't have these absolute experiences and I don't ever see black," so I was really happy when you said it's not necessary, it's not really black. But I just wonder how close or far away I am, and if my superego is so intent on continuing to tell me I don't have the right experience, when maybe I have. And I know you'll say every experience is the right experience, but . . .

AH: Remember why I said many times that the heart knows how far, if it is near or farther away? If it's getting farther away, it will tend to feel discontent and longing. If it's getting nearer, it feels more love and more happiness. That's how you can tell. Nobody else can tell but you, your heart can.

S: But in that moment, I mean, I could feel, it was like the mind couldn't do anything, and so there was just this listening, but I didn't see black, and I didn't see stars blazing, and something in me says, "Well, you were just relaxed," so there wasn't really . . .

AH: Yes, but it sounds like you're wanting confirmation that you're doing it one way or another because you're not sure, and you want me to give you that certainty.

S: That's right. Yeah.

AH: And nobody can. You have to really find out for yourself how come you're uncertain. Because you're comparing your experience with others, with what you hear, and all that. Remember what I said, you just need to find the truth of what's arising in you, and look into that, and let that develop.

S: I'm so good, though, at saying, "No, I'm not having essential experiences" that I didn't want to just minimize this, I wanted to say that I had this experience. My original question to you was going to be: Do you have any tips for someone like me, who . . . ? I mean, I was so shamed to stay with my experience. That is a powerful thing to overcome. It's very, very hard.

AH: Right. But if you can love the truth enough, then it doesn't matter whether there's shame or not.

S: So love includes shame.

AH: Sure. Everything.

S: Okay. Thank you.

S: One of the things I'm noticing that stands between me and my heart is my mind just filling up the space, just doing its job. And it's thinking about the future and what needs to be done, and what's the best decisions I can make. And the second thing that my particular mind is doing a lot is arguing. And right now it's arguing with you. But I've seen it arguing with you, and also arguing with God and with Being, and generally it's just an argumentative type. And one of the things that's come up for me several times is that words seem to be a medium of reification. The word itself seems to, in the moment that it's said, something is fixed, and in a way, it dies. Unless there is breath behind it that gives it life. And you use a lot of words. And sometimes as I listen I can experience how the general energy is moving things in me that are not exposed to words per se, but the medium seems to be a very dominant medium. And what I notice when it comes to the heart is that just a second of presence, or a second of eye contact with you, or my teacher, or my lover, will do a lot more than a whole lecture or two lectures. And I was wondering if there is a medium that can speak directly to the heart rather than take it through my mind, because my mind does get engaged in the conversation.

AH: I think for some people that's true, and the words will entangle their mind, and for some people it might be better to find a different kind of medium. There are people who do all kinds of other things. Music, for instance; we use music. People can use dance of various kinds, or chants. And of course, the personal contact that you mentioned. People are different in that way. So it seems for you, your mind takes over and the words help it to do that. So it might be good for you to see, what is it that speaks to you more directly?

S: Thank you, that's very helpful. I have one other question. Another thing that's been coming up has to do with intimacy. The word came into the talk today, but I've been experimenting with it for a couple of years, and it seems that the real contact, the real experience—I'm not really sure how to say it—comes in a moment of intimacy. And it seems to be in a moment of intimacy with something outside, so it does tend to feel dual—I feel it with somebody or I feel it with a place. And there's a lot of fear around being intimate. I mean, we don't go around being intimate with everything that we interact with. Although with you, I've felt a couple of times that I've walked next to you and I've felt a certain kind of intimacy that wasn't dangerous. And what it's connected with in this particular exercise, the way it's connected in my mind, was that I experience love as like a wild animal that's in a cage, and my mind is just making sure that it doesn't get out and do damage. And that's somehow connected with the issue of the danger surrounding intimacy. And I was wondering if you could help me understand that.

AH: The danger of intimacy?

S: Yeah, it feels like the same kind of danger that the wild animal that I associate with my love can do to others and to itself, just by its wildness and uncontrollability. That the same kind of danger can happen when I'm intimate.

AH: Well, intimacy definitely is very dangerous, true. The deeper the intimacy, the more we dissolve. The less defended, the less protected we are; the more we dissolve, the more we disappear. That's what intimacy means, it means no barriers really. So all our barriers and defenses, which is what we take to define us, are going to dissolve. So intimacy is one way of expressing love, one way that love expresses itself. And intimacy is one of the stages of love. Love and intimacy are not that separate. So if you find sometimes that love can be dangerous, with intimacy too, it's the same thing. And we will work more with intimacy later.

S: I'd like to share something I found very revealing in my experience. When one of my partners was speaking from her mind and kind of complaining about it, my experience of her was one of love and joy, and I just loved her presence. So it made me question what the mind actually is, it made me curious. When I was doing my monologue, I had this Old Testament God basically telling me that the Beloved was not only secret but never to be found, ever, and it was simply not available. And what I got from this was that my mind, it was like being banged on the head—I actually got it that my mind will not lead to the Beloved. It was so obvious. And then my partner encouraged me to see if my heart could be with the Beloved, and it was just a wonderful invitation. And it was almost so easy. However, in the course of my monologue, and in being with my heart, and feeling the fullness and the emptiness, I realized that even though I thought I'd in a sense moved to my heart and made a decision, the mind was still kind of in charge at the end. It just refused to take a back seat for more than ten minutes. So I don't know.

AH: Well, I think it's true, the mind is used to being in the role of the king, the only one that's riding. And the heart makes it possible for the Beloved to be the only one who's riding, but that's not the tendency of the usual mind. And the other thing you said, that the Beloved can never be found, in some sense is true. You can say that you cannot find the Beloved—the Beloved finds you. And when the Beloved finds you, you're gone anyway. So it's not like an experience of finding, like there's somebody who finds something. It's never like that. And also, we've seen that the Beloved is characterized by nonbeingness, and nonbeingness means that there's nothing to be found. So in some very deep way it's true that the Beloved is not findable, because we always find something in particular, and here the mind can't do that because there's nothing; there's no object to be found.

S: Is fidelity to the heart a choice? To this emptiness?

AH: Well, in reality fidelity is not a choice. The heart has inherent fidelity to the truth; it truly loves it. However, when we don't know that, when we're still ignorant or immature, then our heart is divided, and it is useful then to see it as some kind of a choice. Because we do make choices, so in a condition where we still make choices, it is a choice. When we go deeper, we realize that it isn't really a choice and it's never been a choice.

S: In this exercise it really seemed that if the focus is on the emptiness in the heart, then the mind can really be helpful, like the poet in residence that was talked about earlier. But it feels like it requires a turning.

AH: Right. Exactly. The mind can become a useful instrument when it is. And we will work with that a little more too, the relationship of the mind to the heart. I want to end with another poem that's appropriate to what we're exploring. It's called "Love After Love," by Derek Walcott.

> The time will come
> when, with elation
> you will greet yourself arriving
> at your own door, in your own mirror
> and each will smile at the other's welcome,

and say, sit here. Eat.
You will love again the stranger who was yourself.
Give wine. Give bread. Give back your heart
to itself, to the stranger who has loved you

all your life, whom you ignored
for another, who knows you by heart.
Take down the love letters from the bookshelf,

the photographs, the desperate notes,
peel your own image from the mirror.
Sit. Feast on your life.*

---

* Derek Walcott, *Selected Poems of Derek Walcott* (United Kingdom: Faber & Faber, 2009).

FIFTEEN

Divine Darkness

We'll continue now with our exploration of the connection between the mind and the heart. As we've observed, much of the literature and poetry dismisses the mind and says the heart is what's needed. But then we hear poets like Rumi talking about knowing, knowing the secret, and knowing is something we usually associate with the mind. So we need to get a better understanding of what knowing means here, and how it can involve both mind and heart. We need to see exactly how the mind can become an obstacle, and how the heart is able to dissolve that obstacle and behold the secret place and see the treasure.

A good way to do this is to go back to the very beginning, to look at the origination of phenomena, the origination of perception, and the origination of experience. Every culture has its own way of explaining how everything began. In the West we're familiar with the story of creation in the first book of the Bible, the book of Genesis: "In the beginning, God, created the heavens and the earth." Of course, scientists view the beginning very differently with their Big Bang theory. But in a way, science still views the beginning in a similar way to the book of Genesis, because when scientists try to understand the beginning of everything, they also think of it as beginning in the past. Bible scholars think the beginning was around six thousand years ago, and astrophysicists think of it as a few billion years ago, but the principle is the same. It's in the past, somewhere in time.

Regardless of which of those accounts people might favor, the problem from our perspective is that ultimately time doesn't exist. It's a relative concept, and as such, a creation of the mind. So to think of the beginning in terms of time is an artificial concept. Even the astrophysicists are beginning to see that, because they have to accept that when they talk about the Big Bang, they cannot describe it in terms of time and space. As we've already noted, the concepts of time and space are not applicable at the beginning of everything, even though creation myths and science tend to view it as something that happened in the past. But how on earth can we conceive of a beginning if there is no time and space? It seems we need different concepts, ones that go beyond time and space, if we want to understand how the laws of the universe could function at the moment of its birth.

My own belief, which is not the same as knowing, is that if we want to understand the beginning in terms of time, we have to take into consideration the fact that time is not something ultimate. And what that amounts to is that the beginning is happening all the time, ontologically and metaphysically. Everything arises from nothing, as the Big Bang theory proposes, but it's not just at some point in the past—everything is arising from nothing in every instant. It is constant manifestation.

This needn't be just a theoretical proposition. When we're able to recognize that we are the Beloved, we can experience the mystery of continual beginning. We can see then that creation is

Divine Darkness 249

not something that happened once and for all—creation is happening continually. Maybe at some point our scientific theories will include this reality in a way that will help us understand the historical beginning and how time and space are actually created. I don't envisage it being a problem to include continual beginning in a physical theory of the universe. I think it can be formulated easily in mathematical terms, using differential equations to describe rates of change and flow. To describe continual beginning, the equation would show a rate of manifestation instead of a rate of change in time.

We can learn more about the beginning of our own experience if we look at how awareness emerges from the absolute, which is the absolute beginning, the ever-abiding source of everything. When we go into the absolute completely, all the way to the condition of complete cessation, it's usually referred to as the divine slumber or the divine coma. All experience—sensation, perception, and consciousness—is dissolved at that point. The process of awakening out of this coma is a continuum that usually happens quickly, so we don't see all the steps. If it happens more slowly or we get flashes of awareness at different points in the process, we're able to get a better understanding of it. This can reveal more about the subtle relationship between the heart and mind in the discernment of experience, so we'll try and follow the process now.

Before the beginning, there is nothing—no experience at all. So the beginning we're looking at is the beginning of experience, the beginning of perception, and the beginning of consciousness. We can say it's the beginning of awareness, but initially there's no awareness of the awareness. In the very beginning there's no mind, so there's no capacity to know what's happening.

As the bare beginnings of consciousness arise, there is experience and perception, but because the mind is not yet developed, there's no discrimination between the sensory modalities. It's therefore undifferentiated experience, a unified consciousness in which we see, hear, feel, taste, and touch all as one thing. I say we hear, feel, and see, but at this point we don't actually know that there is such a thing as hearing, feeling, and seeing. There isn't the mental discrimination to know that these different modes of perception exist.

This is all similar to the first dawning of consciousness in the newborn infant, when there's no capacity to recognize and discriminate what is being perceived. Another analogy that's easier for us to relate to now is the way we experience the beginning of consciousness as we wake up from sleep, especially if it's a slow awakening from deep sleep. It's like coming out of a coma at first, as we begin to leave complete unconsciousness. Consciousness arises, but there's only the faintest dawning of awareness, so we're barely cognizant of what's happening. There are no clear shapes or forms at first, but as we gradually begin to differentiate color, sound, taste, and feeling, forms and shapes begin to emerge, with different flavors and textures. This is the beginning of mind in the sense that there is some discrimination between the sensory modalities, but there's still no recognition. We can tell there's a color or a taste or a feeling, but we don't know what they are yet—we don't know that this is green, or this is sweet, or this is rough or smooth.

That kind of recognition comes next. Now we know we're seeing black or white, and we know it's smoothness we're feeling. We're not only hearing sounds; we know what the sound is like. With this growing recognition, mind really begins to develop.

The development usually happens very quickly without us noticing it, but sometimes we can catch it and observe how it proceeds. As the mind recognizes and discriminates more and more in the field of awareness, it begins to establish familiar categories, and associative knowledge begins to arise. You recognize that you're in a body, and you're in a particular environment. You know it's your room and it's familiar, and you know you've been sleeping and you're waking up. By now the names for things are coming, and you'll remember your name and know that the thing you're looking at is called a mirror. Mind is already fully present when there is this degree of recognition.

But looking back at the early stage of the process, we can see that a certain kind of recognition—being able to tell what the quality of a perception is—can occur before names and associative knowledge arise. There are inner subjective ways we can experience and discriminate qualities. We know that this is love, or this is sweet, without ever giving it those names—we can distinguish them by recognizing their feel and their particular texture, tone, or flavor. This is the recognition that comes from the heart, and it's a kind of knowing that is before conscious discrimination and differentiation.

So the fact that there's a feel, texture, and flavor to the experience, even though we don't know what it is, indicates that there is heart. We can then say that being able to tell what something is comes from the mind, but there is this first kind of discrimination and knowing that comes from the true mind, which is there before the thinking mind comes in, with all its memories, associations, and labeling. True mind is an expression of being, where the two are inseparable. We know something by being it—and this beingness includes the heart. As the function of discrimination continues to develop, it eventually becomes so dominant that we begin to lose contact with the immediacy of what we are feeling. We then move more toward the kind of mind that is dissociated from the actual feeling, texture, and intimacy of our experience—we are knowing from the usual or ordinary mind.

We can say then that the general tendency is for experience to move more toward mind, but it's important to remember that at the beginning, there is this kind of knowingness in which mind and heart are not separate—there's no differentiation. The differentiation happens gradually, until they are so differentiated that they become dissociated, as two separate modes of perception. The body, with its physical organs and senses, can then differentiate our perception even further. We see with the eyes, hear with the ears, and smell with the nose, and these sensations can be perceived as being completely separate from each other. So the unity of experience in the original consciousness is increasingly differentiated through the mind, and then further through the senses.

This is how experience, especially what we experience in our own field, can diverge into mostly mind knowledge or mostly heart knowledge. Mind knowledge means discrimination, categorization, setting things apart—this is this, and this is different from that—and as it becomes more dominant, it eventually loses touch with inner feeling. When there's more heart knowledge, what is more dominant is the field itself—the pervasive quality of our experience, including feeling, texture, and flavor. But there is still some kind of discrimination—we're able to tell that this is sadness, this is fear, this is love, and this is smooth while that is soft.

It's rare for mind knowledge and heart knowledge to be completely separate from each other, though they can become separated to a large degree. But it's clear that this separation isn't inevitable, because we've seen how heart and mind were originally one, and they can continue to complement each other in the capacity to discriminate experience directly, without the need to think about it. It's only later, as we learn to recognize experience in more and more abstract ways, that ordinary mind becomes dominant. Knowing our experience then becomes a function of memory and association, engaging with concepts and categories, and this makes the knowing retrospective rather than an expression of our direct experience in the now.

Eventually we have the dissociated mind, which we're referring to as the usual or ordinary mind, and that's the mind that the poets tell us to throw away. They don't tell us to throw away the real mind, the original mind that gives us the capacity for real knowing. Many texts and teachings don't say much about the difference between the two types of mind, so the injunction to throw away our mind can seem like we're being asked to throw away our capacity to discriminate and know our experience, which is obviously a vital function. That's the reason many of us don't want to do it, because we can't imagine how we'd be able to operate.

This is why it's important to understand how heart knowledge combines both mind and heart as it discriminates. When we say we have a particular feeling, that can't happen without mind coming into it to some degree, because simply knowing what the particular feeling is means that mind is involved. Some people say, "No, my mind's not involved, I'm just feeling things." Well, if you're feeling without knowing what you're feeling, and just experiencing the feeling itself, then it's true, the mind is not involved. But the moment you know what feeling it is—the moment you're able to discriminate whether it's love or hate, for example—mind must already be involved. We can call this the mind of the heart, and it's only after the capacity for association and conceptualization arises that the mind begins to dissociate from the heart and become what we usually think of as the mind—the abstracted mind of the head.

It takes a great deal of subtlety to distinguish whether our mind is working in conjunction with the heart or has become disconnected from it. It's a matter of degree, and to find out for ourselves, we need to discern whether we're more aware of the texture and intimate feeling of our field, or more aware of the abstracted forms within the field—to the point where we may be missing the field altogether.

So in the process of recognizing and beholding the Beloved, it's only the abstracted mind we need to let go of—the one that's focused on concepts and discrimination and lacks the immediacy and intimacy of feeling. It's that mind that has all the history in it, the memories, associations, and reactions that get in the way of direct experience. As that abstracted mind dissolves and melts away on our journey toward the Beloved, we're no longer so trapped in it, and we're more in touch with our immediate feeling.

But again, because there's still recognition and discrimination, we can see that some kind of mind is still involved. If there was no mind at all, we wouldn't be able to recognize the various forms, qualities, and dimensions that the Beloved manifests itself in, and that's an important part of our process. As the process continues and deepens, however, there's less and less mind there. That means there's less and less discrimination, which is appropriate because the Beloved is completely beyond discrimination. We've seen that the Beloved's nature is before the beginning, before manifestation, and as we begin to apprehend this, our field of awareness and consciousness, and our love, are no longer focused on forms. We're less able to see the separation between forms, and they begin to lose their distinguishing characteristics. Gradually the forms themselves begin to disappear without us even noticing.

As this happens, we feel we know less and less and that we're entering into ever greater and deeper darkness. Many people call this darkness the state of not knowing, or unknowing, but it's only not knowing in the sense that it's not associative knowing—our usual way of knowing by naming, labeling, and memorizing. It is still knowing but of the more direct and intimate kind. And as it deepens further, even this intimate, direct knowing gets subtler and less differentiated, so there's even greater darkness, and greater mystery. We're not unconscious, though—in some sense the experience of our consciousness and awareness can in fact be fuller, deeper, and more intense as we feel the direct immediacy of our experience.

However, we're used to our mind operating at a certain level of consciousness and not at this deeper and more direct level, so each time we go a step further and deeper into the darkness, it feels at first like we don't know anything, and we can't say anything about it. It's similar to when we enter a dark place and can't see anything at first—it takes a while for our eyes to adjust to the darkness. Here we need to get used to this deeper and darker level of consciousness, and then we're able to discern more. We can even begin to say something about it eventually. At first we might say, "I don't know what to say" or "There's nothing to say." But as we stay with it and it becomes more familiar, we become aware that there is some kind of recognition of it, some quality of knowing that we still have, and that there is something we can say about it.

So when we're going through a state of transition and feel we can't say anything about it, that's not necessarily the end of it. By saying something about the darkness eventually, you actually know it, because the saying is not separate from the immediate intouchness with the quality of the experience. In the beginning, we may have heart knowing where the tongue isn't connected with the heart, but in time the two become connected.

As the darkness continues to increase and deepen, and there's less and less discrimination and differentiation, it follows that there's more unification. We're less able to tell things apart, and it's not just forms and concepts that start to merge together as differentiations become blurred—even our sensory modalities begin to merge as the heart and the mind coalesce. So you might at some point feel just pure love and nothing else, and you know it's love even though you're not consciously identifying it as such. It's the way you're behaving that shows that you're experiencing love. You might not be registering your loving behavior, but other people say, "Oh, you seem to be so full of love today!" And you say, "Oh yeah. I didn't realize that." Actually, you did know it, but it was knowing without your mind reflecting on it and thinking about it. And when the movement into the darkness is even deeper and more subtle, at some point there's simply feeling. There's a kind of feel or texture, but the feeling, color, and flavor of your experience become indistinguishable.

We're now getting closer and closer to what has traditionally been called divine darkness. We see that the closer we get to the divine, the Beloved, we experience it as a darkness because there's less discrimination and discernment. The heart mind is still there at first, because we still know the feel, texture, and flavor of our experience, and there's always some kind of mind the moment a quality is set apart or differentiated. But things need to go even further, to a level where the mind is completely dissolved into the heart and we're not able to tell qualities apart. The heart can reach the point where there's a field of sensation with a conscious feel to it, but there's nothing that can be abstracted out, nothing to be discriminated or differentiated.

In some sense we can say that the mind still exists in the darkness even then, because there is still some knowing. But we don't really know anything in particular—we just know. So what do we know? We know the Beloved. But what is it we know about the Beloved? We can't say what else we know—we only know that we know the Beloved. So what is the Beloved? That's the Beloved.

So as the heart goes deeper, it subsumes and melts the mind into it. If anything remains of the mind, it's just the simple fact of knowing, when consciousness and the content of consciousness are the same thing. There's still a mode of experience in which we can discern that the Beloved has its own flavor and texture, but this discernment now has a greater delicacy and subtlety in the increasing darkness. All the sensory modalities regain their elemental nature, reverting to how they were in the original undifferentiated consciousness. And the consciousness becomes pure; it's simply the nature of consciousness as distinct from nonconsciousness.

In this process of submerging and drowning into the deep darkness, there appear flashes, of the kind 'Irāqī calls "divine flashes." They are flashes of brilliance and radiance, and each one is like an explosion of recognition. So even as we're plumbing the darkest depths, there's still a capacity for knowing that erupts in these flashes of insight and recognition. Every once in a while there's a flash of knowingness as we recognize something about the Beloved. We might suddenly see, "Oh, it feels like such intimacy!" and then, "Oh, it's pure love!" Each flash is in some sense mind emerging briefly—it comes and is gone in a flash.

As we go into ever deeper darkness and ever less knowing, there's no end to these flashes. We never get a full and final flash, because the Beloved or the absolute is ultimately unknowable, and no concept could possibly encompass it completely. Each flash, each intuition, each recognition, is like a glimmer of understanding, and then the next moment it's gone, because it's not exactly it. It wasn't wrong; it just wasn't complete. The Beloved is always more mysterious than any insight we might have about it.

So reality reveals itself more and more as the Beloved until that's all that remains. The Beloved reveals itself fully, but the more we come to know it, the more it is a mystery, because that is its very nature. It's natural that the mind wants to dive in and find out more about it, because the mind loves to discriminate and recognize our experience. You see, although we tend to see the heart more as the lover of the truth, in a sense the mind is also a lover—its love and its joy is to know more about reality and discover the truth. Here, the more it finds out, the less it knows. But as the darkness increases and deepens further, the bedazzled mind comes to love and accept even the irresolvable truth of this mystery.

When we say that something is a mystery, we usually think there's something we haven't found out yet—there's something hidden that we need to know more about in order to understand the situation fully. Here there's nothing hidden and yet the mystery remains. The more we know it, the less we know about it. The mystery is completely indeterminable because all logical categories are completely mixed and united. So in the divine darkness, we're no longer looking for something to dispel the mystery; we are embracing and intimately knowing the Beloved as mystery. And that just fires up the love even more. The love becomes deeper and stronger, more passionate and more annihilating, as we go into even greater darkness.

Some people say that this is actually the deepest kind of knowing, because it's the original real knowing of the mind, in which real mind and real heart are just two sides of the same thing. The heart takes us deeper and deeper into the Beloved, knowing it as depth, darkness, and mystery, and confounding the mind's desire to comprehend or conceptualize. The love draws us further in, to the point where the divine flashes appear, and the mind is so bedazzled it can only say, "Wow, isn't that amazing?" The mind has fallen in love. The love is passionate, and as it annihilates the categories of mind and heart, they become one in embracing the unfathomable mystery of the Beloved.

Divine darkness is something that's known in some Western traditions, especially in Christian mysticism. It is frequently associated by Christian mystics with the Father, and the dynamic emergence from it is associated with the Son, or Christ. So here's a passage from *The Mystical Theology*, one of the most well-known texts about divine darkness, by Dionysius the Areopagite. He describes the entering of divine darkness in terms of Moses's ascent of the holy mountain, and he conveys the paradox of knowing by not knowing.

> And then Moses is cut off from both things seen and those who see and enters into the darkness of unknowing, a truly hidden darkness, according to which he shuts his eyes to all

apprehensions that convey knowledge, for he has passed into a realm quite beyond any feeling or seeing. Now, belonging wholly to that which is beyond all, and yet to nothing at all, and being neither himself, nor another, and united in his highest part in passivity with Him who is completely unknowable, he knows by not knowing in a manner that transcends understanding.*

So he knows by not knowing. We think knowing and not knowing are separate, but the deeper we go, they become the same thing. Everything is unified as the heart is unified.

This understanding of the role of mind and heart in true knowing is also known in the Platonic and Neoplatonic traditions. Here's a quote from Plotinus, for example, where the Beloved, or the absolute, is called the first principle.

> The main part of the difficulty [of knowing it] is that awareness of this Principle comes neither by knowing nor by the Intellection that discovers the Intellectual Beings but by a presence overpassing all knowledge.†

So he's saying that you know it through presence, by being it, which is another insight into true knowing. And this being it does have a certain feel, even if there's sometimes a paradoxical feeling that there's absolutely nothing there to feel.

---

* Dionysius, *The Mystical Theology*, quoted in Andrew Louth, *The Origins of the Christian Mystical Tradition: From Plato to Denys* (Clarendon Press, 1983), 173.

† Plotinus, *The Six Enneads*, trans. Stephen Mackenna and B. S. Page (Global Grey, 2018), 845.

And finally, a passage dealing with the ultimate mystery from my book *The Inner Journey Home*.

> Another view is that true nature is inherently a mystery, a pure black light where there is nothing but light, this light preceding not only what we usually know as light, but Being itself. Since its nature is mystery and indetermination, increased intimacy with this dark light will not produce more knowledge; it will instead produce more mystery. To experience mystery is to know the mystery as mystery. It is absolutely empty of any determination, devoid of any quality or form, and so to know is to have no experience. This total absence of experience is not darkness, but rather total and absolute knowledge. It is the absence of all obscuration, but also the absence of all manifestation. Since there is no obscuration, no obstacles, not even the distraction of the forms of manifestation, why would we think of it as ignorance or darkness? Why think of it as a not-knowing or unknowing? Since the transcendent true nature is inherently mysterious and indeterminable, this is the absolute limit of mystery and indetermination. It is absolute knowing. It is the mode of knowledge of transcendent true nature, Being without mirrors, not even the mirror of awareness.*

All these different traditions point to the same paradox. The more we go into the divine darkness, in one sense we know less, but in another sense we know the Beloved more. And we

---

* A. H. Almaas, *The Inner Journey Home: Soul's Realization of the Unity of Reality* (Boston: Shambhala, 2024), 257.

know the Beloved not through thoughts, ideas, and concepts but through the unity of direct touch and feel. That's the unity we've been seeking, and we are now so much the Beloved that our mode of knowing is that of the Beloved. In the Beloved, mind and heart are not two things; they're the same.

So the only way we can begin to know this mystery is by accepting that we can't really know it. The secret can't be known by anyone, because the moment someone knows a secret, it's not a secret anymore. In some sense the secret has to remain hidden from oneself. The Beloved therefore becomes deeper, darker, and more secret, until we reach its utmost secret. The extreme limit of the divine darkness is the divine coma, when all consciousness disappears—there are no more glimmers, no more flashes, no more insights, no more experiences. There's just complete cessation and absolute rest. In some sense that's what the heart wants, to reach its own limit, where there is nothing more to feel. The cessation of not just mind but also heart takes us into the absolute mystery of a delicate, magic enchantment and bedazzlement.

Let's see if we can explore and experience this paradox with an exercise now.

Practice Session:
The Mystery of the Beloved
...

You'll do two repeating questions with a partner. If you don't have a partner to do it with, you can answer in writing.

Each person will spend fifteen minutes responding to the first question repeatedly asked by their partner, and the question is:

What's right about trying to comprehend the Beloved?

This is tricky because it's "What's right . . ." There are deluded reasons and good reasons for trying to comprehend the Beloved, and we want to plumb all of them. You want to be as spontaneous as possible. You might start with things coming out in the usual way for this kind of exercise, but you might get to the point where it becomes just the divine flashes themselves.

And then each takes ten minutes to respond to the second question:

Tell me a way the Beloved is mysterious to you.

Here it's a matter of plumbing the mystery, the darkness instead of the flashes.

. . . . .

Questions and Comments

Student: For me, maybe it's not the discursive mind, but the thinking mind is still very important. You said before to look at our distractions from being with the Beloved, and I looked, and as far as mine was, a lot of always posturing to get positive feedback from others, positive mirroring, so I took it as an aim to try to work with these object relations. And I was sharing it with my teacher, and in the course of the sharing I said that I'm getting some narcissistic wounds but I don't really feel the pain. She said to sense into it, and then I could feel my heart, and I went into the pain in the heart, and then later on, it shifted up to my head across the temples near the forehead. And that night, in meditation, it went from the heart to the head again, and in trying to inquire into it, I said, "My God, the heart is the feeling center, where I feel the pain, the compassion for myself, the woundedness.

And the head is the belief system, that there's something flawed in me, I'm unlovable, unlikable." And I think my whole life has been seeking the positive mirroring to disprove this belief. And so actually, in the meditation I switched from the *kath* center in the belly to the head center, and all of a sudden the pain really focused into the head center. It was just like a laser beam, and I felt it was like a joyous pain, maybe it was because I felt I'd found the culprit. And then I felt heat all over my body right down to my toes. So I felt pretty pleased with myself, if you can say that, that my mind had got me to that place. But then last night in my processing, then the discursive mind took over, and so I was trying to work with it—how much can I mix the pain with my meditative practice? Will I go to clear space, or a genital hole, or black space or something, and have this in there as part of it, to keep it so I don't have to enter into this discursive place? So at least for me this mind is very important, rather than just to stay and try to be with it.

A. H. Almaas: It's very true that mind on all its levels can be useful. It's supposed to be useful—we just don't know how to use it correctly usually, and we forget how to do that. We use our mind frequently for distraction and reification instead of going deeper, but definitely the mind can be used, especially if we have the true inner guidance. That's what we do in this work, in our inquiry we use diamond guidance, which means the capacity to use the normal mind, the thinking mind, to connect with the true mind, to go to true discrimination, and in that way be able to follow the heart. So diamond guidance is the capacity to use the normal mind, with its thinking and associations and memory, because the memory of a certain thing can be useful so we don't have to invent the wheel each time we have an insight. But it's not easy to do that without proper training and guidance—we tend just to follow our thoughts and associations. But we do know how to use it—that's what you were doing. Then of course it can be quite a powerful thing. So it's good to remember that. When we talk about letting go of the mind, we don't mean the mind is never useful, just because of the way we usually use it. But as we go deeper into the experience, there's more of the intimate, direct intouchness with the experience, and the usual mind is less and less needed. If we feel we have to use it at that point, it can become a movement out of the intimacy, although once in a while a certain memory or association can be useful to take us deeper into the experience if the proper guidance is there. So it's like there are different levels of mind, different levels of intellect, and the deeper we go, the more we need to go all the way to the nonconceptual, and diamond guidance actually has a capacity to do that for us. And when we have that kind of precise understanding, even the flashes that appear in the darkness have a crystalline faceted quality. That means we're not only having flashes, but the insights are precise and clear, not just vague intuitions.

S: In the exercise I saw that when I thought I had gotten it about the Beloved, I didn't have it. And when I realized I didn't have it, then I did have it, and I just find that absolutely exasperating. And when it comes up the most is when I'm...
AH: It's because of love.
S: Pardon?
AH: It sounds like somebody's in love. That's the kind of thing you hear about when somebody's in love.
S: I know. I hate that! How are you supposed to talk about this? It comes up when I'm talking about the Work, and usually with

somebody from outside our school who I want to tell something about the work I'm doing. I think I'm fooling them maybe, because I'm giving lip service to the Beloved, but then I looked at it in this exercise and I realized I didn't know who was being fooled, because I don't really know how to be in this state. So I might be doing it and it might actually be having the experience of me, and I'm the one who's being fooled, thinking that I'm fooling them. It's a real mindblower.

AH: Well, after a while you don't mind being fooled, you see. It's called at some point the divine fool. Have you heard that expression? The lover is a divine fool in the sense that to be a fool makes things easier for the heart, you see. But that's true, sometimes you can't tell.

S: I really loved this exercise because I went into the magic, and anything known seemed completely boring—everything was flat, been there, done that. And as the magic kept opening, I saw that the flashes are the eyes of the Beloved. And then I saw the mouth, which was like this inscrutable grin, which I've seen on you quite a few times. And it's like, I know that I can't know that I know, and it was just this essential part of the Beloved's face.

AH: Next thing you probably might see the mole on the other side. That's a sign of beauty in many places.

S: I was really struck the other day when you read from your book *Luminous Night's Journey*, by this process of the layers dissolving, and I was just struck by a certain presence in recognizing this unfolding and opening. And what I was recognizing in doing these exercises was how there's a way in which there is in the face of the bedazzlement something that arises in me that wants to know it, and that obscures it. Somehow that movement becomes a veil.

AH: It's just the same thing as wanting to love it. It's the creation of an object relation, the creation of a relationship—there is a me that loves, and a me that knows. That becomes a duality, so it becomes a veil. It's the same thing. I'm glad you brought that up.

S: So is there some object relation that I need to work through?

AH: Just recognizing that the concept of relationship is the veil here. The duality is a veil. Just to recognize that can intensify the love.

S: I'd like to ask you about the difference between my heart and my belly. Sometimes I feel the love in my heart for the Beloved, and sometimes I also feel, well, like there's a longing in the heart, but sometimes I feel there's a longing in my belly, and it feels like a slightly different quality. When I think about the love for the truth, that feels more like a belly quality, and I was wondering if both the heart and the belly are involved in uniting with the Beloved, or whether it's just the heart, and how they might be related.

AH: Yes, because sometimes we feel wanting not just in the heart. We feel it in the belly, and even in the head, in the mind. And one way of saying it is that your belly has a heart. So does your mind. And your heart has a belly and a mind, just as your mind has a heart and a belly. That's originally an idea of Gurdjieff's, I think, that each center has all three centers in it. Because these are degrees of differentiation basically. Originally they're all the same, and there's the differentiation into three centers, and within that differentiation there can be further differentiations.

S: So you're calling that the heart of my belly. And when the Beloved comes, eventually it all becomes one thing.

AH: Ultimately none of the centers are important, really. You can feel in any part of your body, and you can even think with any part of your body.

S: In one of the exercises I was wondering about the mind obscuring the heart, and I was feeling something about fear being involved in that. But I couldn't feel whether the fear was in my mind or in my heart, and I wondered if... It seems like I feel love in my heart, and I wondered if fear has a location like that or a center related to it.

AH: You see, the heart is sometimes a center, but really the heart is more of a function—it's like the feeling function, which can be anywhere in the body. So to say that fear is in the head or the heart is irrelevant at some point. But fear also has both mind and heart in it, because it has the feeling and the recognition of the feeling. So it can be more mental or more heart—there can be more feeling than just thoughts and the worries about something. That's another kind of differentiation. But the more deeply we go into ourselves, the more we know ourselves, the more we know our soul, these centers lose their importance at some point. They lose their distinctions.

SIXTEEN

Wholeness

Here are two more selections from *The Divine Flashes*. The first one:

> My Chinese darling
> I am with you
> So much that I forget
> Am I you or are you me?
> No, I am I, you are you.
> No, I meant you are me.
> Or rather I am I, you are you
> And you are me!*

And the second:

> The glass grows clear
> The wine grows clear;
> One resembles another,
> All is confused

---

* Fakhruddin 'Iraqi, *Divine Flashes* (Paulist Press, 1982), 82–83.

As if there were wine
And no cup
Or cup
And no wine!*

So what are these speaking to? Well, they're pointing to another veil that we still have to contend with. And to identify the root of the matter, as the saying goes: "If it's not one thing, it's your mother." Now, it might seem like we're going backward if we're bringing that issue up again, but the good news is that it's only coming up because our heart is about to get bigger and we're on the brink of seeing the ultimate truth. You see, although it may seem that we behold the Beloved absolutely now, we don't yet know it fully—the real epiphany is actually still to come.

On our journey of ascent—whether we consider we are moving to the summit or the depth, it's all the same thing—we've had to let go of our attachments to various love objects, including our own selves. That has involved a great deal of loss, grief, and sadness around having to let go of things we love, and also around not yet being completely one with the Beloved. There are many external beloveds that we've had to relinquish, as well as inner beloveds that were obscuring the true inner Beloved. Now our heart has discovered the nature of the absolute Beloved, and we realize just how much we must love it when that love brings us to the point of leaving absolutely everything behind. Because as our heart moves ever closer to the dark luminosity and transcendent mystery of the Beloved, it feels like we're leaving the world and, moreover, the universe as we know it.

---

* Fakhruddin 'Iraqi, *Divine Flashes* (Paulist Press, 1982), 82.

This feels like the greatest loss imaginable, and it's only natural that the prospect of saying farewell to everything we've known brings tremendous grief and sadness. We know we've always loved the world, but we only see it clearly as a love object with this final movement toward the absolute. And we recognize that this is a love object we have an intense attachment to—the world as a whole is a very potent beloved for us. All the same, letting go of our attachment to all manifestation seems to be a requirement if we want to enter the mystery of nonbeing that is its depth and source.

This attachment is a veil in itself, but when we go through it and feel completely unified with the Beloved, even being the absolute, another veil arises that can fragment that unity. We begin to experience a conflict. We've been able to dissolve and merge into the absolute because the heart has recognized that that is its main love, and we've proclaimed, "I love the Beloved more than anything else, including the world." But at this point it becomes clear that the heart is still somewhat divided, and this is revealed in a resurgence of our love for the world. It feels like we're facing a decisive conflict between two powerful loves again—the love for the inner Beloved and its mystery, darkness, and exquisite intimacy, and this reemerging love for the world.

It becomes apparent that regardless of how much we love the nearness and union with the Beloved, we can't help but recognize that we also still love the world. We might feel bad about that becoming such a challenge again, full of sorrow that our fidelity toward the Beloved is still clearly lacking, and we may therefore do our utmost to try to stay only with that love. Or we might find ourselves going back and forth, sometimes loving the Beloved and sometimes loving the world. As we do that, there's joy when we're with the Beloved, but also a sense of loss and sadness, because the other beloved, the world, is not there. And if we're more focused on the world appearing in its full realness and beauty, then we feel we're in danger of losing the absolute, the inner Beloved.

This movement back and forth, this conflict, is one more echo of the familiar conflict we call the rapprochement conflict, which we experienced originally with the separation from mother. As we separated and moved away from her in order to develop greater autonomy and independence, we feared the loss of the intimacy, love, and support we needed from her. The child really wants both, the comfort of dependency as well as independence, but it seems it has to go one way or the other. Neither state is tolerable permanently, however, so the conflict involves going back and forth between the two—the independence, and the rapprochement when the child wants to return to dependency on the mother. And the reason we're talking about mother here is that our experience of this original rapprochement conflict might be complicating the situation now. We feel torn between the final surrender to the Beloved and our love for the world, and we can get more insight into this if we look at how we generally learn to project mother onto the world, and how the world therefore comes to represent mother.

Very early on, in the first few days and weeks of life, our mother's face is all that we see in some sense, and that face becomes the world to us. And even as we learn to strike out on our own and discover our own capacities beyond mother, she is the world we return to whenever we feel insecure. This deep and complete love that we felt toward mother is in contrast to our own development and independence—our autonomy. The rapprochement conflict continues when our desire for autonomy takes us into our deep inner experience, which ultimately means loving our true nature. This leads to us feeling the need to turn away from the world, which replaces mother at this point. So we work on this conflict between attachment and autonomy on many levels, at many stages of our journey, and it can resurface now at this late stage.

So the heart is experiencing division and conflict once more as we go back and forth, between abiding in unification with the absolute, and sadness and grief at the prospect of losing the world. And when I say "the world," that doesn't just mean the physical world but the fundamental world of form—all manifestation of shape, form, or color, whether it be external or internal. The pain is therefore of a different order to what we've known before, because the rapprochement conflict is now taking cosmic proportions.

It feels like an extreme juncture because we seem to be faced with a binary choice—anything other than the dark emptiness of the absolute, anything manifest, is seen as a polarity that's in conflict with it. So although we've recognized that we still love manifest reality, as I said, we may try to suppress or reject this love because it seems to go against our autonomy of self, represented by the inner Beloved. This can be very reminiscent of the desire to push away our mother as we felt the need to find our own independence, so how we feel at this point can reflect a great deal about the earlier rapprochement conflict. Many of us have already worked on this conflict a great deal, and how powerfully it arises now, and how confused we are by it, will depend on how much we've understood and resolved it.

Different people have different ways of resolving the original rapprochement conflict. Some people move more toward the separation and autonomy pole, while others stay closer to dependency on mother. Those who tended toward autonomy then will tend to go toward the absolute now and be willing to lose the world, albeit with much sadness because there's still a conflict. Those who wanted to stay nearer to mother will tend to be pulled more by form and manifestation now, and experience an intensification of the desire to stay with the world. Observing our inclination now can therefore tell us more about how we may have resolved the earlier rapprochement conflict, if we haven't already seen it.

Whichever way we're trying to resolve this conflict now, the most important thing to recognize is that it simply doesn't work. We might decide that the answer is to become completely unattached to the world and only love the absolute, but it doesn't happen. We can let go of our attachments to the world, it's true, but what we find—and this is really the heart of the issue here—is that our love for the world doesn't go away. And that's because that love is real. It's not just an attachment, and it's not just a projection of our symbiotic merging with mother. Acknowledging this can be quite a conflict for committed lovers who have pledged their total love for the Beloved. It's a very deep valley on the path of love, and the pain, anguish, guilt, fear, and hatred that were part of the original rapprochement conflict can reappear in an unexpected way.

As usual on our path, the answer is to simply stay with the conflict and not react by trying to change or eliminate any part of it. If we've already learned to accept and trust that whatever arises is really the doing of the absolute truth, that will help us stay with this conflict now, and we may even begin to see the true resolution. Until we do, the immediate resolution of the conflict between these two loves is the one we've already established—to love the absolute fully and make it our primary love, gradually letting go of the other love objects that have supported us on our journey toward union and dissolution into the dark luminous night. But even though we give the Beloved priority over the world, and the unmanifest priority over the manifest, we accept that our heart is divided because in reality we love them both.

If we allow our love for both to deepen and expand, something unexpected happens—it becomes unified. And then comes the epiphany: We see that we love both the manifest and the unmanifest because they are not two—they are the same. They only appear as two loves because we still have some kind of duality in our mind. We're still seeing the Beloved as something apart from the world, as if there are two separate things: the manifest world on the one hand, and the source—true nature, the Beloved—on the other. But now the heart is about to get bigger and recognize the Beloved in a more complete way. We recognize that the absolute or the Beloved includes everything. It does not exclude anything. It does not exist in contrast with anything.

As we've come ever closer to the Beloved, it's meant shedding everything, letting go of everything, because we'd been focusing on so many things to the exclusion of that absolute nature. But when we behold and then become that luminous nature, and look from its vantage point, we recognize that the world is simply its luminosity. Everything, all the manifest forms we perceive, are nothing but patterns that the radiance of the Beloved assumes. They're not just a reflection of the Beloved—they are emanations.

We realize then that the world and everything that exists is nothing but the body, the heart, and the mind of the Beloved. And we see that the Beloved, the absolute darkness, always has this body, heart, and mind. There's no such thing as a Beloved that's separate from the world, and there's no world that's separate from the absolute Beloved—neither can exist without the other. But even describing it in that way is misleading, as if the two things are somehow connected and united, when in fact they're not and never can be two things.

So we finally see the ultimate truth of reality—the Beloved is absolute nothingness, a condition of complete nonbeing, and at the same time, that nonbeing is the nature of everything. It's like this nonbeingness is stuck inseparably to everything, so it's literally and absolutely the fundamental nature of everything, no matter how big or small.

We can say it's the nature of the body, for instance, so the body's nature is emptiness, nonbeingness. But what does that really mean? Does it include your brain? Yes, it's also the nature of your brain. How about the dendrites, the cells in your brain? What's their nature? It's still the same nonbeingness. How about if we take a molecule from those cells? The nature of that is nonbeing too. And if we take an atom from that molecule, what's the nature of that? Nonbeing. It doesn't matter how infinitesimally small you go, the nature of what you find is this nonbeing. So you can divide the atom into protons, neutrons, and even electrons. What is their nature? It's nonbeing. When you get down to the level of quarks and strings, maybe it's easier to recognize that their nature is pure nothingness. And it's the same with light, which is made of photons. What is their nature? Nonbeing. So wherever you go, from the core to the outermost surface of everything, this nothingness is always there. And this nothingness is the nature of the Beloved, so there's nothing that is not the Beloved.

So while the world and all manifestation is its body, heart, and mind, the Beloved is the very essence, the nature of all of it. When we're simply loving the darkness and emptiness apart from the world, our love is therefore not complete. Yes, we're loving the absolute in a certain way, but we're not seeing the Beloved completely, for what it truly is. We're not loving it in its wholeness, so our love is still divided.

When we see the Beloved in its wholeness now, it's still the darkness and mystery—nothing has changed in that regard. But without adding or taking anything away, we recognize that the mysterious nonbeingness of the absolute, that complete contradiction of all logic, is itself the world and everything in the world. Absolutely. There's not a nanometer of distance between the Beloved and anything in the manifest world.

So it turns out that beneath the apparent division between the world and the Beloved there is only true unity. This brings a liberating insight. We realize why we couldn't reach a final resolution of that division—it's because the division never really existed in the first place. We thought our heart was divided, experiencing two loves, but it was always loving one thing, really—it's just that our dual mind wasn't able to see it that way. When we recognize the unity, we can't say we're either loving the Beloved or loving the world. It's simply not possible to do that if there's no separation in reality and it's all one. So our love is even more whole now; it's unified as one love loving the same thing. And this unified love is no longer something we're striving to develop—it's just an inevitable consequence of seeing the truth of reality, as we experience the absolute, the Beloved, more completely as itself.

When we initially turned our focus away from the external world in order to meet the Beloved, we described it as turning inward, and we've kept calling it the *inner* Beloved. But now that we have the absolute realization of the Beloved, we see that it's not inner. There is no inner and no outer—that's just another dichotomy created by the mind, along with unmanifest and manifest, the world and the absolute, the lover and the Beloved. All the apparent dichotomies are becoming resolved and healed as we see that it's all one thing. Let's be clear, though—we're not saying that the absolute does in fact have some kind of form. No, it's more mysterious than that. The world is a manifestation of form, but that world is also the mystery of absolute nonbeingness. The world is and is not, and the isness and the absence are one and the same thing.

We've seen that the mind struggles with this mysterious unity because it's impossible to understand conceptually, but our heart has known the unity all along. That's why it has always loved both the form and the formless, with what is actually a unified love for the wholeness of nondual reality. So as we move toward the absolute, if we either fear that we're going to have to leave the world behind or experience some kind of world-weariness, it means we're still participating in the duality created by our mind. We still believe that the world is some kind of dispensable add-on to the absolute. It isn't. And just as we discover that the soul is one with the Beloved on our path, we also realize now that the whole world is one with the Beloved. The formless Beloved is there in all possible forms. Whether they are inner or outer forms, they're all expressions of the Beloved and its mystery of nonbeing.

I'll read you something from my journal at this stage of my process, to give you a little more flavor of it.

There was at some point fear, emptiness, and negative merging. The rubber covering I felt over the heart seemed to have hatred in it. It seems that the mental dichotomy between the universe and the absolute makes going to the absolute feel like the loss of everything, the universe. So there's both fear and sadness. At some point I realize there is emptiness in the heart, covered by the rubber, because the unified love of the world and the absolute is no longer allowed to be there. The next day while talking at breakfast, a new state appeared. I felt as if I were everything, in the state of nonconceptual oneness (meaning everything is there without the recognition of it), but I was still the absolute. It felt like a state of unity between the absolute and the world. I had experienced this before as the unity of absolute and logos, but this time there was more of being the state instead of mostly seeing it. There was both a strong and definite sense of beingness with color and harmony, and the sense of absence that is the absolute. I realized that a large part of the conflict for the heart is the mental dichotomy between the world and the absolute, between existence and nonexistence. In this state of absolute unity there is existence, which is world, and nonexistence, which is the absolute. It's the same thing, and it is also me. I realize that a deep sadness emerges if I'm either the absolute or the universe.

So it's time for an exercise to see if you can get the flavor of your own experience at this juncture on the journey.

Practice Session:
The Beloved and the World

...

This will be a fifteen-minute monologue, in groups of two or three if possible, or you can write out your exploration for fifteen minutes if you're alone.

Inquire into your deeply held attitude and positions regarding the relation between the Beloved and the world. You might find out something about that in your early relationship with your mothering person, and your experience of the original rapprochement conflict.

You want to explore your experience of the relation between the world and the Beloved by seeing it in your attitude, your actions, and your feelings, not in terms of what you believe or think. You want to see how that duality is reflected in your own life, in order to see and recognize the subtle underlying position you're taking about it. If we just see it as a theoretical issue, it's not a personal concern, and it needs to become a burning personal concern.

· · · · ·

Questions and Comments

Student: I have always felt some heartful kind of feelings and taken those kinds of feelings to be nearness to the Beloved. In this retreat I have not had any of those feelings. I have had much of what you've described, but whereas in the past I've relied more on a feeling tone, what's been happening here is much more states of presence that have indicated nearness of the Beloved in the way you've described it. It requires a real shift of my perception, so I'm a bit between seats.

A. H. Almaas: Yes. The feeling of nearness means the state is approaching. We feel the approach, but we're not aware of it directly. And then when the nearness is greater, we can be aware of what it is that is near, instead of just a sense of nearness.

S: So then there would be a likelihood that I would experience a more heartful kind of feeling, feelings that I would recognize as heartful feelings.

AH: Yes, that might be so. Either way there'll be heartful feelings, really. But it depends on the person, it depends on the time in the process.

S: So I would need to just move further in this development to expect these other feelings to be indicated?

AH: Maybe. Maybe not. Maybe something else is going on that we need to find out.

S: So we seem to be getting to the heart of the matter, where matter is an expression of the Beloved, and the Beloved is a part of matter, and all is one. Which leads me to ask a question I asked you a number of years ago, which is: What is consciousness, and who is the I that observes, that has some continuity and is aware?

AH: I'm tempted to say, "Here's looking at you, kid!" The awareness is nothing but the Beloved itself.

S: Then why am I . . . is there one Beloved that is all encompassing? Is there an individual Beloved? Is my individual Beloved part of a collective?

AH: So what makes you ask the question? What kind of experience are you referring to that makes you want to ask the question?

S: When I have experiences that at the time have been identified as the absolute, which I now understand was probably the Beloved, there was a consciousness there. There was an observer, an awareness, and I never knew and still don't understand what that is.

AH: So you can say that the Beloved, the light of the Beloved, that radiance of the Beloved, is awareness—the fact that it's radiant means aware—and each soul is an eye, a seeing eye that is an organ of perception for that awareness.

S: I would say they are individual souls.

AH: But they're eyes for the same awareness. So that's one way of saying it. When you understand that, you know why you've been baking all this time, all these years.

S: I've been baking?

AH: Yeah. Baking, roasting, whatever you like. Cooking, ripening—it's developing an organ of perception.

S: What I'm finding the hardest thing for me to grasp is that I am the Beloved, and that seems like the biggest veil for me—that my own self-rejection keeps me from the Beloved.

AH: Self-rejection will definitely do that. So you just see it, and recognize the self-rejection and understand it. Self-rejection creates a kind of separation, and if you recognize the separation, that can intensify the love, and that in turn can burn away the rejection. Instantly, or it might take a while.

S: There's a question I've had building for some time, and in the previous exercise we did, I realized that the place I feel an active reaching out toward the world, in a loving sense, is with what you called mind love, the mind loving to know and understand. I've always had that since I was a kid—that's why I loved science. So when you spoke of the Beloved inside, and the heart, I realized that that's literally a sore place for me. So in a way, the drive I've had since childhood toward learning and intellectual achievement, and knowing in that sense, appears not to have been in line with my heart, because in my heart not only is there nothing I know that's wonderful to go after there but there's also grief, there's pain. And since I came into this work and allowed myself to feel more of myself than my brain would allow, I guess, it's grief, it's tears, it's heartbreak, feeling terribly small and alone, worthless, unlovable. And it's gone on, it's been constant, where I'll cry for hours sometimes, and I often cry in triads. It's a very intense experience, and at the peak of it, it wipes out my mind, which is a wonderful surrender and I lose all the tension in my body. And there's compassion in there, and I think I've had that since the beginning of the work, that experience of compassion. But I don't have experiences of the absolute. I did have an experience of the black about three weeks ago, which took away self-hate, which was really... I mean, I weigh about a quarter of what I used to weigh, and I hated God and I hated everything with a sort of childish tantrum thing that I could see. And that hasn't come back, but I still have grief of an undiminished intensity. And I don't know if this has something to do with the primal break from unity. It feels very deep. It feels like the most true thing I know. And it's precious to me and intimate and private in that way, and it also has a sense of, from that place I want to take away all pain. There's almost a cessation in it, but maybe this is my early... maybe I want to take away my mother's pain to get the holding. But I don't know how to manage when I'm too out of the experience to interpret these things. And so I'm asking... you haven't spoken too much about compassion in this. I know the things you're talking about are sort of more advanced than that, but my best sense of what the inner Beloved is for me is this sense of sadness that feels so personal. There's an intense longing but the object is not well defined . . . It's just a longing to feel held and loved somehow. How would you advise me to use what you've taught here and seek the inner Beloved? Am I on the right track? Is there anything happening here relating to this topic?

AH: Let the sadness get bigger, and deeper, and the heartache—let it get even more painful. You're finding out you're in love. That's how it works. So yes, compassion will help us to tolerate the sadness and hurt and all of that, but we don't want it to take it away. So I remember in my process, I was feeling so sad, some kind of depth of sadness, for a long time, and I didn't know what it was for a long time. I was probably feeling it unconsciously before that, but consciously it was probably continuous for about fifteen years, and it didn't finally stop until the complete beholding of the Beloved. And I don't regret it. I'm glad it didn't stop till then.

S: So strap in for a hard shish kebab and oceans of tears.

AH: Right. Exactly.

SEVENTEEN

The Unity of Love

We'll begin with something from *Divine Flashes* again. It's a mixture of prose and poetry.

Love is the lover's essence, nor could this essence cease to be, however his attachments may flit from beloved to beloved.

> Shift, transfer your heart where you will—
> Love belongs but to the First Beloved.

Love where you may, you will have loved Him; turn your face whatever way, it turns toward Him—even if you know it not.

> Everyone drawn to a beloved
> must be subject to him.
> All are subject to Thee
> but know it not.

The poet means to say,

> Whether they know Thee or not
> all creatures of the world
> now and forever-without-end
> bend but toward Thee.
> All love for someone else
> is but a whiff
> Of Thy perfume:
> none else can be loved.

It is not so much wrong as impossible to love other than Him, for whatever we love (aside from that love, which springs from the very essence of the lover, the cause of which is unknown), we love either for its beauty, or its goodness—and both of these belong to Him alone.

> The beauty of each lovely boy
> each comely girl
> derives from His—
> on loan.*

We've been on a journey from polygamy to monogamy, after seeing that having many beloveds in the world—be they people, things, situations, or activities—was in conflict with the need to focus our love on the inner Beloved. This is something that has to be resolved if we are serious about our inner journey.

There are two resolutions to the conflict: one commensurate with the path, and one commensurate with realization. On the

---

* Fakhruddīn 'Irāqī, *Divine Flashes* (Paulist Press, 1982), 85.

path, the only thing that works is to unify our love by withdrawing it from all our other beloveds and making the ultimate Beloved primary. If all other loves become secondary, that opens the way for us to recognize, behold, and ultimately unite with the true Beloved of the heart.

We've seen that this resolution on the path is not the final and true resolution, however—it's just the best we could do at that stage. With the true resolution of realization we're able to abide in the wholeness of the true Beloved and recognize that it is not something separate from the world. Only then can we see that the world is nothing but a manifestation of the Beloved, a revelation and expression of its beauty and richness. The Beloved is an infinite treasure, and the many qualities and facets of this treasure are constantly being revealed in the myriad forms and possibilities of the manifest world.

In this station of realization, it's clear to us that the Beloved and the world are not two things, and not even two sides of the same thing. They are one and the same, and knowing this brings a fuller and more complete resolution of the conflict between our love for the inner Beloved and our love for the myriad beloveds. We find that our love can be unified and our heart undivided even as we are loving other people or things as well as the inner Beloved. Before, loving both always felt like a division of the heart and its love, but with the realization of the wholeness and nonduality of reality, we see that this apparent division of our love is just an illusion, just as the duality is an illusion. Whatever person, object, situation, or activity we love in the world, we can't help but recognize now that in loving that, we are loving the Beloved. They are not two loves but one and the same love. As 'Irāqī says, "none else can be loved," and that's because there is nothing else to love.

So our love always belongs to the ultimate Beloved, and if we find ourselves loving the beauty, loveliness, and goodness of some of its particular manifestations in the world, we know that these qualities are only "on loan"—they are particular transient expressions of the Beloved's mystery, beauty, majesty, and richness, and not something separate from it.

When we are in this station, we can allow our love free rein, and love deeply, passionately, and sweetly, without any conflict. How could there be conflict if we know that our beloveds and the Beloved aren't separate things? So there's no guilt about apparently abandoning the unmanifest Beloved as we're drawn to the manifest world, because we know they are one. There's no longer any separation between the inner and the outer, the formless and the form. This means there can be all kinds of love—emotional, spiritual, physical, or aesthetic—and we know that they are all an expression of our love for the Beloved.

Whatever we love, we know it's simply because it reminds us of the Beloved. All our love objects are just the face that the Beloved is taking, a particular way it is revealing some of its qualities in the moment. By loving someone, we are loving the Beloved, and it's because we love the Beloved that we love that someone. We realize now that we are actually monogamous even when we might appear to be polygamous because in reality there is no polytheism, only monotheism.

So as well as resolving any apparent conflict now, this resolution also helps us understand that the heart was never really divided in the first place—our polygamy was always at heart a manifestation of the inherent unity of love. From the beginning, the heart was always faithful to the true fullness of the Beloved, the ultimate reality of all manifestation—we just didn't know it consciously. And we cannot be conscious of this underlying fidelity if we're not conscious of the depth, subtlety, and wholeness of the transcendent Beloved. Without knowing that, we become fixated on the particular forms the Beloved is veiled in, and we're unable to see the Beloved through the veils.

Even before this realization, we might sometimes have sensed that the Beloved is being revealed to us in some particular forms. Perhaps there are things that have always reminded the heart of the Beloved somehow—the aesthetic beauty of an object, the quality of sweetness of a person, or the blissful pleasure we get from engaging in some activity. And as we said earlier, it can simply be chocolate ice cream, or a car. Something about all these things opens the heart, and when the heart is open, it can't help but love. So to varying degrees, in that love we get a partial and transient taste of what it's like to be with the Beloved, because as we're beginning to see now, in truth they are all faces of the Beloved—even the chocolate ice cream.

It's a partial and transient taste because we're not yet fully seeing the mystery of the ultimate Beloved underlying absolutely everything that appears—for the most part we're still separating the manifestation of the Beloved from the essence of the Beloved. The heart may be recognizing the Beloved in all the forms we see, but the mind is not. The mind is still dual, seeing things from the perspective of external divisions and separateness. And if we don't truly see that all appearance is just a manifestation of the Beloved, we see these things primarily as what we think they are. We take their reified and objectified form to be reality and love that, when it's not true. They aren't the source of the love—it just appears that way to us if we can't see that the source is something else, something deeper. So we don't realize that the beautiful face we love is really expressing a deeper beauty and significance that is the true source of our love. We often say we find this or that person, this or that object, or this or that activity "divine," which shows that they remind us of the Beloved. But because we still don't recognize the underlying unity of things, we think the forms themselves are the source of the divinity.

So when we don't see the underlying unity, we continue to see divided, disconnected objects, and as we know only too well now, the contentment and satisfaction some of them might give us in this disconnected state is only partial and transient. The heart isn't satisfied by it because it wants the completeness and wholeness of the one Beloved. Only when we see that wholeness do we really see that the Beloved is inherent in everything in the manifest world. It may be easier for us to recognize that the Beloved is inherent in what we find beautiful, but the fact that people can love not only beautiful things and beautiful people but also all kinds of strange and odd things, shows that everything is manifesting the face of the Beloved. Even the things most of us think are odd, ugly, and weird—somebody loves them.

This all becomes clear in the station of recognizing the unity of the unmanifest Beloved and all its manifestations, which allows the ultimate resolution of our conflict. But let's be clear, it is by no means an easy station to abide in, and there are two main reasons why. First, it's not easy because of the tenacious power of duality. The tendency to reify and objectify the manifest forms of the Beloved will remain for a very long time, even though we've seen through it. In loving a particular beloved, there's always the danger that we'll isolate and separate that particular form from the depth and essence of the Beloved, and love it just for its appearance and form. We then forget once more that we only love it because we're loving the inner Beloved through it. And if we forget that, the inner Beloved will disappear because our fidelity has been broken. Whenever the reification and objectification of our love takes hold again, separating our love objects from the depth and essence of the ultimate Beloved, the experience of polygamy returns, along with its division and discontent. Our fidelity to the inner Beloved therefore needs to be established over and over again, and this requires a great deal of commitment, as well as much subtle discrimination.

The other danger we face is that of loving only the inner Beloved and rejecting our external loves. We might want to move only toward the inner depth, the silence, and the blissful peace of formlessness, at the expense of loving the forms in which the Beloved manifests in the world. That means we're limiting the Beloved and making it something separate from the world again, no longer recognizing that whatever we see is the face of the Beloved. This will reinstate the division and conflict, and renew the rapprochement complex we discussed earlier.

So I want to stress that just because we've seen the wholeness of the Beloved and felt the unity of love, that doesn't mean we will always know now that all our beloveds are really an expression of the true Beloved. When we're still on the path, we can't assume it's enough to simply keep that in mind and not worry about it all too much—you know, "Okay, I'll love whatever I want to love and just go for it, because it's all the Beloved really." It doesn't work like that. We still have to continue on the path the way we've been working before. We still have to actively work on our fidelity and commitment to the inner Beloved and be vigilant of the pitfalls and delusions about what it is that we are loving. If we don't remain vigilant, we can easily fall back in love with reified and objectified forms in a way that's disconnected and dissociated from the inner Beloved. And then no matter how much we tell ourselves that we know it's all unity, our unconscious experience will be one of division.

So the resolution only works if we can truly remember the unity. If we can't, we have to be honest about it and go back to making the inner Beloved the primary Beloved. That is still a kind of resolution, and it means there is hope for our heart. Our heart will eventually rediscover the true harmony, contentment, and completeness of the unity that is without conflict, where there is no need to renounce or give precedence to one love over another.

When we feel our intimate love for the inner Beloved and truly recognize the ubiquity of its mystery, beauty, subtlety, and exquisiteness, we can't help but also love other people, life, and the world. And as we love the world, as we love people, as we love our life, we can't help but see the inner Beloved in all of it, and love it even more passionately and more deeply. When that happens, you can't help but melt and dissolve and annihilate, along with all the illusory division and separation.

Our heart is ripened and mature at this point. Its journey is complete, and it is fully unified. And as we reach this state more and more, we may find that our outer beloveds actually increase in number. That's understandable if we're feeling an innate love for the whole world and everyone in it. We might still love some people and things in a particularly intense and personal way, but if we see the Beloved in everyone and everything, of course we will feel love for them all. So here, even more than before, when we're talking about love, it doesn't just mean what you feel for your lover or partner. The love flows out toward your family, friends, acquaintances, activities, work, and interests. It's a total love for your whole life, because the heart is always finding its Beloved in every part of it—your cat, your furniture, the trees, all of your environment, and the sun in the sky. The love encompasses more and more and more, and so there is more joy, happiness, and celebration. The heart's desire is fulfilled every time we love something, because we recognize that it is the ultimate Beloved.

This is an exquisite condition of unity and wholeness. It's possible to be in this condition to varying degrees of course, and we might begin to enter it before we behold the ultimate absolute mystery itself. So with one particular person or thing, we might see that what we love is really an expression of the true nature of the inner Beloved. And we might begin to recognize more consciously the various qualities that we cherish in some of our beloveds—the purity, the beauty, the strength, and the magnificence—and how they appear to us in these worldly forms as a reflection of qualities that come from the Beloved. When the Beloved finally appears in its mysterious depth and emptiness, in its absolute truth and wholeness, this recognition becomes more precise, and as it extends to encompass everything we behold, the unity of love is then complete.

We learned the secret of the heart some time ago, that the intensity of the love itself can annihilate duality, and this is how loving the many has become the same as loving the one. We see now that the reason love can take us from duality to nonduality in this way is that from the very beginning, love is an expression of nonduality. Our love is always unified because it originates from the primal unity. Love may appear to us as a duality at first because everyone talks about love that way, and the languages we learn make it appear that love is an expression of separateness and division, with a tendency toward multiplicity, polygamy, and polytheism. In reality, the division is only apparent and the multiplicity isn't real. We only perceive it because we are not seeing the truth of things.

It's therefore a matter of dissolving the apparent duality and multiplicity of love through an intensification and deepening of it, which will reveal more of its true nature and source. As the love reveals its true nature and source to be the Beloved and nothing else, it reveals its true unity. This unity is the true condition, the nonduality and wholeness that we experience in the Beloved. And as that breaks through and begins to touch us more, it gives our human life deeper richness and meaning. The love we have, the compassion we have, the power we have, the intelligence we have, the caring we can experience, and the excellence we can accomplish—all these are just flashes of the Beloved appearing through the world of sleep, the usual world in which we're not awake to the truth.

The way of love is to basically follow our love of these flashes, allowing them to reveal more and more of the nature of the ultimate light from which the flashes come, as the manifestation of the Beloved and the true reality of love.

So the greatest task is to establish and then maintain our faithfulness and fidelity to the Beloved, so that we remain in union to the extent that we can love the world and its forms without any splitting of our love for the Beloved. Let's do an exercise now to find out where we are in that respect.

PRACTICE SECTION
THE BELOVED AND YOUR BELOVEDS—
CONFLICT OR RESOLUTION?

. . .

You'll do a fifteen-minute monologue, in groups of two or three if possible, or you can write out your exploration for fifteen minutes if you're alone.

Explore your experience of loving the absolute Beloved, your inner nature, and also loving other beloveds. Where are you now in terms of resolving the potential conflict between the two poles—the outer and the inner, the manifest and the unmanifest, and the form and the formless? Explore whether and how much you forget the inner Beloved when you turn to these beloveds, or vice versa. See if you can appreciate and get a feel of the ongoing dilemma, and the difficulties you might still be having with this conflict, because it can show you something important about where you are on the inner journey of love.

. . . . .

Questions and Comments

Student: For me it's always been easier to go to the inner. I don't find it easy to go back to the outer world again after a retreat, and I have a definite tendency to see the outer as a threat. I'm waiting for a catastrophe to happen and it's all very dangerous out there. And in this monologue, I was feeling the whole structure just shaking, and starting to feel the Beloved in the outer, seeing the people around me not as somebody I have to watch out for. It doesn't feel solid. It all feels vibrational around me right now, and I like it!

A. H. Almaas: It reminds me of much of the sacred art and iconography, where the absolute and the world are represented as the *yab-yum*, a god and a goddess in an embrace. That's really the idea, that that embrace is a unity.

S: I have a question that is about sexuality, how that fits in with our topic. Particularly, it seems to me that I've done very little exploration on that here, that there is a kind of sexuality that is pretty easily integrated with the Beloved, seeing the beauty and all of that. But then there also seems to be a kind of animal soul sexuality that has a lot of longing and lusting and all of that wanting in it, and I have a sense that it is possible somehow also to integrate it. But I have no understanding of it at all. So I wondered if you might say something about sex.

AH: It has to do with integrating the sexuality with the heart. The more there is heart in the sexuality, the more that the animal sexuality becomes just one dimension of it, instead of it being the only thing. So really the integration of the heart is what transforms sexuality in general, without losing the animal part—the animal part just becomes more of the passion and the energy.

S: Could you say something about that, the integration of the animal and the ...

AH: I don't know what to do beside demonstrating it.

S: That's okay!

AH: What I mean is that originally, from early on as infants, desire and love are the same thing. They don't differentiate. And in the reintegration, the desire and love become the same thing again. So desire is not separate from love. So giving and taking are like two sides of the same thing, and that's what I meant by the embrace. The embrace, the interpenetration, the interaction, is expressing the unity on all the levels, which brings in specific energy, the sexual energy. The sexual energy in that place is not just the animal—the lust and the physical part—but it has a tenderness, a sweetness, and a passion and a depth to it, and the animal part turns out to be an expression of the same love, except it's oriented more externally, more toward the object, and not recognizing it as an expression of the true Beloved. And the more we do that, the more it becomes the love of an object, and that brings in the division, which is then a limitation of the love and even of the sexuality itself.

S: I never thought I would get to the place where I understood from experience what you meant by loving the pain. A couple of times after these teachings my heart has been so open, and then last night it closed again and I couldn't feel anything, and I inquired and did all the things I thought to do and nothing much worked, and after the monologues I started to feel pain. And I could feel something, and I felt gratitude for that. But what came up after that was a really strong recognition of how helpless I feel in the opening when it comes, and when it goes, and how helpless I feel when I can't feel my heart.
AH: Right. We just feel the helplessness. It's true, feeling the pain opens our heart. It tends to do that.
S: That sounds like the next big challenge.
AH: To embrace the pain?
S: Yes.
AH: Yes, to embrace the hurt. That's how we embrace our heart, one of the ways we do it. Sounds great.

S: It's sort of a follow-up from my question after the previous talk, and also about dualism and about pain and accepting it. The night before I asked the question and your response was that I could work with the diamond mind, I was questioning the pain and trying to stay with it instead of going into the digression of the mind. And then after talking to you, last night I decided that it's really a nonduality, the mind, space and my mind, and so I decided to try to stay with the pain but go into some space, so I went into some clear space. I could feel the pain in my head because I wanted to stay with it to get rid of it or to try to work with this, which came up with my belief system that I'm unlovable. And so I was able to stay with the pain, so then I went to the genital hole space and I felt the pain there. The pain became sort of exquisite. It was very sharp, but as had just been mentioned, it felt like a good feeling that I had it. And then when I went to the second stage of black space, the pain was there. It was not as intense, but like more solid—it had a texture, like it was solid and brown and almost cancerous. And I thought, "Now I can stay with it, and I can metabolize it." And then the diamond mind kicked in and said, "This is dualism, this is rejection," and to embrace it. So I embraced it, and within a very short time this brown mass turned into clear white space.

AH: I find that embracing any experience in terms of how we feel it always transforms it. It's usually the direction.

S: During the retreat I've been wondering about nonbeing and being, manifestation being one, and how the arising of manifestation occurs. And we've been talking just now about sexuality, and it seems like from sexual embrace there's the arising of a human soul, and when we speak of the nonbeing, we speak of the Beloved. Because I'm curious how from nonbeing being occurs. And is that somehow the initial movement from nonbeing to being, the movement of love, or the arising of the first touch of love, and at the heart of all manifestation is this movement of love?

AH: In what context are you asking how nonbeing becomes being?

S: Well, I feel that if nonbeing and being are at the same time, then I'm existing but I'm not existing, and I wonder, if there's nonbeing, why existence at all? But it seems like there's some place where one moves from one to the other. Maybe I'm asking for a boundary that doesn't exist.

AH: That's true. It doesn't. It's not like there is being and nonbeing. Being and nonbeing are just an attempt to refer to reality. Reality is really mysterious. So when we try to describe it, we'll say it's both being and nonbeing, but that doesn't actually mean that there's being and nonbeing stuck to each other. It's really the same thing. And it defies our mind, our reason. It doesn't make sense to our reason. So being and nonbeing is an attempt at seeing some of the ways it manifests, some of its facets.

S: I wonder whether you could help me with clarifying something around cessation. Maybe tell me the steps or how you experience that. It's like I've been trying to stay awake to the experience that is coming, and in this witnessing of the other monologues, I experienced it as an ongoing melting that seemed to dissolve form, and I had the sense that if I could stay awake, gradually everything would disappear but I would somehow still be awake rather than fall asleep. I had the sense that at a certain point my body started to recognize something that it recognizes at night, and then it goes, "Oh, it's time to sleep," and then it just falls over. And during these talks there have been times when I would be gone, and just recognized that in coming back, but my body didn't collapse, my posture was still straight. And there were other times when I would be gone and then I'd come back through my posture collapsing. So there seems to be something about sleep and nonsleep and awakeness, and I somehow couldn't stay cognizant enough to follow the steps close enough to this cessation to feel that I can understand it, so I wonder whether it can be understood and whether you could help me with that.

AH: It seems to me you're already seeing it. As you say, it's a gradual melting and dissolving. Sometimes it happens and you're not even aware that there's melting, you just disappear. But to be aware of it means to just see the gradually dissolving and disappearing into nothing, and that can go two ways. The dissolving can be so complete that you lose consciousness, as you said, and come back one way or another, or the dissolving can happen by revealing the emptiness that's underlying everything. And in that case you won't lose consciousness, you won't lose awareness.

S: So in that case you would just experience the emptiness and feel awake, still with the capacity to experience, and the object of the experience would be the emptiness.

AH: Right. But there won't be just emptiness. If it's just emptiness there'll be no experience. There's always form, otherwise you can't be awake.

S: So if that form dissolves, then the consciousness is all gone, and then you only realize it when you come back?

AH: Right. But as I said, it's possible to be aware of the emptiness underlying all the forms, and see and recognize that emptiness is everywhere, but there are forms happening that are not separate from the emptiness. And then you can be awake.

S: So the sense of the possibility to be awake without there being consciousness, that's actually true, that can happen that you're awake but you have no consciousness.

AH: There cannot be consciousness or awareness if there's no manifestation at all, no awareness of manifestation. Awareness of manifestation and awareness go together. They're the same thing.

EIGHTEEN

Intimacy

We'll start with another piece from *Divine Flashes*—a final flash. Some of you have probably already caught on that the Beloved is a flasher.

> I have a friend
> whose form is body and soul
> —but which body, what soul?
> The Universe is His form;
> every fair meaning,
> every fair form
> I gaze upon—
> that is His form.*

We've seen that the Beloved is not only every fair form but even what we consider ugly forms. All manifestation is a manifestation of the Beloved's beauty and richness, including what we think is negative, difficult, or painful. It might seem paradoxical

---

* Fakhruddīn 'Irāqī, *Divine Flashes* (Paulist Press, 1982), 88.

sometimes and not make any sense to us, but there's no corner of the universe that the Beloved can't be found in. To know and behold the Beloved completely means to see that, and know that nothing is excluded from the true and exquisite condition of unity and wholeness.

But there's an even deeper mystery and magic to this unity, which is revealed when we recognize that the essence of this mysterious reality is nonbeing and nothingness—the complete absence of anything. So yes, from one perspective we can say that the many things we see are all just expressions of the Beloved. But from the true perspective of the Beloved, it's not like that. There aren't actually many things—there's just one thing, the nothingness, which doesn't have any form, shape, or size. How could true nothingness, nonbeingness, and formlessness have a form, shape, and size? It can't, because nothingness doesn't have any extent—it would need to be something in order to extend. So this absolute formlessness and nothingness is very mysterious and paradoxical, and it challenges some of the fundamental positions and beliefs we have about reality—what we consider to *be* reality, and not just our beliefs about it.

One way we might begin to understand the mystery of reality is to see that when we really investigate it, we don't find any solidity, any concreteness. The manifestation we perceive is just the appearance of things—their nature is actually nothing. And the fact that there's absolutely nothing there means that there are no obstructions within the experience of it—there's nothing in the way. Because the formlessness is absolute, even the form of space disappears, and that means there's nothing between you and me. We're all manifestations of the same truth, and that truth is what's between you and me. And that truth is nothingness.

The way we usually see it is that you're over there and I'm here. But for the Beloved, no, no. There's no over there and no here—that's just how things appear. In reality, it's all in one place, and it's all the Beloved. In this nothing there can't be any distance between anything, so there's nothing between you and anything else in the universe—no barriers, no walls. It's a condition of no separateness because it's a condition of absolute nothingness. Everything is this absolute mystery of nothingness and nonbeing, and it's not even an emanation of that nonbeing—it is simply nonbeing itself. The Beloved can therefore be seen as boundless and infinite, but it can also be seen as just one infinitesimal point.

The experience of this condition, the experience of the wholeness of the Beloved, is therefore a complete disappearance, a pure annihilation of what's between one thing and another. It's like my inside and your inside are the same thing—it's the same inside, and this inside has no sides, no walls holding it in. So by being in touch with my depth, which means I'm in touch with my nature as the Beloved, I'm also in touch with your depth. I'm not only feeling the depth of my heart, I'm also feeling the depth of your heart. It's the same depth, because it's the same heart, with absolutely nothing in between and no distance that separates.

It's not really something to think about and describe in words because the words won't make any sense. You need to feel into it, and you might then realize that you're feeling everything from the inside. Your nature is the complete unobstructedness of nonbeing, and that is the nature of everything, so there can't be any barrier or obstruction between my heart and your heart, and no obscuration—there's just absolute nothingness.

It means I'm in touch with you in the deepest way you can be in touch with yourself. In some sense this seems magical, but only if you look at it from the normal perspective, where we take the world to be the objects that we see. From that perspective, we question how there can be nothing in between everything. But if we simply experience that truth and feel the complete emptiness, freedom, and spaciousness of this nothingness, we can feel that there's no obstruction anywhere, from one end to the other. What feels here and what feels over there is the same thing. We could say it's not really there, it's all here, but in fact, here and there lose their meaning—they become united.

This is something we learn every time we experience our true nature in its different manifestations and dimensions. We always come closer to this truth—that when we experience true nature, we feel a deep knowing of other people and the world because we know it all from the inside, at the depth of its nature. And now we're reaching this mystery at the level of the absolute dimension of true nature, where there are no objects and no concepts—only nothingness. Our love has taken the heart to the place where there is no possibility of separateness and distance, and so the sense of nearness is absolute and complete. There is zero distance between you and the Beloved, and since absolutely everything is the Beloved, there's no distance between you and everything else.

This condition is often referred to as unobstructedness or transparency, but in terms of the heart, in the language of love, it feels like we're completely in touch with all of existence. The heart is completely open, completely delicate, and completely soft—so soft, delicate, and open that it's deeply in touch with everything and everyone. But it's not like one is in touch with the other. There is no other. There's no separateness and no duality in this intouchness, so no obstruction or limitation whatsoever—there's just the experience of immediacy, of being in touch with everything as one unified thing. And because it's all one thing, to say you're in touch with everything doesn't actually make sense. It's more like the whole world is the heart and you're feeling it from inside. You could say it's inside your own heart, but that heart is the whole world, feeling itself without any obstructions or barriers.

The best word to describe this condition, using the language of love, is "intimacy." When we experience ourselves as forms and manifestations, while knowing we are the absolute and that the Beloved is our nature, a central way we experience ourselves is by being totally intimate with all of reality. Nearness has become union, and that leads to something that isn't just nearness, but intimacy. There's always increasing intimacy with the nearness of love, but when we arrive at the Beloved, we understand that absolute, true intimacy is the state of complete intouchness with everything and everybody.

So we're not talking about intimacy from the usual perspective of two people interacting and coming closer. True, absolute intimacy is how love is experienced when there are not two, when we are in this place where there is no distance and no separateness. When you know that nothingness is our nature and inner reality, we can't say that there is one person loving the other. There's just a sense of tenderness, sweetness, delicacy, and appreciativeness that isn't directed one way or another—it just is. This intimacy has the sense of being connected, but it's not a connection between two things. It is more like an open feeling of the heart—all hearts have become one heart, which is completely open and unobstructed. There's just an empty space that has the delicate soft feeling of the heart.

So there is love. There is sweetness. There is softness. There is smoothness. There is an exquisite delicacy and refinement and vulnerability, which is completely inseparable from this openness and spaciousness and emptiness. It's like the emptiness becomes a loving emptiness, and the love becomes a spacious love. Then there is quiet, peace, silence, and stillness—and this silence, this stillness, has a secrecy and the sense of exquisite intimacy.

This is the intimacy that we've always strived for with the ones we love. When we're in love, how intimate do we want to be? Maybe there's some intimacy on the phone, but it's not enough, and texting or emailing is even less intimate. We want to close the geographical distance, so we meet, have a date, and get closer. That's more intimate. Then you meet again and have more time together, go for a walk and talk for hours. And that opens up another dimension of intimacy. And of course, you want to overcome more of the physical separation and get more intimate physically, so you hug and kiss. But that's not enough. It just makes you hungry for more, complete physical intimacy, so you take off all your clothes. That's good, but it's still not enough you notice. Maybe you make love, but when you make love in those early passionate stages, what you're really wanting is to go inside the skin of the other—you want to remove the shell of the body so that the heart and the soul can be completely one. So the body is obviously something that will always make you feel separate from your lover, and you can overcome some of that by making love and melting in a pleasurable way. But it's never enough, and you still feel driven to find what you really want—the complete intimacy that is how you actually are at the depth.

So when the geographical distance is gone, when the clothes are gone, when the physical boundaries feel gone, and when all the emotional and mental boundaries are gone—when everything is gone and there is no obstruction whatsoever—then there's intimacy. And in this total intimacy, you don't say anything. You don't say,

"I love you"—it feels too intimate to say that. Of course I love you, and you know it, so why say it? This state of intimacy cannot be expressed, and any attempt to do so just diminishes it. It's just there, and usually it's quiet, with nothing happening. Not busy thinking about anything or making plans. Just being there.

So we're learning what intimacy is when love and the Beloved become one—lover, Beloved, and love are all the same. They're not separate, and there's no distinction between them in this exquisite intouchness. We can feel that with one person or the whole universe because it is the nature of everything.

As I said before, in Sufi terminology the word *ashk* is used for love, which includes the meaning of gravitational pull. That pull leads to *kurb*, which means nearness, and that then leads to *uns*, which is intimacy. Intimacy isn't an exact translation of the word *uns*, however. *Uns* has a richer meaning than just intimacy because it also has the meaning of joy and happiness. It also has the sense of familiarity, because if people are this intimate, they know each other completely, and so there's nothing to say. It's that kind of familiarity where intimacy needs no words.

Let's see if we can get a sense of our own experience of intimacy, with an exercise.

Practice Session: Intimacy

• • •

You'll do just one repeating question with a partner, each of you spending fifteen minutes asking the question. If you don't have a partner to do it with, you can answer in writing. The question is:

Tell me how you experience intimacy.

Just say spontaneously how you experience and feel it.

· · · · ·

Questions and Comments

Student: I was touching the experience of intimacy with the other, and by answering the question, a state of deepening intimacy arose, and by not resisting, by not manipulating, by not doing anything, it felt like the other came into the space, and what I consider me became thinner and thinner and less and less. And then when the exercise was over, we were hugging, and interestingly in the hugging there was a sadness coming up for me, a very curious sadness arose, as if touching the body made me aware again that there's a level in which it can't be consummated, on the level of the body, that kind of intimacy.

A. H. Almaas: Very true. In time, the body itself becomes subsumed into that intimate place, so it pervades the body too.

S: Recently I experienced my dog passing away, and I had quite a number of moments before she passed where I was gazing into her eyes, and I experienced true intimacy during that time. And being with humans who have passed away, in their last moments, I felt that same peacefulness and that lack of boundaries. And my question is, with cessation, annihilation, is there that same experience during that time?

AH: As intimacy?

S: Yes.

AH: The experience of cessation is more of a disappearing, annihilating. It can have intimacy as part of it, but not necessarily. And intimacy at the depth we're talking about, because there are many degrees as we know, it requires that the cessation has already happened, because in that intimacy there is emptiness. And sometimes the cessation, as we experience ourselves dissolving in the Beloved, sometimes we experience it as a deepening intimacy that culminates finally in the cessation.

S: I notice that in the experiencing of intimacy, it's as though it's paradoxical, because it's as though some subtle fluidic substance arises that annihilates distance and in which I start to feel myself dissolving. I was wondering if you had any comment about that.
AH: Sounds right. The inner solvent appears and dissolves things. That's what happens with intimacy. The more intimacy, the more dissolving, and we can experience the dissolving agent in one way or another. It is more like a fluid than anything else, but it really is a nothing, which flows like a fluid. A river of nothing. And that's why it annihilates.

So we've been wanting intimacy with the Beloved, but it's only when we finally behold and dissolve in the Beloved that we find pure intimacy. Reality itself is pure intimacy. It can be delicate and sweet. It can be spacious and open. It has that exquisite quality of the heart in terms of tenderness and softness, an exquisiteness of feeling, because love and intimacy are the same thing. It's a love that is completely disappearing, and the disappearance is always soft and delicate, fluffy and sensitive.

About the Diamond Approach

The Diamond Approach® is a contemporary path of spiritual realization emerging within and informed by the specific time we live in. It brings forth a unique view, understanding, and application of ancient spiritual wisdom and contemporary psychological knowledge to help us discover and embody our essential nature as we live our complex, modern lives.

The Diamond Approach is taught in groups and private sessions around the world (the United States, Canada, Australia, New Zealand, Asia, the Netherlands, Germany, Italy, Great Britain, Scandinavia, and more) by ordained minister/teachers.

Please visit https://www.diamondapproach.org/ for more information.

Diamond Approach is a registered service mark of the Ridhwan Foundation.

Ridhwan Foundation
P.O. Box 10114
Berkeley, California 94709-5114

Credits

Excerpts from *Divine Flashes*, from The Classics of Western Spirituality, by Fakhr al-Dīn Ibrāhīm 'Irāqī, translated and introduced by William C. Chittick and Peter L. Wilson, Copyright © 1982 by the Missionary Society of St. Paul the Apostle in the State of New York, Paulist Press, Inc., New York/Mahwah, NJ. Used with permission of Paulist Press. www.paulistpress.com.

Excerpts from *A Garden Beyond Paradise: The Mystical Poetry of Rumi*, translated by Jonathan Star and Shahram Shiva, copyright © 1992 by Jonathan Star. Reprinted by permission of the translator.

Excerpts from *The Kabir Book: Forty-Four of the Ecstatic Poems of Kabir* by Kabir, translated by Robert Bly, © 1976 by Beacon Press, permission conveyed through Copyright Clearance Center, Inc. Used with permission of Beacon Press.

"Love After Love" from *The Poetry of Derek Walcott 1948–2013* by Derek Walcott, selected by Glyn Maxwell, copyright © 2014 by Derek Walcott. Reprinted by permission of Farrar, Straus and Giroux and Faber and Faber, Ltd. All rights reserved.

INDEX

Abraham, 32–33
absence
  absolute, 233, 261, 279
  Beloved as, 232
  of love, 100, 102, 105
  presence and, 51, 237
absolute, the, xvii, 189–90, 206,
    238, 271, 296
  absolute knowing and, 261
  awareness emerging from, 249
  Beloved appearing as, 96, 176, 214
  gender attributions and, 194–95
  heart as true abode of, 214–21,
    222
  intimacy and 306
  magnificent power of, 187–88
  as nature of everything, 188,
    190–92, 275–79
  yearning for, 177–78
  See also Beloved, inner
absolute dimension, 176, 197, 305
absorption, 224
animal soul, 38–39, 180–81,
    296–97
annihilation
  into the Beloved, 213–14, 215, 219
  of duality, 293–94
  of mind in heart, 8, 56–57, 69,
    203, 204, 228, 257
  passionate love and, 175–76,
    185, 188, 190–91, 200, 203–6,
    259
  yearning for, 140–42, 177
  See also cessation
attachment
  letting go of, 99, 102–5, 119, 172,
    270–71
  to love objects, 48, 51
  rapprochement conflict and,
    272–74
attraction
  magnetic love and, 124–27, 129
  power of, 122–27
  unity and, 123–25
autonomy
  inner fidelity and, 50–51
  personal essence and, 48
  rapprochement conflict and,
    272–74
  true aloneness and, 73, 91

awareness
   beginning of, 249–50
   path of, 81, 82
   as radiance of the Beloved, 282

bedazzlement, 190, 204–5, 219, 236–37
beginning
   of everything, 247–48
   of experience, 249–54
   mystery of continual, 248–49
Beloved, inner
   annihilation into, 175–76, 185, 190–91, 200, 203–6, 293–94
   awakening to complete and pure love for, 171–77
   beholding, in various ways, 185–93
   conflict of loving both world and, 271–75
   confusing human love with love for, 119–30
   cultural influences on experiences of, 85–89
   difficulties of naming, 54–58
   difficulty talking about, 176, 187
   divided loyalty of heart and, 25–34
   as divine darkness, 255–62, 258–59
   eliminating notion of relationship and, 45–46, 200–204, 214
   emptiness and nonbeingness of, 140–48, 155–56, 157, 186–87, 231–35, 276–78, 303–6
   formless nature of, 72, 113, 122, 209, 231, 303
   heart as true abode of, 214–21
   heart opening and (*see* opening of heart)
   heart's discontent and, 6, 7, 23–24, 82–83, 117, 185, 198
   heart's primordial knowing of, 23–25, 70–71
   impersonal aspects of, 75–76
   as intangible and unfathomable, 7, 23, 37, 186–87, 208, 238, 258
   intimacy and unity and, 305–8
   jealousy and, 27, 49, 111, 112–13, 135
   letting go of ways of knowing, 69–70
   longing for, xix–xx, 21–22, 24, 28–29, 52, 53, 57, 84, 110–11, 177–78
   losing everything to, 66–75, 270–71
   magnetic love and, 124–27
   mature love and, 6, 7, 21, 35–36
   mind as barrier to, 228–39, 277–78, 289
   monogamous requirements of, 26–28, 32–33, 49–51
   moving beyond notions of divinity and, 88–93, 109–10
   mysteriousness of, xx, 53–55, 99, 102, 140, 174–75, 186–87

mystical poverty and, 99–107
names for, xvii–xviii, 24, 40–41, 111
as nature of everything, 188, 190–92, 198, 216, 235, 275–79, 302–3
nondual love and, 204–6
object relations and, 91, 119, 201, 202–3
personal essence and, 48
as primary love of the heart, 50–51, 67, 83–84, 94–95, 121
rending veils that obscure, 168–76
seeing, everywhere, 112
true mind's knowing of, 254–59
true nature and, 41–42, 82–83
unity of all existence and, 90, 113–14
unity of love and, 49–50, 69, 185, 277–79, 286–94
world in unity with, 275–79
yearning to disappear into, 140–48, 155–62
See also absolute, the
Big Bang theory, 209, 237, 247–48
black holes, 208–9
Bly, Robert, 17
bodhichitta, 156
boundlessness, of the Beloved, 1, 91, 304
brokenheartedness, 22, 31, 118, 217

cessation
death wish and, 157–62
as dissolving and melting, 299–300
divine darkness and, 262
intimacy and, 309–10
nirvana and, 156
regressive wish and, 142–48
of self, 156–57, 171
as union with the Beloved, 163–64
yearning for, 140–48, 155–62, 171
childhood experiences
of the Beloved, 150–51
dawning of consciousness, 250
death wish and, 159–60
early images of God, 89–90, 93
feelings of yearning and, 120–21
history of loss, 73–74
infants in separate bedrooms, 43
letting go of object relations and, 91–92
path of love and, 31
rapprochement conflict, 272–74
regressive wish and, 141–48
separation and, 68–69
structuring of soul and, 168
Christian mysticism, 42, 259
"Clay Jug, The" (Kabir), 17
compassion
Beloved and, 217, 294
perspective of, 82
sadness and, 284

consciousness
    cessation and, 300–301
    development of, 249–54
    purification of, 257
    that experiences the Beloved, 281–82
courage, moving beyond notions of divinity and, 90–91, 95
creation stories, 247–49
crystal heart, 105–6
cultural influences
    divine images and concepts and, 85–89
    personal relationships and, 42–44

Dante, 41
dark night of the soul, 71, 104, 119
darkness
    Beloved as absolute, 276, 277
    divine, 255–62
    inner mystery and, 176
    luminous night and, 219, 236, 270
    primal cavity and, 143–45
death wish, 157–62
depression, 72, 118, 161
depth psychology, 143, 144
desire, love and, 19, 21, 127, 296–97
    See also longing/yearning
devotional path, xviii, 41–42, 82.
    See also love, path of
Diamond Approach, 1–2, 170
diamond guidance, 264–65
diamond vehicle, 174
Dionysius the Areopagite, 259–60
direct experience
    of the Beloved, 186, 230
    heart and, 229
discontent
    of the heart, 4–11, 82–83, 117, 185, 198
    longing for the Beloved and, 23–24
Divan-i Shams-i Tabrizi (Nicholson), 167
divided heart, 9
    path of love and, 25–34, 170
    safety and, 35
    between world and the Beloved, 271–75
divine coma, 249, 262
divine darkness
    absolute rest and, 262
    deepest knowing and, 255–62
    great mystery of, 255, 258–59, 261
divine flashes, 257–58, 259
Divine Flashes ('Irāqī), 65–66, 183–84, 197, 213, 269–70, 285–86, 302
divinity
    cultural influences on experiences of, 85–89
    moving beyond familiar notions of, 88–93
    as oneness and unity, 90

of pure and complete love,
173–74
relationship with soul, 123–24
"Don't Leave Me Unbaked"
(Rumi), 137–38
duality
lover and the Beloved and,
198–205, 232
love's annihilation of, 293–94
reification and, 289–91
relational love and, 200–203
of world and the Beloved,
275–76

ecstatic love
Beloved and, 21, 199–200
opening of heart and, 30, 47,
84–85
See also passionate love
emptiness
awareness of, 103
of the Beloved, 140, 186–87,
231–35
of divine darkness, 261
of heart as natural condition,
103, 105, 171
intimacy and, 307
See also nonbeingness
emptying the heart
Beloved as heart-thief and, 216
deep longing and, 22
inner fidelity and, 51
mystical poverty and, 99–107,
109, 119–20, 177, 186, 214, 231

of objects of love, xix–xx,
67–71, 83, 85, 99–101
passionate love and, xx
removing idols and, 33, 36, 56,
62, 100
soul and, 103–5
enlightenment
heart's desire for, xviii, 156
path of love and, 41
power of love and, 123–24, 125
experience, development of,
249–54

fidelity of the heart, 245
fear of loss and, 66–75
true autonomy and, 50–51
unity of love and, 185, 277–79,
288–89, 291–92
flame, soul and, 110
form
as emanations of the Beloved,
275–76
world as manifestation of, 273,
278
See also names and images
formlessness
of the Beloved, 72, 113, 122, 209,
231
heart's devotion to, 65–66, 69,
83–84, 85
mysteriousness of, 303
surrendering to, 141
Freud, Sigmund, 23, 143–44, 159–60
friend, as name for Beloved, 55

Garden Beyond Paradise, A
(Rumi), 97–98, 137
Genesis, 247–48
God
   cultural influences and, 86–89
   moving beyond familiar
      notions of, 88–93
   names for, 55
   as not loving, 59–60
   Sufi house of, 32–33, 100
gravitational pull of love, 308
   unity and, 124–27, 199
grief
   loss and, 270–71, 273
   yearning and, 117–18
guest, as name for the Beloved,
   40–41, 51, 55
"Guest, The" (Kabir), 8
"Guest Arrives Only at Night,
   The," 8

habits, impact on the work, 82
habitual structures, inquiry into,
   169–74
heart
   as abode of absolute reality, 221
   alienation from true nature, 54
   annihilating mind in, 8, 56–57,
      69, 203, 204, 228, 257
   barriers to fidelity of, 66–75
   Beloved as primary love of, 50–
      51, 67, 83–84, 94–95, 121, 185
   condition of "no," 100–101, 103
   conflict of loving world and the

      Beloved, 271–75
   direct experience and, 229
   discontent of, 4–11, 23, 82–83,
      117, 185, 198
   divided loyalty of, 9, 25–34, 170,
      271–75
   divine darkness and, 256–57, 259
   emptying objects of (*see* empty-
      ing the heart)
   as human characteristic, 82
   as locus of soul, 23
   longing to disappear, 155–57
   mind's obstruction of, 229–39
   nonduality and, 198–99
   opening of (*see* opening of heart)
   orgiastic nature of, 19–21, 82
   polygamous nature of, 3–4,
      8–9, 13, 23
   as presence of essence, 174
   primordial knowing of the
      Beloved, 23–25, 30, 70–71,
      236–37
   recognition of the Beloved's
      emptiness, 234–35
   sexuality and, 296–97
   as true abode of the Beloved,
      214–21
   true mind and, 251–54, 260, 262
   unity of love and, 185, 275,
      277–79, 288–89, 291–92
   See also fidelity of the heart; love
heart, path of the, xvii, xviii, 39,
   197, 203–5
   brief summary of, 83–84

Index 321

direct teaching for, xix
as tempestuous, 84–85
See also love, path of
heart knowledge, development of, 249–54
holy spirit, 224
human beings, as characterized by heart, 82–83
human love
  confusing with love for the Beloved, 119–30
  divided loyalty of, 25–34
  falling in love, 124, 126, 131
  incompleteness of, xix, 3–7, 23
  inherent limitations of, 35–36, 37, 46
  objects of, 2–7, 9, 18–19, 23
  orgiastic nature of, 19–21
  passionate love vs., xix–xx
  power of attraction and, 122–27
  stages of, 52
  See also love; personal relationships
humility
  moving beyond notions of divinity and, 91
  path of love and, 29–30, 53, 171

idols, removing from the heart, 33, 36, 56, 62, 100
images. *See* names and images
Inner Journey Home, The, 261
inquiry
  method of, 1–2, 264
  path of love and, 2
  into structure of personality, 169–74
instincts
  animal soul and, 38–39
  limitations of, 19
intimacy
  cessation and, 309–10
  danger and, 243–44
  nonduality and, 237
  unity of love and, 305–8
'Irāqī, Fakhruddīn, 187, 203, 216, 257, 285–86, 287
  poems of, 65–66, 183–84, 197, 213, 269–70, 285–86, 302

jealousy, Beloved and, 27, 49, 111, 112–13, 135
Jesus, 101
Jewish mysticism, 42
joyfulness, path of love and, 72

Kaaba, 32–33, 62, 100
Kabir, 21, 41, 51, 53, 55, 118, 230
  poems of, 17, 40, 72, 115, 117, 154, 158, 227–28
knowing
  development of, 249–54
  of divine darkness, 255–62
  as divine flashes, 257–58, 259
  with heart and mind together, 251–54, 260, 262
  through presence, 260
  transcending, 260

loneliness, aloneness vs., 73
longing/yearning
   for the Beloved, xix–xx, 21–22, 24, 28–29, 52, 53, 57, 84, 110–11, 177–78
   for cessation, 140–48, 155–62, 171
   childhood associations of, 120–21
   different qualities of, 140
   discriminating between human and the Beloved, 119–30
   for enlightenment, 156
   in human love, 19
   moving beyond notions of divinity and, 90
   pure forms of, 120, 128–29, 155, 170–71
   regressive wish and, 142–47
   separation and, 86, 117–18
loss
   alienation as, 82
   of all familiar support, 66–75, 270–71, 273
   mystical poverty and, 101
love
   annihilating power of, 175–76, 185, 190–91, 203–6, 219, 293–94
   beyond notion of relationship, 200–204, 213–14
   changing nature of, 15
   condition of "no," 100–101, 103, 108–9
   divine darkness and, 259
   fundamental role of, 2–3
   intimacy and, 305–8
   language of, xviii, 29, 116–17, 199, 201, 308
   magnetic, 124–27, 199
   nonduality and, 198–200
   objects of (*see* objects of love)
   power of, and enlightenment, 123–24, 125
   Stupa love, 173–75, 189
   See also heart; human love; passionate love
love, path of
   awakening to complete and pure love, 171–77
   bridging duality and nonduality and, 198–205, 293–94
   differentiating personal relationships from, 41–42, 44–46, 48
   divided loyalty of heart and, 25–34
   ecstatic love and, 84–85
   fear of losing everything on, 66–75, 270–71
   humility and, 29–30, 53, 171
   as inner journey, 6, 7–9, 17–18, 23
   as long and challenging, 31, 51–54, 139, 184
   mystical poverty and, 99–107
   opening of heart and, 47, 84
   painful feelings and, 30–31, 66–75, 88–89, 118–19, 282–84

path of inquiry and, 2
path of warrior and, 80
pride and, 29
relational aspect of, 200–203
renouncing objects of love and, 71, 287
sacrifice and, 70–75
separation and, 68–69
spiritual journey as, 1
summary of stages of, xix–xxi, 83–84, 170–74, 184–85, 213–14
traditions following, 41–42
true realization and, 286–94
See also heart, path of the; unity of love
"Love After Love" (Walcott), 245–46
Love Unveiled, 1, 167
lover and Beloved
love's obliteration of, 204
sacrifice and, 70, 78, 80
unity of, 189, 191
working with duality of, 198–205, 232
luminous night, Beloved as, xx, 186–88, 214, 219–20, 236, 270, 275
Luminous Night's Journey, 7, 105–6, 177–78, 205–6

magnetic love, 124–27, 129, 199
mature love, 5–6
Beloved and, 6, 7, 21, 35–36

earthly, 4, 35–36
ecstasy and, 21
meaning
essence and, 65, 66, 77
search for, xviii
mind
abstract concepts of, 116–17
annihilating, in the heart, 8, 56–57, 69, 203, 204, 228, 257
as barrier to the Beloved, 228–39, 277–78, 289
bedazzlement of, 236–37, 258–59
development of, 249–54
functions of, 207, 228–31, 235–36, 244, 264–65
as human characteristic, 82
object relations and, 201, 202–3
obstruction of the heart, 229–39
true knowing of the Beloved, 254–59, 260, 262
two types of, 251–54
mind knowledge, development of, 249–54
monogamy
Beloved and, 26–28, 32–33, 49–51
unity of love and, 286–88
monotheism, 33, 288
Moses, 259–60
mother, rapprochement conflict and, 272–74
Muhammad, 33, 34, 36

mysteriousness
 of absolute nothingness, 303–6
 of the Beloved, xx, 53–55, 99, 102, 140, 174–75, 186–87
 of divine darkness, 255, 258–59, 261
mystical poverty, xx, 71
 emptiness of heart and, 103–7, 119–20, 177, 186, 206, 214, 231
 opening of heart and, 108–9
 yearning and, 128, 171
Mystical Theology, The (Dionysius the Areopagite), 259–60

names and images
 for the Beloved, xvii–xviii, 24, 40–41, 86
 cultural influences on divine, 85–89
 experiencing the Beloved without, 65–66, 69, 72, 91–93, 109–10, 209, 231
 knowing without, 251
 reification of the Beloved and, 54–58, 92, 171
narcissism, Beloved and, 217
Nature, Beloved appearing through, 77
Nicholson, R. A., 167
nirvana, desire for, 156
nirvana principle, 159–60
nonattachment, heart of, 105
nonbeingness
 absolute mystery of, 303–6
 beingness and, 298–99
 Beloved and, 155–56, 157, 186–87, 235, 245, 276–78
 as essence of form, 233
 letting go of everything and, 271
 ultimate truth and, 139–40
 yearning for, 140–48, 155–62
nonconceptuality, Beloved and, 231
Nondual Love, 1, 158
nonduality
 annihilation and, 204–6
 beholding the Beloved and, 230
 intimacy and immediacy and, 237
 language of love and, 116
 moving beyond, 127
 path of love and, 198–205, 293–94
 of ultimate truth and love, 116, 198
nothingness
 absolute mystery of, 303–6
 divine slumber and, 249
 everything arising from, 248–49
 See also emptiness
nuclear family, development of, 43

object relations, 11
 Beloved and, 91, 119, 201, 202–3
 longing and, 121
 moving beyond notions of God and, 91–92
 self-destructiveness and, 159–60

objectification process, 148–49
objects of love
  attachment to, 48, 51, 99, 270–71
  beliefs about having many, 107–8
  Beloved as primary, 49–50, 67, 121, 275, 287, 292
  characteristics of earthly, 2–7, 9, 18–19, 23
  divided heart and competing, 25–27, 34, 35–36
  as expressions of the Beloved, 288–90, 292–93
  heart divesting itself of, xix–xx, 67–71, 83, 85, 99–107, 119, 287
  projecting onto the Beloved, 119
  world as, 271–75
"One Whisper of the Beloved" (Rumi), 97–98
opening of heart
  ecstatic love and, 30, 47
  impact on sense of self, 210
  mystical poverty and, 108–9
  painful feelings and, 30–32, 297
  path of love and, 47, 84
optimizing force, 149–50
orgiastic experience
  Beloved and, 25
  of heart, 19–21, 82
  opening of heart and, 30

painful feelings
  cessation as relief from, 141–42
  embracing, 297–98
  grief and yearning, 117–18
  losing everything and, 66–75, 270–71, 273
  moving beyond notions of divinity and, 88–89
  opening of heart and, 30–31, 282–84, 297
passionate love, 29
  annihilation and, 175–76, 185, 188, 190–91, 200, 203–6, 213–14, 215, 219, 259
  deep longing and, 57, 120–21, 128, 141
  for secret one, 8
  as spiritual stirring, xviii, xix–xx
peak experience, 168
personal essence
  Beloved and, 48
  Stupa love and, 174
personal relationships
  cultural differences and, 42–44
  differentiating from path of love, 41–42, 44–46, 48
  impact of heart's inner fidelity on, 67–68, 69
  modern challenges for, 53–54
  personal essence and, 48
  as spiritual path, 42, 44–46
  teacher/student, 126
  usefulness of settled, 44, 122, 131–32
  See also human love

personality, inquiry into habitual structure of, 169–74
Plotinus, 260
poetry
    language of love and, xviii, 116–17
    mystical language and, 112, 238–39
polygamy of heart, 3–4, 8–9, 170
    as barrier to the Beloved, 26–28, 32–33, 291
    as deep truth, 23
    fear of, 13
    unity of love and, 288–89
polymorphously perverse, 23
polytheism, 32–33, 288, 294
pomegranate love, 190, 200
practice sessions
    barriers to fidelity of the heart, 75
    beholding the Beloved, 192–93
    Beloved and the world, 280
    Beloved and your beloveds—conflict or resolution, 295
    biography of the heart's loves and discontents, 9–11
    confusing love for the Beloved with human love, 129–30
    divided loyalty of heart, 34
    going beyond the divinity you've known, 93
    heart and the Beloved, 222
    identifying as the lover of the Beloved, 207
    images of the inner Beloved, 57–58
    intimacy, 308–9
    mind obstructing the heart, 239
    mystery of the Beloved, 262–63
    staying faithful to the inner Beloved, 107–8
    wish for cessation, 147–48
    yearning for the Beloved and the wish for cessation, 162–63
    your love for the Beloved, 179
presence
    absence and, 51, 237
    Beloved as, 87, 90, 235
    knowing through, 260
pride, path of love and, 29
primal cavity, regressive wish and, 143–48, 158
primary and secondary love objects, 4, 28, 49–50, 67, 121, 275, 287, 292
primordial and symbiotic relationship, 133–34
privacy, Beloved and, 176

rapprochement conflict, 272–74
realization
    cessation and, 163–64
    true unity of love and, 49–50, 69, 286–94
reason and logic, limitations of, 230–31, 237–38
recognition, development of, 250–51

regressive wish, for cessation, 142–48, 158
reification
  duality and, 289–91
  of true nature, 55–57, 77, 82
repetition compulsion, 159–60
Rumi, 41, 53, 112, 161, 238, 239, 247
  poems of, 97–98, 104, 137–38, 139, 140, 167, 226
  Shams al-Din and, 44–46

sacredness, Beloved and, 176
sacrifice
  path of love and, 70–75
  suicide of ego identity and, 79
science, modern, 247–49
secret, Beloved as, 8, 40–41, 176
self
  awakening to complete and pure love, 171–77
  cessation of, 156–57, 171
  emptiness of heart and, 103, 104, 105
  inquiry into habitual structure of, 169–74
  magnetic love and, 126
  open heart and sense of, 210
  soul and, 168–69, 172
  transformation of, 170, 217
self-destructiveness, 159–60, 161
self-knowledge, search for, xviii
selflessness, of pure love, 126
self-preservation, divided heart and, 35

separation
  alienation as, 82
  attraction and, 123
  duality and, 116, 200–203
  longing and, 86, 117–18
  of lover and the Beloved, 198
  path of love and, 68–69, 73, 171, 176
sexuality, 296–97
Shams al-Din, 44–46
soul
  death wish of, 158–59, 160–62
  emptiness of heart and, 103–5
  flame as awakening of, 110
  individuation of, 48
  practices for opening, 168–70
  relationship with divine, 123–24
  structured self as part of, 168, 172
  surrendering of, 141
  transformation of, 217
  in union with the Beloved, 164
  yearning of, 120, 170–71
spiritual practices, limitations of, 168–69
spiritual resolve (*himma*), 38, 65
St. John of the Cross, xx
Stupa love, 189
  awakening of, 171–77
suffering, seeking end to, xviii, 141–42, 156
Sufism, 38, 111
  house of God, 32–33, 100
  path of love and, 42, 215, 308
suicide, 79, 161

symbiotic relationship, 133

time and space, 237, 248–49
transitional objects, 43
true nature
    absolute dimension of, 305
    consequences of not knowing, 6–7
    developing relationship with, 41–42, 46
    earthly love and, 35–36
    heart as locus of, 23, 221
    heart's alienation from, 54
    inherent mystery of, 261
    many facets of, 81–82
    privacy and, 176
    reification of, 55–57, 77, 82
    reunification with, 197–98
    seeing the Beloved as, 82–83
trust, moving beyond notions of divinity and, 90–91

ultimate truth
    Beloved and, 209, 276
    different names and paths to, xvii–xviii
    nonbeingness and, 139–40
    nonduality and, 116, 198
    power of attraction and, 123–25
    Stupa love and, 174
unity
    attraction and, 123–25
    Beloved and, 90, 113–14, 287–94
    Beloved and world as, 275–79, 302–3
    gravitational pull and, 124–27
    nonduality and, 198–99
unity of love, 38
    challenges to, 290–92
    fidelity of the heart and, 185, 277–79, 288–89, 291–92
    increased outer beloveds and, 292–93
    intimacy and, 305–8
    of lover and the Beloved, 189, 191
    realization of, 49–50, 69, 286–94
    true monogamy and, 286–88

vulnerability
    intimacy and unity and, 306–7
    love and, 14–15, 18, 20
    opening of heart and, 30
    path of love and, 52–53, 172

Walcott, Derek, 245–46
wholeness, unity of love and, 275–79, 287–94, 304
will, path of, 81, 95
world
    as object of love, 271–75
    realness of loving, 274
    as unity with the Beloved, 275–79, 287–94, 302–3, 306

Books by A. H. Almaas

Essence with *The Elixir of Enlightenment*
Facets of Unity
The Inner Journey Home
Luminous Night's Journey
The Power of Divine Eros
Runaway Realization
Alchemy of Freedom

Diamond Mind Series

Volume 1. The Void
Volume 2. The Pearl Beyond Price
Volume 3. The Point of Existence

Diamond Heart Series

Book One. Elements of the Real in Man
Book Two. The Freedom to Be
Book Three. Being and the Meaning of Life
Book Four. Indestructible Innocence
Book Five. Inexhaustible Mystery

Diamond Body Series

Spacecruiser Inquiry
Brilliancy
The Unfolding Now

The Journey of Spiritual Love Series

Love Unveiled
Nondual Love
The Inner Beloved